THE BENEFITS OF PROVIDENCE

THE BENEFITS OF PROVIDENCE

A NEW LOOK AT DIVINE SOVEREIGNTY

JAMES S. SPIEGEL

CROSSWAY BOOKS

A PUBLISHING MINISTRY OF
GOOD NEWS PUBLISHERS
WHEATON, ILLINOIS

Library of Congress Cataloging-in-Publication Data
Spiegel, James S., 1963-
 The benefits of providence : a new look at divine sovereignty /
James S. Spiegel.
  p. cm.
 Includes bibliographical references.
 ISBN 1-58134-616-6
 1. Providence and government of God. II. Title.
BT135.S74 2005
231.5—dc22   2005006013

ML		15	14	13	12	11	10	09	08	07	06	05
15	14	13	12	11	10	9	8	7	6	5	4	3	2	1

FOR
BAILEY, SAMUEL, AND MAGDALENE

CONTENTS

"We do not want merely to see beauty, though,
God knows, even that is bounty enough.
We want something else which can hardly be put
into words—to be united with the beauty we see,
to pass into it, to receive it into ourselves,
to bathe in it, to become part of it."

C. S. Lewis,
The Weight of Glory

PREFACE

For as long as I can remember I have sensed the presence of God. From the time I was a toddler, listening to my mother tell me about God, I recognized that the world is rich with manifestations of the divine. Even as a rebellious teenager, wishing that I could be a law unto myself, I could not shake this feeling. As I have matured, this sense of God's presence has grown more acute, even as it flowered into what I regard as a personal acquaintance with God, along with a full-fledged theology of his attributes and works. Today my sense is no longer merely that God is *here* with me, but that he is everywhere, within and without, sustaining all things, that he guides every event in human history, and that he is coordinating all aspects of the cosmos toward a glorious end. I believe that God's work in the world is thoroughly intimate and redemptive. In short, I confess, with the great Christian minds Augustine, Anselm, Aquinas, Luther, Calvin, and Edwards, that God is entirely sovereign and perfectly good, the holy and omnipotent Lord of all. And I confess with the apostle Paul, along with the Stoic poet whom he quotes, that in God "we live and move and have our being" (Acts 17:28).

For centuries Christians have affirmed the sovereignty of God. But recent generations have seen a falloff of commitment to this doctrine. For a variety of reasons, many Christians have opted to depart from the great tradition affirming meticulous divine governance of the world. Most disturbing is the growing popularity of openness theology, which represents the nadir of the long slide from orthodoxy. This is a perilous move for the church and doubly tragic. We are witnessing the rejection of a doctrine that is both biblically anchored and practically beneficial.

And in its stead, thousands are embracing what may be regarded as heresy, the implications of which are practically devastating. The words of Jeremiah come to mind: "My people have committed two sins: They have forsaken me, the spring of living water, and have dug their own cisterns, broken cisterns that cannot hold water" (Jer. 2:13).

This book aims to contribute to the growing body of literature critical of the latest alternatives to the orthodox Christian doctrine of divine providence. When you get down to it, of course, the issue at hand is not just the maintenance of sound doctrine but also the nature of God. The current dispute over openness theology is essentially a debate about who God is and therefore could not be more urgent, nor the implications more significant.

In the book of Philippians Paul exhorts, "continue to work out your salvation with fear and trembling, for it is God who works in you to will and to act according to his good purpose" (2:12-13). Another book of mine (*How to Be Good in a World Gone Bad*, Kregel, 2004) focuses on how we are to "work out" our salvation. At various points throughout the present volume, especially in the final chapter, I affirm and apply the notion that it is God who works in us "to will and to act according to his good purpose." Just how both can be true—how we can be morally accountable and at the same time the work in us can be divinely orchestrated—is mysterious, but this is nonetheless the plain teaching of Scripture. Perhaps here we must simply affirm with the writer of Deuteronomy, "the secret things belong to the LORD" (29:29).

Yet Christian theologians and philosophers are called to inquire, if at times tentatively, into even the most hallowed domains of human knowledge. We are called not simply to rest in the dogmas of the past—however profound and well-established—but to explore new inroads to orthodoxy, to articulate afresh the verities of the faith, and to reinspire the people of God with the core teachings of our tradition. This is the daunting adventure of Christian scholarship, and this book exemplifies this effort. It is written in full conviction that our forebears were correct in affirming the meticulous providence of God, that this doctrine is both faithful to Scripture and a boon to personal virtue, and that there yet remain many creative avenues of expression of this doctrine to exalt the mind and encourage the heart.

Portions of this book are reworkings or expansions of some previously published articles. Many sections of Chapters 1 and 2 originally appeared in my essay "Does God Take Risks?," a chapter in *God Under Fire: Modern Scholarship Reinvents God* (Zondervan, 2002). Parts of Chapter 3 are drawn from my essay "Towards a New Aesthetic Vision for the Christian Liberal Arts College," *Christian Scholar's Review* 28:3 (Spring 1999). And some sections of Chapter 4 first appeared in "A Berkeleyan Approach to the Problem of Induction," *Science and Christian Belief* 10:1 (April 1998), while other portions were drawn from "The Philosophical Theology of Theistic Evolutionism," *Philosophia Christi*, Series II, 4:1 (Spring 2002). My thanks go to these publishers for permission to reprint those materials here.

I am grateful for my wonderful colleagues at Taylor University, especially those in the Department of Biblical Studies, Christian Education and Philosophy, who have been a steady encouragement to me in all my scholarly endeavors. And I want to thank my colleagues in the broader Christian philosophical and theological communities who have inspired me in so many ways. Lastly, I am thankful to my wife, Amy, who is a constant support and encouragement to me in all that I do. Next to Christ himself, she remains the clearest expression of God's gracious providence in my life. Our children—Bailey, Samuel, and Magdalene— are likewise standing testaments to providence. I dedicate this book to them in the hope that they, too, will one day see themselves as characters in the divine artwork, saved by grace, and willing servants of our sovereign Lord.

INTRODUCTION:
WHY PROVIDENCE MATTERS

A few years ago my university invited a seminary professor to speak to our students. Just prior to his lecture, he and a colleague of mine struck up a conversation that eventually turned to the doctrine of divine sovereignty. Soon they both recognized that they held very different views about the extent of God's providential governance of the world. "Well," one of them concluded, "we just worship different Gods." The other nodded in agreement, saying, "Yes, we sure do." The conversation ended there.

At the time I found this exchange to be rather curious, perhaps even a bit melodramatic. How could these two intelligent, devout Christian men agree that they worshiped different deities just because of their differing doctrines of providence? My colleague believed God to be completely sovereign over creation, ordaining all things that come to pass. The visiting scholar maintained that God passively allows many things to happen, even limiting his own knowledge about the future. To both men these divergent conceptions of divine providence were sufficient grounds for denying they worshiped the same God. Was their shared assessment correct?

However one answers that question, this anecdote illustrates the fact that the doctrine of providence is a fundamental theological issue. The extent to which God controls the world is of vital importance both to our personal lives and to numerous related Christian doctrines. For example, one's doctrine of providence directly affects one's view of human freedom. This, in turn, influences the way one conceives of human responsibility. One's views on these issues also shape one's approach to God's relationship to human sin and suffering. And the doctrine of providence affects one's take on various moral attributes of God, including his wisdom, kindness, justice, mercy, and love. These are not trivial theological matters but momentous issues that affect believers at a basic level.

In 1 Timothy 4:16 Paul writes, "watch your life and doctrine closely. Persevere in them, because if you do, you will save both yourself and your hearers." This is just one of many biblical passages that emphasize the importance of sound doctrine, but this exhortation goes further than most in linking sound doctrine with salvation. Indeed, as the wayward theologies of many cults and even terrorist networks tragically demonstrate, bad doctrine can destroy lives and even escort people to hell. While perhaps not as pivotal as the doctrines of the Trinity, the divine incarnation, the resurrection of Christ, or the authority of Scripture, the doctrine of providence is crucial to Christian faith and practice. Misconceptions and misapplications of the concept of divine sovereignty can be personally devastating and can even distort one's perspectives on these more basic theological issues.

The classical Christian view of providence affirms God's exhaustive foreknowledge and complete control over the cosmos. Because God is omniscient, he knows the future as well as the past and the present. And because God is perfectly good and wise, we can be confident that he governs the world perfectly. Regardless of how things might appear at times, we can rest in the assurance that God will achieve all of his purposes for history and our individual lives. The promise that "in all things God works for the good of those who love him, who have been called according to his purpose" (Rom. 8:28) speaks directly to the fact that God is at work in every detail of the believer's life, redeeming even the most painful experiences for the believer's own good and for God's glory. This is the high view of providence.

The last century has seen significant erosion of the high view of providence. Liberal theologians of various stripes have critiqued this orthodox doctrine, and in recent years challenges have been raised even in evangelical circles. The perspective known as openness theology continues to grow in popularity, in spite of its grossly unbiblical tenets. Its proponents, known as open theists, claim a high view of Scripture and defend their perspective using a wide array of arguments that have persuaded many Christians that God neither knows the whole future nor completely controls the world. In creating and governing the world, open theists tell us, God takes risks. Because of the extent of human freedom, even God cannot always predict what we will do next. Thus it occasionally happens that God's plans are frustrated, his expectations are disappointed, his hopes are dashed, and his judgments are mistaken. Such belief in divine risk, as touted by open theists, constitutes the essence of a low view of providence.

My purpose in this book is to provide a broad defense of the high view of providence, both through critical analysis of the low view of providence and through constructive application of the high view. My critical aim is to demonstrate that the concept of divine risk contradicts the plain teaching of Scripture and that the major arguments against the high view are flawed. My constructive aim is to reveal some significant benefits of the high view of providence, both of a theoretical and practical nature. Thus the overarching thesis of this book is that *there are many good reasons to accept the high view of providence and no good reasons to reject it.*

In the first chapter I survey the standard perspectives on divine providence. These include three versions of the high view: Augustinianism, Molinism, and simple divine foreknowledge. I critique the latter two views, both of which regard God's foreknowledge as logically prior to his providential decrees. Thus, for the remainder of the book I assume the Augustinian perspective to be the strongest version of the high view of providence. Nonetheless, I invite advocates of Molinism and simple divine foreknowledge to explore the many benefits of the high view of providence, as their views are amenable to much of my constructive project. I also review the low view of providence in the first chapter, examining openness theology as well as its historical precursors: process theology, political liberation theology, and feminist theology.

In Chapter 2 I assess the high and low views of providence in light of Scripture, concluding that the low view is biblically unwarranted and that the high view enjoys significant biblical support. In so doing, I use openness theology as the representative of all versions of the low view of providence, because it is currently the most popular among these perspectives. Moreover, open theists are the most concerned to argue from Scripture, and many of them even subscribe to biblical inerrancy. I consider the open theists' central arguments for their view and rebut each of these. I examine the philosophical motivations for their perspective, showing why the concept of divine risk is unnecessary. And I identify some historical and cultural factors that account for the rise of this errant theology in the first place.

In Chapter 3 I discuss the orthodox doctrine of divine conservation of the cosmos, noting how it implies an Augustinian view of providence. From here I explore several major implications of this perspective, specifically regarding the laws of nature, the concept of miracle, and the whole domain of aesthetics. With regard to the latter, I develop the idea of the world as an aesthetic phenomenon and God as a cosmic artist. I expand this aesthetic model in light of some contemporary aesthetic theories, specifically proposing that the cosmic art is fundamentally an act of divine expression and communication. This model prepares the way for further critical applications regarding the issue of divine emotion and the problem of evil, which I take up in Chapters 5 and 6 respectively.

In Chapter 4 I apply the high view of providence to the practice of science. I discuss four issues, two of which are methodological and two of which are substantive. The methodological issues are the notorious problem of induction and the debate over methodological naturalism. I show how the high view of providence dissolves the problem of induction and undermines methodological naturalism. This latter implication, I note, diminishes the grounds for embracing an evolutionary perspective on the substantive issue of origins. The other substantive issue I examine is the contemporary debate over the nature of human consciousness. After surveying the major theories of mind, I show that the high view of providence has some surprisingly useful applications to this issue, offering hope for a satisfactory account of consciousness where all the current theories fail.

In Chapter 5 I explore the matter of divine emotion based on the aesthetic model spelled out in the third chapter. After looking at the standard views, divine passibilism and impassibilism, I propose an alternative that incorporates the insights and avoids the major shortcomings of each: divine *omnipathism*. This is the idea that God experiences all emotions eternally and immutably. I develop the concept of omnipathos in a way that parallels some of the other classical attributes of God, specifically omniscience and omnipresence. I also discuss the major theories of emotion and show how each of them can be applied to a conception of God as omnipathic.

In Chapter 6 I discuss the problem of evil, showing how the high view of providence offers many significant resources for dealing with this perennial issue. I review many of the major theodicies and demonstrate why they fail to adequately account for God's permission of evil. The approach favored by the high view of providence is the "greater good" theodicy, which emphasizes God's redemptive use of human suffering and even immorality. I explore several applications of this perspective, as related to character building, solidarity with Christ, and beatific vision. And I present a biblical case for divine sovereignty over moral evil.

Finally, in Chapter 7 I apply the high view of providence to numerous moral and devotional matters. I argue that the high view naturally enhances the nurturing of such moral virtues as humility, faith, courage, and patience. Moreover, I explain how the high view provides the believer with a more universal right of complaint to God about personal trials. And, likewise, I show how the believer has better grounds for the privilege of thanking God for his blessings. I conclude by applying the high view of providence to the spiritual disciplines and the practice of evangelism.

My intent in this book is to present a long-standing theological doctrine in a fresh way that demonstrates its explanatory power, illustrates its conceptual depth and versatility, and proves its practical utility. I hope for the reader that all of these considerations will converge to make a persuasive case (if one wants to call it that) for the high view of providence. There are many wonderful benefits in taking this view, and there is a significant toll to be paid by those who reject it in favor of the low view of providence. I am convinced that the high view is a boon to both academic inquiry and personal faith. If this book goes some distance in demonstrating this, then my efforts will have been worthwhile.

1

TWO VIEWS OF DIVINE PROVIDENCE

Generally speaking, the doctrine of divine providence affirms that God "provides" for his creatures. The Lord not only created the entire universe—he also prudently manages it. All theists, Christians included, agree about this much. Just what divine management of the world entails, however, is widely disputed. Does God actively determine every event that comes to pass? Or does he passively allow some events to happen? If the latter, are there some occurrences that God does not anticipate that actually surprise him? These are not idle questions, as was noted in the Introduction. One's take on this issue deeply influences one's worldview and personal life, coloring the way one sees current events, church history, and cultural trends, as well as one's personal relationships, career choices, and moral decision-making. In short, the doctrine of providence is fundamental to one's way of living.

AN OVERVIEW OF STANDARD PERSPECTIVES

One may take a more or less strong view of providence, depending upon just how much control of the cosmos God is thought to have. For the purposes of our discussion, I will distinguish between "high" and "low" views of providence, where the former affirm significantly greater divine control of the world than do the latter. What has come to be called "classical theism" or, more specifically, the classical view of providence says that God's control of the cosmos is absolute. On this view, everything happens according to a meticulous divine plan, including the free actions of human beings. God is always and everywhere working out this plan, and even the most nefarious deeds of human beings somehow, mysteriously, contribute to his purposes. Because God's cosmic blueprint is fixed down to the last detail, his foreknowledge is exhaustive. He knows the past, present, and future completely. In fact, strictly speaking, since God is not bound by time, he does not have to wait for events in our future to unfold. He knows them from all eternity because they are eternally decreed. The divine design for history, too, is eternal, based on God's chief end in creation: to glorify himself.

The classical view regards God's plan for history as logically prior to his knowledge of it. However, some proponents of the high view of providence reverse this order, seeing God's foreknowledge as logically prior to his plan for creation. Among those who take this approach are advocates of (1) simple divine foreknowledge and (2) divine middle knowledge. Proponents of simple foreknowledge (SF) maintain that God has exhaustive knowledge of future events and that his sovereign governance of the world is based on this foreknowledge. By placing God's foreknowledge ahead of his decrees for history, SF aims to safeguard human freedom. And by locating the causal origins of sin in the wills of free creatures, SF provides help in responding to the problem of evil.

However, because SF seems to suggest that the future is determined (how else could God know the future with certainty?), the concept of divine middle knowledge was devised to avoid this implication. According to divine middle knowledge (MK), from eternity God considered all of the possible worlds that he might create. Among those that contain free beings, God considered what all of these beings *would* do with their creaturely freedom (as opposed to what they *will* do, according to SF), and he selected the world he deemed best, all things considered. As in the classical model, MK affirms exhaustive divine foreknowledge. But like SF, MK denies that this foreknowledge is premised on divine decree. The perceived benefits of MK are the same as for SF. God can carry out his purposes while preserving a sense of human freedom, and since sin causally originates in human wills, rather than in divine decree, God is in no way culpable.

What all versions of the high view of providence affirm together is divine *omniprescience*: God knows the future exhaustively. Moreover, since either God decrees according to this knowledge or his knowledge is based on his fixed decrees, God's control over the world is complete. There is no risk involved in his creative activity. What I am calling the "low" view of providence essentially denies this claim and affirms the reality of divine risk. Proponents of this perspective insist that divine omniprescience cannot be squared with genuine human freedom, and they deny that even softer versions of the high view (SF and MK) provide a sufficient buffer against the problem of evil. These two problems, say defenders of the low view, fundamentally undermine Christian belief in the relationality of God. Accordingly, they propose that God took risks in creating the world, and his moment-to-moment governance of creation is likewise replete with risky acts. God does not perfectly know what the future will bring, they say, because the choices of free creatures are not entirely predictable, even by a divine being.

THE HIGH VIEW OF DIVINE PROVIDENCE

The purpose of this chapter is to explain in some detail the two major perspectives on divine providence: the high view of providence, which affirms exhaustive divine foreknowledge and denies divine risk, and the low view of providence, which denies exhaustive divine foreknowledge and affirms divine risk.[1]

The Classical View of Providence

What is now called the classical view of divine providence was first explicitly articulated by St. Augustine. According to Augustine, God possesses infallible knowledge of all events throughout the course of history. God has complete foreknowledge, but he does not apprehend the future as we do, "for he does not pass from this to that by transition of thought, but beholds all things with absolute unchangeableness; so that . . . those things which emerge in time . . . are by him comprehended in his stable and eternal presence."[2] God, then, is not essentially a temporal being. He enters into time, but he is not limited by it. So there is no

---

[1] For a good analysis of two versions of the high view of providence (viz. Augustinianism and Molinism), see Thomas Flint's analysis in "Two Accounts of Providence," in *Divine and Human Action: Essays in the Metaphysics of Theism*, ed. Thomas V. Morris (Ithaca, N.Y.: Cornell University Press, 1988), 147-181.

[2] Augustine, *The City of God*, trans. Marcus Dods (New York: Hafner, 1948), 1:460.

increase in his knowledge, as "all that was to be in time, what and when we were to ask of him, to whose asking and to what requests he should hearken or not hearken, were known to him beforehand without any beginning."[3]

God's exhaustive foreknowledge, Augustine maintains, implies the predetermination of all things, including human actions. Human wills, he says, "have just so much power as God willed and foreknew that they should have. . . . Whatever they are to do, they are most assuredly to do, for He whose foreknowledge is infallible foreknew that they would have the power to do it. . . ."[4] Furthermore, Augustine insists that this divine foreknowledge and the determinism it implies are consistent with human freedom. God granted us a genuine power to will our actions, which is sufficient to secure our moral responsibility. Thus, "we are by no means compelled, either, retaining the prescience of God, to take away the freedom of the will, or, retaining the freedom of the will, to deny that He is prescient of future things, which is impious. But we embrace both. We faithfully and sincerely confess both. The former, that we may believe well; the latter, that we may live well. . . ."[5] So Augustine espoused an early version of *compatibilism*, the view that determinism and human freedom (and therefore moral responsibility) are logically compatible.

The Augustinian model of providence in particular, and the doctrine of God generally, was embraced and reiterated by the most preeminent Christian theologians and biblical scholars over the course of the next 1,500 years. St. Anselm, for example, affirmed that God is not bound by time, confessing that God "dost not exist in space or time, but all things exist in thee. For nothing contains thee, but thou containest all."[6] In consequence of this, Anselm reasoned, God must also be "impassible." That is, God does not experience emotions as human beings do. We passionately experience God, but God himself has no passions.[7]

Continuing the Augustinian tradition, Thomas Aquinas explicated a doctrine of God that featured a high view of providence. Divine omni-

---

[3] Augustine, *The Trinity*, trans. John Burnaby, in *Augustine: Later Works* (Philadelphia: Westminster Press, 1955), 8:152.
[4] Augustine, *The City of God*, 1:194-195.
[5] Ibid., 1:196.
[6] Anselm, *Proslogium*, in *Basic Writings*, trans. S. N. Deane (La Salle, Ill.: Open Court, 1962), 71.
[7] Anselm holds, perhaps paradoxically, that God is both compassionate and passionless. He writes, "How . . . art thou compassionate and not compassionate, O Lord, unless because thou art compassionate in terms of our experience, and not compassionate in terms of thy being" (ibid., 59).

science, he maintained, includes all things actual and potential: "God knows all things whatsoever that in any way are. . . . Whatever therefore can be made, or thought, or said by the creature, as also whatever He Himself can do, all are known to God, although they are not actual."[8] But Aquinas is careful to point out that divine knowledge is not merely passive. Rather, "the knowledge of God is the cause of things. For the knowledge of God is to all creatures what the knowledge of the artificer is to things made by his art."[9] Such divine knowledge as the cause of things he calls the "knowledge of approbation."

So God is, as it were, a cosmic artist, directing the world down to every last detail, as "the causality of God . . . extends to all being."[10] This includes human beings, who differ from "natural things" by their capacity to deliberate and freely choose courses of action. And, Aquinas adds, "since the very act of free will is traced to God as a cause, it necessarily follows that everything happening from the exercise of free will must be subject to divine providence."[11] In this way, Aquinas, like Augustine before him, affirms both human freedom and theological determinism. The two teachings are compatible, he maintains, "for human providence is included under the providence of God."[12]

With the Protestant Reformation came a new emphasis on divine providence, applied in particular to the matter of salvation. Martin Luther emphatically reiterated the classical doctrine of God, saying, "it is . . . essentially necessary and wholesome for Christians to know that God foreknows nothing contingently, but that he foresees, purposes and does all things according to His immutable, eternal and infallible will."[13] God's perfect foreknowledge, again, follows upon his active governance of the world. As his creatures, "we are subject to God's working by mere passive necessity."[14] So when it comes to salvation and moral goodness, we are utterly at God's mercy. Luther compares the will of each human being to a beast of burden. "If God rides it, it wills and goes whence God

---

[8] Thomas Aquinas, *Summa Theologica*, trans. English Dominican Fathers (New York: Benziger Brothers, 1947), 1:79.
[9] Ibid., 1:78.
[10] Ibid., 1:122.
[11] Ibid., 1:123.
[12] Ibid.
[13] Martin Luther, *The Bondage of the Will*, in Ernst F. Winter, *Erasmus—Luther: Discourse on Free Will*, trans. Ernst F. Winter (New York: Frederick Ungar, 1961), 106.
[14] Ibid., 130.

wills. . . . If Satan rides, it wills and goes where Satan wills. Nor may it choose to which rider it will run, nor which it will seek. But the riders themselves contend who shall have and hold it."[15]

Luther was quite aware that this view of providence invites criticism regarding the problem of evil. If God controls human wills, then how can we be blamed for our wrong choices? And doesn't God's sovereignty over evil threaten his own goodness? Luther's approach to the matter is typical among classical theologians. He prefers simply to affirm as a biblical fact both divine sovereignty and divine goodness in the face of human evil, rather than to explain *how* they are compatible. "When God works in and by evil man, evil deeds result. Yet God cannot do evil Himself, for he is good. He uses evil instruments. . . . The fault which accounts for evil being done when God moves to action lies in these instruments which God does not allow to lie idle. . . ."[16] So God's actions are not to be measured or evaluated by us. On the contrary, his will "is itself the measure of all things." God's will is perfect; so "what takes place must be right, because He so wills it."[17]

It was after a millennium of such frank confessions of theological determinism that John Calvin reiterated the doctrine. Yet today it is his name that is most typically identified with it. Calvin asserts, "there is no erratic power, or action, or motion in creatures, but that they are governed by God's secret plan in such a way that nothing happens except what is knowingly and willingly decreed by him."[18] All divine decrees are for the purpose of bringing about God's own glory. Calvin's is a deeply theocentric theology, but his deterministic framework is not so austere as to ignore the obvious human benefits of this doctrine, for "in times of adversity believers [may] comfort themselves with the solace that they suffer nothing except by God's ordinance and command, for they are under his hand."[19]

There is no place in Christian theology for "chance" or "fortune," Calvin maintained. In fact he considered these to be "pagan terms." Still even those who affirm divine sovereignty sometimes make the mistake

---

[15] Ibid., 112.

[16] Ibid., 130.

[17] Ibid.

[18] John Calvin, *Institutes of the Christian Religion*, trans. Ford Lewis Battles (Philadelphia: Westminster Press, 1960), 1:201.

[19] Ibid., 1:200.

of using such expressions, the reason being that "God's providence does not always meet us in its naked form, but God in a sense clothes it with the means employed."[20] These are the "instruments" to which Luther referred, otherwise known as *secondary causes* used by God to accomplish his will on earth. This includes not only the "natural" evils that befall us but also those deliberately caused by other human beings. Even these "moral" evils "are so governed by [God's] providence that they are borne by it straight to their appointed end."[21] As for the problem of evil, Calvin, again with Luther, eschews the notion that there is any problem of the sort, just because God is absolutely sovereign and therefore can do whatever he wants with his creatures. For this reason, Calvin declares, "it is sheer folly that many dare with greater license to call God's works to account, and to examine his secret plans, and to pass as rash a sentence on matters unknown as they would on the deeds of mortal men."[22]

The Puritan theologian Jonathan Edwards fashioned a thoroughgoing classical theology in the Augustinian tradition. Like those before him, he affirmed God's essential atemporality, declaring that "there is no succession in God's knowledge, and the manner of his knowledge is to us inconceivable."[23] He also affirmed the doctrine of exhaustive divine foreknowledge, which includes the voluntary actions of human beings. And divine foreknowledge of all events, Edwards argues, implies the predetermination of all things. For if the prior knowledge of the event is infallible, "then it is impossible it should ever be otherwise . . . and this is the same thing as to say, it is impossible but that the event should come to pass: and this is the same as to say that its coming to pass is *necessary*."[24] Edwards, too, affirms the impassibility of God, reasoning that if God has predetermined all things, he cannot be surprised, disappointed, or grieved as human beings are.[25]

Like others in the Augustinian tradition, Edwards takes a compat-

---

[20] Ibid., 1:216.

[21] Ibid., 1:207.

[22] Ibid., 1:211-212.

[23] Jonathan Edwards, *Freedom of the Will*, in *The Works of Jonathan Edwards* (Edinburgh: Banner of Truth, 1974), 1:38.

[24] Ibid., 1:38-39 (emphasis his).

[25] Edwards asserts that "there is no such thing *truly* as any pain, or grief, or trouble in God" (*Remarks on Important Theological Controversies, op. cit.,* 2:529).

ibilist approach to the issue of human freedom, but he develops a much more rigorous philosophical account than any of his predecessors. He defines freedom as the ability to act according to one's choice, as opposed to the libertarian approach endorsed by Arminian theologians. Either the movement of one's will is caused by one's motives or its choices are uncaused and therefore arbitrary. If one's choices are arbitrary, then one can hardly be morally responsible. So rather than undermining human moral responsibility, Edwards argues, determination of the will preserves it. The Arminian view, on the other hand, unwittingly sabotages moral responsibility by implying that freedom requires an absence of a cause for volition.[26]

Simple Divine Foreknowledge

Despite its long and venerable history,[27] the classical or "Augustinian" view of providence has come under fire from those who take the libertarian approach to human freedom. Specifically, this is the view that defines a free act as one that is solely determined by the person's will. A free person, therefore, has the *power of contrary choice*. In other words, a person has acted freely only if given precisely the same circumstances, one could have chosen differently from what he or she actually chose. Critics of the Augustinian view argue that if God has decreed the whole of history, including human choices, then we cannot have the power of contrary choice. But, of course, Scripture clearly teaches that God foreordains events in history. So what alternative is there for the libertarian who wishes to avoid the fatalist conclusion that humans are not really free?

The doctrine of simple divine foreknowledge (SF) reverses the relation between divine foreknowledge and foreordination as affirmed by the Augustinian view, so that instead God's decrees are based upon his foreknowledge of events. SF affirms that God's knowledge of the future, like his knowledge of the past, is absolute. Even Jacob Arminius was unwavering on this point, declaring that "the understanding of God is certain and infallible; so that he sees certainly and infallibly, even, things

---

[26] Jonathan Edwards, *Freedom of the Will*, op. cit., 1:13-30.

[27] My survey of the classical view highlights only some of the more outstanding figures. Scores of others could have been included, particularly since the eighteenth century, including Charles Hodge, B. B. Warfield, Charles Spurgeon, Louis Berkhof, and John Murray.

future and contingent, whether he sees them in their causes or in themselves."[28] John Wesley also took this perspective, even as applied to the free choices of human beings: "God foreknew those in every nation who would believe, from the beginning of the world to the consummation of all things."[29] Such exhaustive foreknowledge precludes the possibility of divine risk in creating the world, which is why I am categorizing SF as a version of the high view of providence as I have defined it.

Proponents of SF claim that their view preserves human freedom by locating the origin of our actions in human wills, as opposed to the decrees of God.[30] Additionally, they say, this has the salutary effect of shielding God from accusations of evil. After all, if God's knowledge is logically consequent to our choices, then his providential activity is not the ultimate source of our immorality or of the suffering that follows from it. God merely foresaw our free choices, both good and evil; he did not cause them.

The doctrine of simple divine foreknowledge might appear to be a handy way of dealing with some serious objections to the Augustinian view of providence. But it actually creates more problems than it solves, and I will summarize just a few of these. First, SF makes divine foreknowledge providentially useless. Proponents of SF insist that God ordains events on the basis of his prescience. But the very notion is incoherent, since his foreknowledge is certain and infallible. Therefore, the events foreseen by him are unalterable, and thus his knowledge of them cannot be used to truly influence them. As William Hasker puts it, "it is clear that God's foreknowledge cannot be used either to *bring about* the occurrence of a foreknown event or to *prevent* such an event from occurring. . . . In the logical order of dependence of events, one might say, by the 'time' God knows something will happen, it is 'too late' either to *bring about* its happening or to *prevent* it from happening."[31]

But SF is not only incoherent—it also has devastating implications regarding the nature of God. For one thing, SF undermines divine free-

---

[28] Jacob Arminius, "Disputation 17," in *Writings*, trans. James Nichols (Grand Rapids, Mich.: Baker, 1956), 2:37.

[29] John Wesley, "On Predestination," in *The Works of John Wesley*, third edition (Peabody, Mass.: Hendrickson, 1991), 6:226.

[30] For a good contemporary exposition of this view, see David P. Hunt, "Divine Providence and Simple Foreknowledge," *Faith and Philosophy* 10:3 (July 1993): 394-414.

[31] William Hasker, *God, Time, and Knowledge* (Ithaca, N.Y.: Cornell University Press, 1989), 57-58.

dom. If God has known from eternity all of the actions he will perform in history, then it is impossible for him to act in contradiction to this knowledge. He can neither refrain from performing actions he has foreseen himself performing, nor perform actions that he has not foreseen himself performing. All of his actions for all of history are bound and determined. And, of course, this means that God is not free.[32]

Such divine determinism further implies that God is not omnipotent, assuming the SF proponent's libertarian definition of freedom as the power of contrary choice. Given this view, an omnipotent being is one who, at least, has the power to refrain from performing some actions he actually performs or to perform some actions he actually refrains from performing. On the SF view, God has no such power. His certain and infallible knowledge of the future necessitates his acting in all of the ways foreseen by him. He has no power to act otherwise, so he is not omnipotent.[33]

There are yet more devastating implications regarding God's goodness. To be morally responsible, an agent must act on the basis of intentions and a decision to perform actions because the agent deems them to be good. But if God is bound to act as he does by what he foresees himself doing, then his actions are not the result of his intentions and decisions to perform good acts. And, notes Richard R. La Croix, "even if all of God's acts are in fact good, it cannot be because of the goodness of those acts that God performs them and, hence, God's intrinsic goodness cannot consist, even in part, in the fact that God performs all of the acts that he does perform on the grounds that they are good."[34] This clearly implies that God is not intrinsically good.

Finally, SF undercuts the personhood of God. The capacity for intentional action based on reasons and motives is essential to personhood. But by affirming that God's activity is necessitated by his foreknowledge, SF precludes the possibility of God acting on the basis

---

[32] This is precisely the problem that motivated Luis de Molina to devise his theory of middle knowledge, to be discussed next. Molina writes, "I [do not] understand very well how complete freedom would be preserved in God if, before the act of His will, He foreknew which part it was going to be turned toward. For if such knowledge existed, then He would in no way be able to choose the opposite part; thus, if He foreknew before that determination which part His will was going to be turned toward, then I do not see at what point He had the freedom to choose the opposite part" (*On Divine Foreknowledge*, trans. Alfred J. Freddoso [Ithaca, N.Y.: Cornell University Press, 1988], 171).

[33] I borrow this criticism (and those that follow) from Richard R. La Croix. See his "Omniprescience and Divine Determinism," *Religious Studies* 12:3 (1976): 374ff.

[34] Ibid., 376.

of reasons and motives. Hence, this view implicitly denies that God is a person.

Suppose the defender of SF tries to avoid these implications by appealing to God's atemporality. Since God is outside of time, one might say, he never truly "*foresees*" anything. Thus, God is not bound in advance of his providential activity. Unfortunately for SF, such a move either fails to solve the problems noted above or collapses SF into the Augustinian doctrine of providence. This is because given divine atemporalism, either God's decrees depend upon his perfect knowledge or vice versa. If the former, then all of the devastating implications of SF remain (again, assuming libertarianism), since God's actions are still determined by what he knows. If the latter, then SF is abandoned in favor of the Augustinian doctrine that God knows on the basis of his decrees. So the problem with SF has not to do with a particular view of God's relation to time but with the notion that God's foreknowledge is logically prior to his providential decrees.

These are just some of the intolerable implications of the SF claim that God's foreknowledge is logically prior to his decrees. In their attempt to solve some admittedly difficult problems, proponents of SF forfeit some basic attributes of God—his freedom, power, goodness, and personhood.

The Molinist View of Providence

The doctrine of divine middle knowledge, also known as Molinism, aims to overcome the sorts of problems that plague SF. This theory dates back to the sixteenth century when it was devised by Jesuit theologians, most prominently Luis de Molina, after whom the theory is named.[35] Molinists distinguish between three different logical moments of divine knowledge. On the one hand, God has knowledge of all the possible worlds he could create, including all of the different beings he could make and all of their actions. This is what Molinists call God's *natural knowledge*, for he is aware of all possible worlds by his very nature. In addition to his natural knowledge God knows completely the world he

---

[35] See Molina, *op. cit.* For recent expositions of Molinism, see William Lane Craig, *The Only Wise God: The Compatibility of Divine Foreknowledge and Human Freedom* (Grand Rapids, Mich.: Baker, 1987) and Thomas P. Flint, *Divine Providence: The Molinist Account* (Ithaca, N.Y.: Cornell University Press, 1988).

has actually brought into existence, inclusive of all future events. Such knowledge is the result of God's own free act of creation and thus is referred to as his *free knowledge*.

Now in addition to God's natural knowledge of possible worlds and his free knowledge of the actual world, he also possesses knowledge of which worlds he could create that are consistent with creaturely freedom. For only some possible worlds contain genuinely free beings. And God has complete knowledge of what all free beings *would* do in those various possible worlds. Such truths are known as *counterfactuals*—hypothetical propositions about what *would* be the case if something else were the case. Molinists call such hypotheticals regarding free human choices *counterfactuals of freedom*. And they refer to God's knowledge of these as divine *middle knowledge*, for like free knowledge it is not essential to God's nature, but like natural knowledge it is logically "prior to any free act of God's will." [36] God chose to create the world he did based upon his middle knowledge of how free beings would act in various circumstances. [37]

The Molinist perspective aims to preserve a strong notion of divine sovereignty. God's plan for the world is guaranteed fulfillment because he knew prior to creation just what every person in that world would do in every circumstance that would arise. But the freedom of all human beings is also respected. For God's middle knowledge of how they would freely act forms the basis of his choice in creation, not vice versa. Molinists embrace a libertarian conception of freedom, and their view is largely an attempt to reconcile a high view of providence with this view of freedom. The result is that Molinists are even able to affirm divine predestination. But, as in SF, they do so by asserting the logical priority of God's foreknowledge to his predetermining of the elect.

While Molinists are to be commended for their concern to guard the high view of providence and make sense of human freedom and responsibility, the doctrine of divine middle knowledge is deeply problematic. The central difficulty with Molinism concerns the truth-value of so-called counterfactuals of freedom. In any instance of knowledge, what a person knows is grounded in some fact. If I know the Detroit Lions won last

---

[36] Luis de Molina, *op. cit.*, 168.
[37] Some biblical texts seem to provide direct support for the doctrine of divine middle knowledge. See, for example, 1 Sam. 23:6-13 and Matt. 11:20-24.

Sunday, it is because there is some fact of the matter (i.e., the Lions winning) to which my knowledge corresponds. But on this analysis, the future actions of persons with libertarian freedom cannot be known, for there simply is no fact of the matter to be known. If a free person has the power either to perform an act or refrain from performing it, then her action is indeterminate until she has performed it. Thus, even God cannot know what a free creature *would* do, for there is no factual ground for such knowledge. This problem, known as the "grounding objection," is widely recognized as devastating to Molinism.[38]

Some Molinists, such as William Lane Craig, try to overcome this problem by insisting that counterfactuals of freedom such as "S would do X in circumstance C" are analogous to future-tense statements such as "S *will* do X in circumstance C." Craig notes that in the latter instance, it is not necessary that the circumstances in question actually exist but only that they will exist. Similarly, he says, "at the time at which counterfactual statements are true, it is not required that the circumstances or actions referred to actually exist." All that is required, says Craig, is "that such actions *would* be taken if the specified circumstances *were* to exist."[39]

However, Craig's response really just begs the question, for here he simply insists that counterfactuals of freedom have truth-value. But this is precisely the question at issue. The only way that counterfactuals of freedom can have truth-value is if they denote some determinate fact, which by definition they do not. And it is here that the analogy with future tense statements is off the mark. A statement such as "S will do X" does denote something determinate, though it has yet to occur. If in fact S will certainly do X, then the statement is true now, in spite of the fact that S has not yet done X. The same cannot be said about the statement "S would do X in circumstance C," at least given a libertarian perspective, because the person's freedom leaves it open as to whether or not this statement is true. There just is no fact to which the statement can correspond, and hence the statement cannot have a truth-value, so it cannot be an item of knowledge, even for God.[40]

---

[38] For good articulations of this objection see Robert M. Adams, "Middle Knowledge and the Problem of Evil," *American Philosophical Quarterly* 14:2 (April 1977): 109-117 and Steven B. Cowan, "The Grounding Objection to Middle Knowledge Revisited," *Religious Studies* 39:1 (2003): 93-102.

[39] William Lane Craig, *op. cit.*, 140 (his emphasis).

[40] For a related but distinct criticism of the doctrine of middle knowledge, see William Hasker, *op. cit.*, 39-52.

It seems that the core idea within Molinism is incoherent. They regard conditionals such as "S would do X in circumstance C" as having the same logical status as statements such as "S did do X" or "S will do X." Simply put, they treat counterfactuals as if they were factual. The only way out for the Molinist is to recognize that what God foresees *is* indeed factual, that for God our future is as certain as what is past or present. But, of course, to affirm this is to reject Molinism.

I conclude that simple divine foreknowledge and divine middle knowledge are not plausible alternatives to the Augustinian doctrine of meticulous providence. Therefore, for the remainder of this book I will be concerned with a specifically Augustinian perspective. And some of the applications that I make in the latter part of this book will fit more naturally with this view. However, despite my rejection of both simple foreknowledge and middle knowledge, proponents of both perspectives may still affirm most of the particular benefits of providence discussed in this book. I do not mean to exclude members of these other camps. I do, however, mean to exclude advocates of the low view of providence, as will soon become obvious. I aim to demonstrate that those who believe in divine risk lose out on many theoretical and practical benefits of divine providence.

Essential Features of the High View of Providence

In light of the preceding survey, the primary tenets of the high view of providence (Augustinianism as well as SF and MK) may be summarized as follows:

1) *Exhaustive divine foreknowledge*: God knows every true proposition, and he cannot be mistaken in any of his beliefs. Since God is not limited by time, events that will occur in our future are already known to him, even as certainly as he knows past events. Augustinians and proponents of SF and MK differ as to which is logically prior, God's knowledge or his determination of the future. But they agree that all events in history, including the volitions of free human beings, were fully known by God before he created the world. So God cannot be surprised by anything that happens.

2) *Divine control*: God sovereignly controls the world. Augustinians regard this as involving immediate, active control of all world events,

including human choices. SF and MK allow for such control to be understood in terms of divine permission of particular events, though given God's foreknowledge or middle knowledge, he created the world knowing precisely how and when those events would occur. So whether the details of history are directly or indirectly governed, divine control over the world is absolute.

3) *Divine purpose*: God governs his creation intentionally, directing the details of the universe with the highest end in view, his own glory. Moreover, God acts redemptively in history on behalf of his people, the church of Christ. God loves, forgives, protects, preserves, and will ultimately reward us. Augustinians unabashedly assert that God predestines some for eternal life and others for destruction. Proponents of SF and MK affirm predestination but only as a consequence of divine foreknowledge, as God created the world knowing who will or would obtain eternal life.

4) *Divine sovereignty over evil*: Suffering and immorality are sovereignly governed by God. Although undesirable in themselves, God works to use these things for the betterment of his people and the advancement of his own glory. Augustinians and proponents of SF and MK disagree about the mode of divine control over evil, but both camps assert that God knowingly and intentionally created a world in which such evils were bound to occur.

As corollaries to these essential tenets, the high view of providence entails that: (a) divine omniscience is inclusive of all free human choices, (b) God's ultimate plan for the world is guaranteed to succeed, because he is the cosmic sovereign, and (c) whatever sin or suffering occurs in the world is somehow consistent with God's ultimate plan for the world. Of course, some serious philosophical and theological questions arise in light of (a) and (c). For instance, how can human freedom and moral responsibility be reconciled with the high view? Whether the future is divinely predetermined or merely exhaustively foreknown by God, the appearance of freedom in our choices might seem to be illusory. And how can one affirm God's goodness while at the same time affirming that God wills sin and suffering in the world? If God really hates sin, then this seems to rule out the possibility that he could foreordain immoral actions. It is just such thorny problems that have motivated contemporary reconsiderations of the doctrine of divine providence, as we shall see in the next section.

THE LOW VIEW OF DIVINE PROVIDENCE

Like the high view of providence, the low view comes in varying degrees, admitting more or less divine control.[41] But the claim that all versions make in common, and which is definitive for the categories employed here, is that *God takes risks*. As I am using these terms, the low view of providence affirms, while the high view denies, that God is a risk-taker.

Before surveying several varieties of the low view, it will be helpful to clarify the concept of risk-taking. What does it mean to say that one "takes a risk" in performing an action? There are at least three conditions required for an act to be properly considered risky: (a) the agent must not know (in advance) all of the effects of the agent's act, (b) the agent must not completely control all of the effects of the act, and (c) there must be some real possibility of harm or loss resulting from performance of the act, whether that misfortune befalls the agent himself or herself or persons for whom the agent cares. To summarize this definition, we might say that *a risky act is one that might result in unforeseeable and uncontrollable misfortune*. Given this understanding of risk, it is clear that proponents of the high view of divine providence deny that God is a risk-taker. Augustinians, Molinists, and proponents of simple divine foreknowledge would, however, characterize their rejection of (a) and (b) differently, as we have seen.

So the high view of providence denies that God takes risks. Historically, this has been the predominant position of Christians on the matter, though every era of church history has seen critics of this view. However, in the twentieth century the high view of providence was subjected to especially fierce critique by scholars from diverse theological camps. In recent years this criticism has even crept into evangelical theological circles, a noteworthy fact in itself. Some members of the most conservative camp of Christian theology now accept teachings formerly

---

[41] I do not mean this terminology to prejudice the discussion, through any association between "high" and "good" or "low" and "bad." I considered using other terms to denote the distinction I am making here, but other candidates (such as "strong" and "weak") seemed even more problematic. Hence, I have chosen these terms, albeit with some dissatisfaction, because they are descriptive, convenient, and the least apparently prejudicial among potentially serviceable terms.

considered heretical by mainstream Christian thinkers. I am referring to the central claims of openness theology: that God does not know the future exhaustively, that he can be mistaken in his beliefs and even have his plans thwarted by humans. Such ideas are not new in Christian theology, as liberal theologians have entertained them for generations. However, proponents of these ideas have typically denied the absolute authority of Scripture. What is unique about openness theology is that its proponents confess scriptural authority, many even affirming biblical inerrancy. Yet its substantive claims about divine providence are much in line with its liberal theological precursors. Let us review these precursors briefly, as this will provide some helpful historical background to openness theology.

Process Theology

The idea that God changes in diverse ways as a result of his relation to the world is the main distinctive of process theology. The founder of this movement, philosopher Alfred North Whitehead, distinguished between two aspects of a "dipolar" divine nature—a "primordial" nature and a "consequent" nature. According to Whitehead, the primordial nature of God is "free, complete . . . eternal, actually deficient, and unconscious," whereas the consequent side of God's nature "is determined, incomplete . . . 'everlasting,' fully actual, and conscious."[42] Although God is distinct from the world, he does not really transcend the world. He is *with* and *in* the world, changing and growing through his interaction with the world. Similarly, the world itself is "impotent to achieve actuality apart from the completed ideal harmony, which is God."[43] So both God and the world are actualized through each other's influence.

But how can God be perfect and yet change? Charles Hartshorne further developed the idea of a dipolar, changing God in such a way as to address this common objection to process theology. Hartshorne redefines divine perfection to mean that God is "better than any individual other than himself."[44] He says, "God is *perfect in love*, but never-completed, *ever growing*, (partly through our efforts) in the joy, the richness

---

[42] Alfred North Whitehead, *Process and Reality* (New York: The Free Press, 1978), 345.
[43] Alfred North Whitehead, *Religion in the Making* (New York: New American Library, 1974), 115.
[44] Charles Hartshorne, *Reality as Social Process* (Glencoe, Ill.: The Free Press, 1953), 157.

of his life, and this without end through all the infinite future."[45] So God is surpassable, but only by himself. As for God's knowledge, he anticipates the future as we do. He "know[s] future events only in their character as indefinite, or more or less problematic, nebulous, incomplete as to details."[46] God is able to predict the future, as humans do, only probabilistically, seeing "the range of possible things among which what happens will be a selection."[47] So God grows in understanding as he experiences the world with us, but this does not rule out divine omniscience, according to Hartshorne, since "omniscience does not mean the total absence of growth or change."[48] His explanation for so truncating the doctrine of divine omniscience is: "This seems to be the only view of God's knowledge that does not make human freedom impossible."[49]

When working out the doctrine of God, all process theists pay close attention to the implications of the doctrine regarding relevance to human life and significance. To be fully relational, process theologian Schubert Ogden maintains, "God must enjoy real internal relations to all our actions and so be affected by them in his own actual being."[50] In this regard, he conceives of God as the "supremely relative reality" as well as absolute reality. God is essentially social, but to be so, Ogden reasons, he must also be temporal, experiencing events within time just as human beings do.[51]

So the God of process theism is a far cry from the God of orthodox Christianity.[52] Whereas the latter is independent of the world, unchanged by historical events, and essentially atemporal, the former is dependent upon the world, conditioned by events, and essentially temporal. God, in this view, is neither sovereign nor creator of the world, but he influences the world, even as the world influences him.[53]

---

[45] Ibid., 156 (emphasis his).
[46] Ibid., 158.
[47] Ibid., 161.
[48] Ibid., 158.
[49] Ibid., 162.
[50] Schubert Ogden, *The Reality of God* (New York: Harper and Row, 1963), 47.
[51] Ibid., 63.
[52] For an excellent summary and critique of process theology or, as it is sometimes called, "panentheism," see Norman Geisler's *Encyclopedia of Christian Apologetics* (Grand Rapids, Mich.: Baker, 1999), 576-580. For a more thorough critical analysis, see Eric C. Rust's *Evolutionary Philosophies and Contemporary Theology* (Philadelphia: Westminster Press, 1969).
[53] Process theist John Cobb sums it up this way: "The character of the world is influenced by God, but it is not determined by him, and the world in its turn contributes novelty and richness to the divine experience." From *God and the World* (Philadelphia: Westminster Press, 1969), 80.

Political Liberation Theology

The liberation theology movement of the 1970s and 80s was a further departure from historic Christian thought, as some influential Latin scholars used theology to work toward radical political change. In this movement, the focus and purpose of theological scholarship shifted from understanding the nature of God to the practical function of freeing the oppressed, particularly Latin Americans who were victimized by an exploitative capitalistic economic system. Many liberationists argued that this requires the defeat of capitalism and justifies the use of violence to free the oppressed. In some cases, political revolution was countenanced. The more extreme liberation theologians even espoused wedding Marxism to their Christian theology.[54]

A leading figure in this movement was Gustavo Gutierrez. Unlike most of his fellow liberationists, Gutierrez strove to make a biblical case for his theology, but his rejection of the traditional approach to divine providence, in favor of an anthropocentric view of history, is nonetheless evident. Gutierrez endorses "a historical vision in which mankind assumes control of its own destiny."[55] "In this perspective," he argues, "the unfolding of all of man's dimensions is demanded—a man who makes himself throughout his life and throughout history. The gradual conquest of true freedom leads to the creation of a new man and a qualitatively different society."[56] This vision for a new society is, for liberationists, defined in terms of freedom. Thus, Leonardo Boff proclaims, "total liberation and its attendant freedom is the essence of God's kingdom."[57] For liberationists this freedom is an emancipation from oppression and other forms of suffering that are constituted by unjust relations between human beings.[58]

As in Latin liberation theology, black liberation theologians focus

---

[54] See Jose P. Miranda, *Marx and the Bible: A Critique of the Philosophy of Oppression*, trans. John Eagleson (Maryknoll, N.Y.: Orbis Books, 1974) and *Communism in the Bible*, trans. Robert R. Barr (Eugene, Ore.: Wipf & Stock Publishers, 2004).

[55] Gustavo Gutierrez, *A Theology of Liberation*, trans. Caridad Inda and John Eagleson (Maryknoll, N.Y.: Orbis Books, 1973), 25.

[56] Ibid., 36-37.

[57] Leonardo Boff, *Jesus Christ Liberator: A Critical Christology for Our Time* (Maryknoll, N.Y.: Orbis Books, 1978), 281.

[58] For critical discussions of liberation theology from an evangelical perspective, see Humberto Belli and Ronald Nash, *Beyond Liberation Theology* (Grand Rapids, Mich.: Baker Books, 1992) and Raymond C. Hundley's *Radical Liberation Theology: An Evangelical Response* (Wilmore, Ken.: Bristol Books, 1987).

heavily on relief of suffering, specifically the oppression of African-Americans by the white American majority. This emphasis often informs their doctrine of God. A case in point is James Cone, who writes, "despite the emphasis on future redemption in present suffering, black theology cannot accept any view of God that even *indirectly* places divine approval on human suffering."[59] Given this restriction, Cone reasons that "Providence . . . is not a statement about the future. It does not mean that all things will work out for the best for those who love God. Providence is a statement about present reality—the reality of the liberation of the oppressed."[60] And he adds: "It is within this context that divine omnipotence should be interpreted. Omnipotence does not refer to God's absolute power to accomplish what he wants."[61] Instead, Cone prefers to see God's power as concerned solely with liberation of the oppressed.

Feminist Theology

Like political liberationists, feminist theologians focus on the problem of human oppression. But rather than simply rejecting the Augustinian view of providence, they see this perspective itself as the *source* of much oppression. In particular, they critique the tendency to conceive of God as dominating rather than working with the world, as is manifest in the traditional metaphors for God, such as "king," "ruler," and "sovereign." Sallie McFague writes that this "monarchical model is dangerous in our time: it encourages a sense of distance from the world . . . and it supports attitudes of either domination of the world or passivity toward it."[62] Feminists underscore the mutuality and reciprocity in God's relations with his creatures. Their metaphors of choice, therefore, include God as "mother," "lover," "healer," and "friend."

The advantage of such terminology is that it points up the intimacy of God's relationship to us. As Anne Carr explains, "feminist images of God as mother, sister, and friend suggest that God's self-limitation is such

---

[59] James Cone, "God Is Black," in *Lift Every Voice: Constructing Christian Theologies from the Underside*, eds. Susan B. Thistlethwaite and Mary P. Engel (San Francisco: Harper Collins, 1990), 93 (emphasis his).
[60] Ibid.
[61] Ibid.
[62] Sallie McFague, *Models of God* (Philadelphia: Fortress Press, 1987), 69.

that in a relational and incarnational framework God's power is *in humans* as embodied human agents. God's liberating action occurs through human power and action that imitates the persuasive, nonviolent power of God. . . ."[63] McFague explores the more radical alternative conception of the world as "God's body" or, less fancifully, as "the self-expression of God."[64] Such a model, she notes, "emphasizes God's willingness to suffer for and with the world, even to the point of personal risk."[65]

The suffering of God is a recurrent theme within feminist theology. Since God cares for and loves his people, who themselves so often experience injury and grief, God's loving nature guarantees that he will participate in that suffering. So, Carr writes, "the compassionate God of the experience of women means *a suffering God*."[66] It also entails the pain of personal loss for God, for as McFague notes, "a lover feels the pain of the beloved deep within himself and would undergo any sacrifice to relieve the pain."[67] Such suffering, she adds, "is not salvific but it is inevitable: it is a risk incurred by all who confront evil by siding with those who suffer and are oppressed."[68]

Many other aspects of the feminist doctrine of God are configured in light of this emphasis on divine compassion and suffering. For instance, according to Elizabeth Johnson, "speaking of the suffering God from a feminist liberation perspective entails reshaping the notion of omnipotence."[69] She advocates "seeing love as the shape in which divine power appears."[70] Rather than conceiving of divine power as essentially controlling or overpowering, she develops a model emphasizing God's power as "relational, persuasive, erotic, connected, loving, playful, empowering. . . ."[71]

Thus, like process theists, feminist theologians reject classical theism. But, like political liberation theologians, they approach the doctrine

---

[63] Anne Carr, *Transforming Grace* (New York: Continuum, 1988), 152, emphasis hers.

[64] Sallie McFague, *op. cit.*, 72.

[65] Ibid.

[66] Anne Carr, *op. cit.*, 152 (emphasis hers).

[67] Sallie McFague, "The Ethic of God as Mother, Lover and Friend," in *Feminist Theology: A Reader*, ed. Ann Loades (Louisville: Westminster Press, 1990), 264.

[68] Ibid.

[69] Elizabeth Johnson, *She Who Is* (New York: Crossroad, 1992), 269.

[70] Ibid.

[71] Ibid., 270.

of God less metaphysically, stressing the social and moral dimensions of God's relationship to the world. The feminist theologians emphasize such themes as the cooperative work of God (concerned primarily with ending oppression), the liberating power of God, the suffering love of God, and the compassionate, comforting presence of God with his creatures. All of these themes are aspects of the broader feminist emphasis on the relationality of God, a vital concern they share with process theists and political liberationists.[72]

Openness Theology

None of the process theists, liberation theologians, or feminist thinkers mentioned in the preceding survey could be categorized as evangelical in their orientation.[73] That proponents of openness theology (or "open theism" as it is sometimes called) often regard themselves as evangelicals is what is distinctive about this most recent anti-classical theological movement.[74] Open theists share many aspects of their doctrine of God with some of the scholars just discussed. It would be naive to think these similarities are entirely coincidental. But whether or not their unorthodox doctrines are borrowed directly from these alternative theologies, open theists believe their position is not only consistent with evangelical conviction but, in fact, required by it.

To summarize the open view of providence is to see just how closely akin it is to the other low theologies of providence just discussed. Open theists maintain that: (1) God is bound by time and does not entirely know the future, (2) God's power is limited by human freedom, (3) God fundamentally opposes all human suffering, while (4) God himself suf-

---

[72] For an excellent critical assessment of feminist theology, see Mary A. Kassian, *The Feminist Gospel: The Movement to Unite Feminism with the Church* (Wheaton, Ill.: Crossway Books, 1992).

[73] By "evangelical" I intend to imply, at least, a commitment to the view that the Bible is absolutely authoritative, infallibly trustworthy on all matters to which it speaks. Although most of the open theists I identify in this section regard themselves as evangelicals, some of them do not. Still, it is worth noting their claims, if only because their influence is being significantly felt within the evangelical fold.

[74] I have two terminological disclaimers to make here. First, the general tags "openness theology" and "open theism" are not precise labels, nor are the other terms I have used above—"process theology," "liberation theology," and "feminist theology." The diversity of opinion among scholars typically given these labels makes neat and uncontestable grouping impossible. Nevertheless there is enough uniformity of opinion to justify use of these terms to gather scholars together under single names for ease of discussion. Second, many open theists prefer the appellation "relational theism" for their view. I have decided against usage of this designation only because such terminology might suggest that those of the Augustinian persuasion do not affirm the relationality of God, which, on the contrary, all in fact do.

fers as his involvement with the world leads to divine surprise, disappointment, sorrow, anger, and other real passions.

Open theists emphasize God's relational nature. Accordingly, they eschew the Augustinian perspective because they deem it to be irreconcilable with the belief that God maintains real personal relationships with human beings.[75] John Sanders, for instance, prefers to call his view "relational theism," meaning by this "any model of the divine-human relationship that includes genuine give-and-take relations between God and humans such that there is receptivity and a degree of contingency in God. In give-and-take relationships God receives and does not merely give."[76] Similarly, David Basinger maintains that the scriptural portrait is that of "a God who interacts with his creation in the sense that he responds to what he experiences in an attempt to bring about his desired goals."[77] Like process theists, open theists defend a dipolar theism, where God's nature may be conceived as both "actual" and "potential." God is not only absolute, necessary, eternal, and changeless but is *also* relative, contingent, temporal, and changing, insofar as he relates and responds to his creation.[78] Such a view implies a comprehensive recasting of the doctrine of God.

In openness theology divine relationality entails that God cannot be omniscient as traditionally understood. Open theists reject the notion that God has exhaustive knowledge of all events past, present, and future. Instead they affirm that "God knows everything about the future which it is logically possible for him to know."[79] Future free human actions are not knowable in advance by any being, so they cannot be included among the things that God knows. Therefore, open theists affirm divine "present knowledge," whereby, as David Basinger puts it, "God's infallible knowledge extends over everything that is (or has been)

---

[75] Vincent Brummer's theological "model of love" has been very influential among some open theists and has helped to stimulate this emphasis on God's relational nature. See *The Model of Love: A Study in Philosophical Theology* (New York: Cambridge University Press, 1993) and *Speaking of a Personal God: An Essay in Philosophical Theology* (New York: Cambridge University Press, 1992).

[76] John Sanders, *The God Who Risks: A Theology of Providence* (Downers Grove, Ill.: InterVarsity Press, 1998), 12.

[77] David Basinger, "Can an Evangelical Christian Justifiably Deny God's Exhaustive Knowledge of the Future?" *Christian Scholar's Review* 25:2 (December 1995): 142.

[78] See Richard Rice's assertion of this essential common ground between process theism and open theism in *God's Foreknowledge and Man's Free Will* (Minneapolis: Bethany House, 1980), 33.

[79] William Hasker, *op. cit.*, 187.

actual and that which follows deterministically from it," excluding any future states of affairs that involve free human choices.[80]

This modified view of divine omniscience also allows for randomness. Sanders asserts that "God makes room for indeterminacy or chance. Though God sustains everything in existence, he does not determine the results of all actions or events, even at the subatomic level."[81] The open theists see this element of caprice as a source of potential good. As T. J. Gorringe sees it, "many advantages attach to a universe where chance is a fundamental factor. The unexpected stimulates our creative potential and 'provides both the stimulus and the testing to promote our spiritual evolution.'"[82]

Openness theology also modifies the traditional understanding of divine omnipotence. God's power is restricted by the freedom of human beings. And the fulfillment of his plans for history is dependent upon the choices we make. Therefore, like process theology, openness theology affirms that human beings and God work together to achieve God's ends. "Some important things are left in the hands of humanity as God's co-creators such that we are to collaborate with God in the achievement of the divine project."[83] In many particulars, therefore, the course of history is finally contingent upon human choices rather than on divine wisdom. But, the open theists reassure us, this need not cause us fear. For, as Clark Pinnock notes, "God is omnicompetent in relation to any circumstance that arises and is unable to be defeated in any ultimate sense."[84]

Such assurances are not meant to guarantee that God will not fail in some of his projects. On the contrary, to the open theists, biblical history clearly shows that God is sometimes disappointed and frustrated.[85] Sanders sums up God's efforts to accomplish his goals: "God persuades, commands, gives comfort and sometimes brings judgment in order to get humans to sign on to his project. God genuinely wrestles with his

---

[80] David Basinger, "Can an Evangelical Christian Justifiably Deny God's Exhaustive Knowledge of the Future?" 134. Richard Swinburne defends a similarly temporally restricted account of divine omniscience in *The Coherence of Theism* (Oxford: Oxford University Press, 1993), 167-183.

[81] John Sanders, *op. cit.*, 215.

[82] T. J. Gorringe, *God's Theatre: A Theology of Providence* (London: SCM Press, 1991), 14. Gorringe quotes D. J. Bartholomew from *God of Chance* (London: SCM Press, 1984), 98.

[83] John Sanders, *op. cit.*, 44.

[84] Clark Pinnock, "God's Sovereignty in Today's World," *Theology Today* 53:1 (April 1996): 21.

[85] See Richard Rice's "Biblical Support for a New Perspective," in *The Openness of God: A Biblical Challenge to the Traditional Understanding of God* (Downers Grove, Ill.: InterVarsity Press, 1994), 56.

human creatures. Sometimes God gets everything he wants, and sometimes he does not."[86] This is the essence of the "risk model" of providence endorsed by Sanders and his fellow open theists. The outcome of any event is not determined in advance. God neither controls nor knows all of the future. He waits eagerly to see what will happen next, just as we do. This is why Sanders can seriously ask, "Is God a fool? Will his attempts at restoration succeed?" His answer is: "Only the history of God's activity and the human response to it will tell."[87] However, Sanders admits, "sometimes God's plans do not bring about the desired result and must be judged a failure."[88]

Implied in the concept of divine risk is the notion that God is an essentially temporal being, dwelling entirely inside time with his creatures (a view shared by process and liberation theologians). But it is not solely from the other aspects of their doctrine of God that open theists infer God's temporal nature. They also base their case on biblical descriptions of divine action in the world. William Hasker argues, "if God is truly timeless, so that temporal determinations of 'before' and 'after' do not apply to him, then how can God *act* in time, as the Scriptures say that he does?"[89] Rice's reasoning is similar: "To say that God acts . . . means that it makes sense to use the words *before* and *after* when we talk about him. God makes decisions and then he acts. . . . After God acts, the universe is different and God's experience of the universe is different. The concept of divine action thus involves divine temporality."[90] Although insisting that God is time-bound, open theists do not necessarily oppose usage of the term "eternal" to describe him. They simply understand it to mean that he always has and always will exist.[91]

There is a further motive for the open theists' rejection of divine atemporalism. As Richard Rice observes, "there seems . . . to be no way

---

[86] John Sanders, *op. cit.*, 60.
[87] Ibid., 49. Elsewhere, he states that "in the risk model everything does not happen precisely as God intends. God experiences setbacks and even defeats. Given the sort of world God created, there is opportunity to question the divine wisdom. Even if we cannot blame God for evil, we can still wonder whether it was worth the risk of embarking on the project" (p. 183).
[88] Ibid., 88.
[89] William Hasker, "A Philosophical Perspective," *The Openness of God*, 128.
[90] Richard Rice, "Biblical Support for a New Perspective," *The Openness of God*, 36.
[91] See, for example, Clark Pinnock's discussion of God's eternity in "Systematic Theology," in *The Openness of God*, 119-121. For a rigorous defense of the temporality of God, see Nicholas Wolterstorff's "God Everlasting," in *God and the Good*, eds. Clifton Orlebeke and Lewis Smedes (Grand Rapids, Mich.: Eerdmans, 1975).

to avoid making God responsible for evil if we accept the usual view of God's relation to time."[92] If God is outside time, then he knows the future as well as the past. This implies that God knew all the evil that would occur before the creation of the world. Thus, open theists affirm instead that God is within time and that God did not know in advance that human beings would sin. So, says Rice, "God is responsible only for the possibility of evil (simply because he created morally free beings). But He is not responsible for the actuality of evil. The creatures are entirely to blame for that."[93]

Openness theology affirms that God is fundamentally opposed not only to moral evil but to human suffering of all kinds. God works continually to relieve pain and suffering in all its forms, whether caused by human beings or not. And we who are involved in the work of God contribute to that redemptive project. On this point the open theists follow the feminists and liberation theologians. Together they affirm that God's battle against evil is a real struggle, with real defeats for God along the way. For, as Gregory Boyd asserts, "God must work with, and battle against, other created beings. While none of these beings can ever match God's own power, each has some degree of genuine influence within the cosmos."[94]

Because terrible suffering occurs in the lives of the people he loves, God himself suffers, say the open theists. Here, too, they agree with the liberationists and feminists, but their defense of the doctrine is more biblically based. As Pinnock explains, "the suffering or pathos of God is a strong biblical theme. . . . God suffers when there is a broken relationship between humanity and himself. . . . God is not cool and collected but is deeply involved and can be wounded."[95] Herein lies another key element of "risk" in God's creation of a world of free beings. Not only does such a world pose the possibility of creaturely suffering but also of divine suffering. In creation God risked regarding his people and himself.

To sum up the open theists' view of providence, they affirm divine

---

[92] Richard Rice, *God's Foreknowledge and Man's Free Will*, 51.

[93] Ibid., 51-52. Similarly, Pinnock asserts that "God may be responsible for creating a world with moral agents capable of rebelling, but God is not to blame for what human beings do with their freedom" ("God's Sovereignty in Today's World," 19).

[94] Gregory Boyd, *God at War: The Bible and Spiritual Conflict* (Downers Grove, Ill.: InterVarsity Press, 1997), 20.

[95] Clark Pinnock, "Systematic Theology," *The Openness of God*, 118.

sovereignty only in a very broad sense. God elected to create human beings free and to allow history to proceed on its own without controlling every detail. He neither perfectly knows nor directly controls all of history. In openness theology divine providence involves, first, divine *responsiveness*. As Rice says, "Providence involves God's creative response to events as they happen."[96] Of course, God does not respond to all events but only to some. For this reason, this view might be described as a "containment" view of sovereignty. Secondly, providence entails divine *accountability*. "God is," Sanders claims, "in control in the sense that God and God alone is responsible for initiating the divine project and for establishing the rules under which the game operates."[97] And, as already noted, providence involves divine *risk*, which as Basinger points out, may be understood in at least two senses: "God is a risk-taker in the sense that he commits himself to a course of action without full knowledge of the outcome; and God is a risk-taker in the sense that he adopts certain overall strategies—for example, the granting of significant freedom—which create the potential for the occurrence of events that he wishes would not occur."[98]

CONCLUSION

My aim in this chapter has been to survey the major views of divine providence. I have distinguished two principal perspectives, based on their affirmation or denial of divine risk. What I am calling the high view of providence denies that God takes risks and affirms God's exhaustive foreknowledge and complete control of the world. The low view of providence, on the other hand, denies exhaustive divine foreknowledge and affirms the reality of divine risk. There are multiple versions of each perspective. Proponents of the high view include Augustinians, Molinists, and advocates of simple divine foreknowledge. I argued that both the Molinist and simple foreknowledge perspectives are fatally flawed, but I welcome proponents of these views to affirm many of the constructive aspects of this book nonetheless.

The low view of providence is a relatively recent phenomenon in the

---

[96] Richard Rice, *God's Foreknowledge and Man's Free Will*, 73.
[97] John Sanders, *op. cit.*, 215.
[98] David Basinger, *The Case for Free Will Theism* (Downers Grove, Ill.: InterVarsity Press, 1996), 48.

history of theology, at least as a concerted theological movement. Openness theology is an increasingly popular version of the low view. As with its precursors, there are significant philosophical concerns driving this perspective, most significantly the problem of human freedom and the problem of reconciling God's goodness with sin and suffering. In the next chapter I will examine some other factors that have contributed to the rise of openness theology. This will form a part of my larger task to critically assess the low view of providence.

2

ASSESSMENT OF THE TWO VIEWS OF PROVIDENCE

In the previous chapter two basic perspectives on divine providence were distinguished. The high view of providence affirms God's complete control over creation, which entails exhaustive divine foreknowledge and purposeful control over all that happens in the world. Three principal versions of this view were discussed: Augustinianism, Molinism, and simple divine foreknowledge. The former affirms meticulous divine governance of the cosmos, while the others place logical priority on God's foreknowledge. I argued that Molinism and the simple foreknowledge perspective suffer serious conceptual problems that should incline proponents of the high view to favor the Augustinian variety. Accordingly, in the constructive portions of this book (Chapters 3-7), I will assume and apply the Augustinian perspective. Even so, I will also assume that these other views remain live options for proponents of the high view, and their proponents may readily affirm many of the constructive claims that follow in this book.

The other main view of divine providence affirms the reality of divine risk. Process theology, liberation theology, feminist theology, and openness theology each deny exhaustive divine foreknowledge and affirm that God's activity in the world is such that it might result in unforeseeable and uncontrollable misfortune. In this chapter I aim to show that this perspective is unbiblical, but in doing so I will focus upon openness theology. I will do so for two reasons. First, currently more popular than other views affirming divine risk, openness theology is considered by many Christians to be a compelling theological alternative. There is a pressing need to correct this mistaken impression. Second, unlike process, liberationist, and feminist theologians, open theists assume Scripture to be absolutely authoritative, and they strive to prove that their view is biblical. Given this assumption, they maintain the low view of providence to be more reasonable than the high view. Let us, then, take a closer look at their biblical arguments to see if this is the case.

OPEN THEIST BIBLICAL ARGUMENTS

In the first chapter we surveyed the major themes in openness theology. Here I want to summarize the arguments they use to justify their belief in divine risk or what I am calling the low view of providence. Their primary arguments appeal to the following:

(1) *Conditional statements*. Sometimes God's instructions to his people in the Old Testament are framed in the form of "if-then" statements, such as in Nehemiah 1:8-9 where the Lord says to the Israelites, "if you are unfaithful, I will scatter you among the nations, but if you return to me and obey my commands, then even if your exiled people are at the farthest horizon, I will gather them from there and bring them to the place I have chosen as a dwelling place for my name." (See also Exod. 4:8-9 and Lev. 26.) Such language seems to indicate that there is uncertainty as to how the Israelites will behave, that the future is open, and that God himself is not sure about the outcome. Elsewhere God speaks about the future using such terms as "perhaps" and "maybe" (for example, Ezek. 12:3 and Jer. 26:3). Again, these are not expressions one would expect from a God who knows the future exhaustively.

(2) *Divine regretting and relenting*. Scripture sometimes speaks of God grieving over a turn of events and regretting some of his own actions, such as his creation of human beings (Gen. 6:6) and his making Saul king (1 Sam. 15:11). Divine regrets suggest that history was not determined in advance or perfectly foreknown. Still other passages indicate that God relents from plans he has made, as he declares through Jeremiah: "If at any time I announce that a nation or kingdom is to be uprooted, torn down and destroyed, and if that nation I warned repents

of its evil, then I will relent and not inflict on it the disaster I had planned" (Jer. 18:7-8). (See also Exod. 32:14, Isa. 38:1-5, Joel 2:13, Amos 7:1-6, and Jonah 3:10.) These narratives seem to describe a God who is genuinely responsive to human choices and who, therefore, is essentially temporal.

(3) *Petitionary prayer.* The Bible enjoins us to make requests of God. As Jesus says, "Ask and it will be given to you; seek and you will find; knock and the door will be opened to you. For everyone who asks receives; he who seeks finds; and to him who knocks, the door will be opened" (Matt. 7:7-8). And James says "you do not have, because you do not ask God" (Jas. 4:2).[1] But if such prayers are to be meaningful and effective, then there must be a real possibility of a literal divine response. Therefore, in the words of Pinnock, "prayer proves that the future is open and not closed. It shows that future events are not predetermined and fixed."[2]

(4) *Divine ignorance and error.* Biblical narrative depicts God as learning new truths on various occasions, such as when he says to Abraham, "Now I know that you fear God, because you have not withheld from me your son, your only son" (Gen. 22:12). And, according to some open theists, God occasionally makes mistakes.[3] For example, when commenting on the wanton behavior of his people, God says, "I thought that after she had done all this she would return to me but she did not" (Jer. 3:7; see also Jer. 32:35). These passages suggest that even God is subject to false beliefs about the future. If this is so, then, indeed, the future is not predetermined, and the doctrine of divine omniscience does need reworking along the lines suggested by open theists.

Divine Atemporalism and Sempiternalism

I will respond to each of these arguments in turn. But first an important preliminary issue must be discussed, specifically that of God's relationship to time.[4] The open theists' belief that God is bound by time, known

---

[1] See also Phil. 4:6.

[2] Clark Pinnock, "God Limits His Knowledge," in *Predestination and Free Will*, ed. David Basinger and Randall Basinger (Downers Grove, Ill.: InterVarsity Press, 1986), 152.

[3] See, for example, John Sanders's *The God Who Risks: A Theology of Providence* (Downers Grove, Ill.: InterVarsity Press, 1998), 129-137, 205-206. Sanders supplements this argument with the claim that some biblical prophecies are not fulfilled.

[4] I will discuss the issue of God's relationship to time in much greater detail in Chapter Five.

as *sempiternalism*, is a crucial tenet of their perspective. For if God is not essentially temporal, then he cannot literally "respond" to historical events, as open theists claim. There are several reasons for rejecting the sempiternalist view. First, as Paul Helm has argued, God is not essentially a spatial being, so he cannot be essentially temporal.[5] The arguments that prove God to be spaceless are from a logical standpoint strictly parallel to arguments that prove him timeless. Conversely, arguments for sempiternalism are analogous to arguments that God is essentially spatial. Regarding the question of God's relation to time and space, then, there is logical parity. Either God is spaceless and timeless, or he is essentially spatial and temporal. Thus, open theists must choose between admitting divine *atemporalism* or admitting that God is an essentially spatial being. The latter option is obviously absurd, so they must surrender their sempiternalism.

Secondly, the Bible's descriptions of God's acting in time and his acting in space should be interpreted analogously. Spatial metaphors are used in the Bible to describe God, and certain of his activities take place in space. For instance, in 2 Samuel God declares, "I have not dwelt in a house from the day I brought the Israelites up out of Egypt to this day. I have been moving from place to place with a tent as my dwelling" (7:6). In many other passages, the "hands," "arm," "mouth," "feet," and "nostrils" of God are referred to, as are his actions in space, such as dwelling in temples and cities and performing miraculous acts of parting seas, healing bodies, and impregnating a virgin. But neither spatial metaphors nor accounts of God's spatial activities should be taken to imply that God is bound by space. Rather, they communicate to us something about God's nature and show that he can and does perform actions in the spatial realm. So why suppose that analogous temporal descriptions of God and his actions in time are sufficient to show that he is essentially temporal? Rather, temporal descriptions of God should be interpreted as showing that he enters and acts in time, not that he is bound by it.[6]

---

[5] Paul Helm, "God and Spacelessness," *Philosophy* 55 (1980): 211-221.
[6] On this point see Hugh J. McCann, "The God Beyond Time," *Philosophy of Religion*, second edition, ed. Louis Pojman (Belmont, Calif.: Wadsworth, 1994), 232.

Conditional Statements

We are now in a position to evaluate the key biblical arguments employed by the open theists. Consider the "if-then" conditional statements and promises used by God. Do such expressions really imply that the future is undetermined or even unknown by him? Not at all. Rather, they serve some valuable functions pertaining to moral theology. First, conditional statements are means of instructing people about God's moral will and informing them as to the consequences of their actions, depending upon what course of action they take. In turn, such conditionals serve to prompt human action of some kind, such as repentance when wrath is threatened. Second, "if-then" promises express general truths about the nature of God's dealings with us, whether or not the conditional antecedent "if" is ever fulfilled. For example, even if no one trusts and obeys God, it remains true that God *would* bless those who trust and obey him. In this sense, conditional statements are timelessly true, applying to God's relations to all people at all times.

In any case, it must be borne in mind that if God is an essentially atemporal being who enters into time to communicate with essentially temporal creatures, then we should expect him to use language that is appropriately condescending. "If-then" conditionals and temporally tensed language (e.g., "now," "then," "before," "after," "yesterday," "tomorrow," etc.) serve as vehicles to assist our understanding and help us relate to God. So it is no surprise that such expressions are used in biblical narrative. How else would a timelessly eternal being communicate with temporal creatures to whom the future is largely unknown?

Divine Relenting and Regretting

A similar approach may be taken for cases of divine relenting and regretting. That such passages are not to be interpreted as literal descriptions of the mind of God follows from the fact that God is not essentially temporal. Moreover, some biblical passages caution us against taking this interpretation, such as 1 Samuel 15:29, which says "the Glory of Israel does not lie or change his mind; for he is not a man, that he should change his mind" (see also Num. 23:19). This is not to say that those passages that describe God as relenting are misleading or false, for they do communicate something very important—namely, the depth of God's compassion and the extent of mercy that he is willing to show to sinful human beings.

Furthermore, as in the case of conditional statements, the point of references to divine relenting is often moral. God makes threats and warns of coming wrath to prompt righteous behavior. Descriptions of divine relenting are simply a powerful way of communicating the usefulness of repentance to avoid that wrath which, without repentance, *would* have been visited upon those God warns. Similarly, references to divine regret should be interpreted as describing God's disapproval of some human behavior, not as an indication that God literally wishes he had not performed some action.

Petitionary Prayer

What of the open theists' appeal to petitionary prayer as evidence for their perspective? What are we to make of the biblical injunction to make requests of God? While God's command should be enough justification for our petitionary prayer, there are two other points worth noting. First, God has ordained prayer as a secondary cause for the accomplishment of his will. So in this sense our petitions really do impact the world.[7] However, God does not *need* our prayers to realize his plans in history and in individual human lives. To believe so would undermine his omnipotence. Nor is he ignorant of our needs such that he must be made aware of them before he can properly assist us. To believe so would undercut his omniscience. Besides, it is clear from Scripture that God foreknows our prayers. For example, consider the narrative in Genesis 20. King Abimelech had taken possession of Sarah, not knowing she was Abraham's wife. After threatening to kill Abimelech, God said to him, "Return the man's wife, for he is a prophet, and he will pray for you and you will live" (v. 7). In the meantime, God closed the wombs of all women in Abimelech's household. But then we learn that "Abraham prayed to God, and God healed Abimelech, his wife and his slave girls so they could have children again" (v. 17).

---

[7] As Aquinas notes, "Divine providence disposes not only what effects shall take place, but also from what causes and in what order these effects shall proceed. Now among other causes human acts are the causes of certain effects." And, of course, prayer is one such act. So, says Aquinas, "we pray, not that we may change the Divine disposition, but that we may impetrate [ask for] that which God has disposed to be fulfilled by our prayers." From *Summa Theologica*, trans. English Dominican Fathers (New York: Benziger Brothers, 1947), 2:1539.

A second crucial function of prayer is its role as a spiritual discipline. As John Calvin says, God "ordained [prayer] not so much for his own sake as for ours,"[8] and the effect it has upon the believer should not be underestimated. Calvin writes:

> It is very important for us to call upon him: First, that our hearts may be fired with a zealous and burning desire ever to seek, love, and serve him, while we become accustomed in every need to flee to him as to a sacred anchor. Secondly, that there may enter our hearts no desire and no wish at all of which we should be ashamed to make him a witness, while we learn to set all our wishes before his eyes, and even to pour out our whole hearts. Thirdly, that we be prepared to receive his benefits with true gratitude of heart and thanksgiving, benefits that our prayer reminds us come from his hand.[9]

Thus, Calvin says, prayer stimulates desire for God, purges shameful desires, and inspires a grateful attitude. Also, to pray is to exercise faith, to remind oneself of one's dependence upon God, to grow in the virtue of humility, and to be directly comforted by the Holy Spirit in the process of prayer.

So petitionary prayer need not change God's mind to be tremendously useful. Anyway, such a notion has absurd implications, as Eleonore Stump has shown in a fascinating treatment of the topic.[10] She argues as follows: It is God's will to bring about the best possible world, and every petitionary prayer enjoins God to perform some action that will change the world for better or worse overall. Now if taking such action will make the world worse overall, then obviously God will decline the request. But if it will make the world better overall, then God would have performed the action anyway, so the request was unnecessary. Therefore, petitionary prayer really does not change God's mind or alter his actions.

Stump offers a second argument suggesting that such a view puts too much power in the hands of human beings for determining other peoples' destinies. Stump asks us to consider the prayers of Monica for her

---

[8] John Calvin, *Institutes of the Christian Religion*, trans. Ford L. Battles (Philadelphia: Westminster Press, 1960), 2:852.

[9] Ibid.

[10] Eleonore Stump, "Petitionary Prayer," *American Philosophical Quarterly* 16:2 (April 1979): 81-91.

son, St. Augustine: "If one supposes that God brought Augustine to Christianity in response to Monica's prayers, what is one to say about Augustine's fate if Monica had not prayed for him? And what does this view commit one to maintain about people who neither pray for themselves nor are prayed for?"[11] The frightening prospect of such a view is that Augustine might not have been saved had his mother not prayed. Hence, it turns out, his eternal destiny (and the fates of the rest of us?) was really in the hands of a mere mortal. Similarly, the fates of those ultimately lost may, to some degree, be blamed on those who never prayed for them. Such a view is both counterintuitive and biblically implausible.

Divine Ignorance and Error

The argument from divine ignorance and error is less frequently made by open theists but must be addressed nonetheless, for it constitutes a direct attack on the doctrine of divine omniscience. As with the other three open theist arguments, this one can be dismissed once it is shown that God is not essentially temporal. Since God is not bound by time, he cannot "come to know" anything. Rather, he knows all things from a timelessly eternal standpoint, the future as well as the past. Therefore, narratives in which God is depicted as apparently learning something new or being mistaken in his beliefs must be taken as nonliteral. They are included in the biblical accounts presumably to underscore God's real interaction with his people within time. Other functions are served by such expressions as well. For example, when he says to Abraham, "Now I know that you fear God" (Gen. 22:12), this communicates to Abraham, and to the reader, that Abraham has proven his faith in action. The point of the story concerns the way Abraham's behavior evidences his commitment to God, not to suggest that God has learned something new.

The open theist argument from divine error is especially disturbing since it does not merely suggest a lack of some knowledge on God's part but affirms actual mistakes God has made: God thinks X is true when actually X is false. The implications of such a doctrine are severe. If God can be epistemically mistaken, then perhaps he can make moral errors as well. If God can falsely believe proposition X is *true*, then might he

---

[11] Ibid, 88.

not also falsely believe act Y is *good*? Thus, even God's prohibitions of such things as stealing and adultery might be mistaken. Or, even more troubling, perhaps God can *act* wrongly, as might be suggested by Genesis 6:6, where God regrets having made human beings. Such is the slippery slope occasioned by the doctrine of divine error. To affirm that God errs in his plans opens the possibility of other blunders, even moral mistakes. This clearly undermines the holiness of God and flouts the biblical portrait of God.[12]

BIBLICAL EVIDENCE FOR THE AUGUSTINIAN VIEW OF PROVIDENCE

Having responded to each of the open theists' arguments and having shown the devastating implications of their view, we will now consider a positive biblical case for the Augustinian view of providence. Earlier we saw how the greatest thinkers in the history of Christian theology—Augustine, Anselm, Aquinas, Luther, Calvin, and Edwards—take this approach. Now let us see *why* there is such agreement on this issue among these formidable theologians.

Evidence for Absolute Divine Sovereignty

In short, Scripture teaches that God is absolutely sovereign. According to the biblical account, God controls the world at every level:

(1) *God is sovereign over the entire cosmos.* God's cosmic sovereignty consists, first, in the fact that he created the universe and he continually sustains it. As Paul writes in Colossians 1:16-17, "by him all things were created. . . . He is before all things, and in him all things hold together." (See also Rev. 4:11 and Job 38—41.) Second, God's cosmic sovereignty consists in his carrying out a plan for the cos-

---

12 The likely counter-reply to this argument by open theists who affirm divine epistemic error is that Scripture so clearly teaches that God is holy and perfectly good that this slippery-slope argument has no force. The Bible itself is our safeguard against compromising the biblical doctrine of God, they will say. But such a response misses the point and in a very ironic way. For the root of the problem with the open theists is that they are willing to reinterpret Scripture to fit their philosophical theology (as will become more apparent later in this chapter). And if they have done so with the doctrines of divine providence, immutability, omnipotence, and omniscience, then we have reason to expect that other elements of the doctrine of God will eventually be targeted. Thus, the essence of the debate between the open theists and classical theists is not just theological but methodological. And, of course, it is historical as well, since these scholars are willing to scuttle centuries of theological consensus in the Christian church in order to accommodate some contemporary philosophical trends.

mos that is subject to no one's will but his own. In Isaiah 46:10 God says, "I make known the end from the beginning, from ancient times, what is still to come. I say: My purpose will stand, and I will do all that I please." Similarly, the psalmist writes, "The LORD does whatever pleases him, in the heavens and on the earth, in the seas and all their depths" (135:6).

(2) *God is sovereign over human history and leaders of nations.* God directs the courses of whole nations, as is clear in such passages as Joshua 24, Jeremiah 18:6, Ezekiel 26:1-6, and Daniel 5:18-21. And he governs those who rule nations, as Proverbs 21:1 makes clear: "The king's heart is in the hand of the LORD; he directs it like a watercourse wherever he pleases." The case of Pharaoh is a vivid example of this. In the face of numerous plagues on his people, he did not let Moses' people go. Rather, as the writer of Exodus states on several occasions, God hardened Pharaoh's heart (Exod. 4:21; 9:12; 10:20; 11:10). And in Exodus 9:16 God explains to Pharaoh, "I have raised you up for this very purpose, that I might show you my power and that my name might be proclaimed in all the earth."

(3) *God is sovereign over particular human choices and "chance" events.* While Scripture emphasizes human moral responsibility and the importance of wise counsel and decision-making, it is also clear that God governs all aspects of human decision-making. Proverbs 16:9 says, "in his heart a man plans his course, but the LORD determines his steps." (See also Prov. 20:24 and Acts 17:26.) Even seemingly random events are divinely controlled, as Proverbs 16:33 says: "the lot is cast into the lap, but its every decision is from the LORD." Indeed, didn't the disciples assume divine sovereignty over chance events when they drew lots to choose Judas's replacement (Acts 1:24-26)?

(4) *God is sovereign over the church and over individual Christians' lives.* Scripture speaks especially clearly to God's care for his people, as the psalmist declares: "All the days ordained for me were written in your book before one of them came to be" (139:16). In the New Testament Paul repeatedly applies a doctrine of meticulous providence to individual salvation, saying that God "chose us in [Christ] before the creation of the world to be holy and blameless in his sight. In love he predestined us to be adopted as his sons through Jesus Christ, in accordance with his pleasure and will" (Eph. 1:4; see also 2 Thess.

2:13). And a little later in Ephesians he asserts that in Christ "we were also chosen, having been predestined according to the plan of him who works out everything in conformity with the purpose of his will" (v. 11). Note that this passage not only affirms the Augustinian view of providence but also offers a three-tiered causal explanation of divine election, moving backwards from specific choice to electing decree to divine purpose: God *chooses* whom he *predestines*, according to *the purpose of his will*.

Paul offers a similar account in Romans, where he declares that "those God foreknew he also predestined to be conformed to the likeness of his Son, that he might be the firstborn among many brothers. And those he predestined, he also called; those he called, he also justified; those he justified, he also glorified" (8:29-30).[13] (Of course, proponents of the high view of providence disagree over whether divine election precedes or follows God's foreknowledge. Here Augustinians differ from Molinists and advocates of simple divine foreknowledge. But this "in-house" debate is actually trivial in comparison to the dispute with the open theists, for the latter deny both divine foreknowledge and divine predestination of the elect.) The doctrine of election is even embedded in the narrative of Acts. In chapter 13 Luke reports that among the Gentiles who heard the gospel message at Antioch, "all who were appointed for eternal life believed" (v. 48). Such language seems inexplicable according to openness theology.

(5) *God is sovereign over suffering and moral evil.* Traditionally, Christians have taken great solace in the biblical teaching that God's sovereignty is not limited, even by suffering and immorality. However counterintuitive this might appear to some, this fact is repeatedly underscored in Scripture. For example, in Exodus 4:11 God assures Moses that not only his speech impediment but all such physical handicaps are his doing. Through Isaiah he says, "I am the LORD, and there is no other. I form the light and create darkness, I bring prosperity and create disaster; I, the LORD, do all these things" (45:6-7).[14] And Jeremiah declares, "though [the Lord] brings grief, he will show compassion, so great is his unfailing love. For he does not willingly bring affliction or grief to the

---

[13] Also, God's foreknowledge and predestination include the fates of unbelievers as well, as passages such as Rom. 9:14-24, Rev. 13:8, and 17:8 reveal.

[14] See also Lam. 3:38 and Amos 3:6.

children of men" (Lam. 3:32-33).[15] This is an especially significant passage, as it affirms both the active hand of God in human affliction *and* divine regret about it. This directly confutes open theists who assume the two are incompatible.

The biblical writers do not flinch in subsuming even the evil actions of sinful human beings under the sovereign influence of God. As was noted above, Pharaoh's evil resistance follows upon the Lord's hardening of his heart. Similarly, Saul's murderous pursuit of David was prompted by "an evil spirit from the LORD" (1 Sam. 19:9; see also 1 Sam. 18:10 and Judges 9:23). And all of Job's sufferings are attributed, in the end, to God himself (Job 42:11), showing that Satan is but a pawn on the world's stage. Finally, there is the passion of Jesus. The scourging, crucifixion, and death of Jesus, as well as his resurrection, were all in God's plan. On the Day of Pentecost Peter says to some fellow Jews that Jesus "was handed over to you by God's set purpose and foreknowledge; and you, with the help of wicked men, put him to death by nailing him to the cross" (Acts 2:23).[16]

Predictive Prophecy and Divine Sovereignty

God's sovereignty over all aspects of creation is further established by predictive prophecy in the Bible. In hundreds of instances God foretells events, often in extraordinary detail, long before they occur. Scores of prophecies are made and fulfilled within the Old Testament period. Over two hundred Old Testament messianic prophecies are fulfilled by Jesus Christ, from the place of his birth to the manner of his death. And some other prophecies are made and fulfilled within the New Testament, such as Jesus' prediction of Peter's threefold denial. This is powerful evidence that either God has predetermined history or, at least, he has exhaustive knowledge of the future.

Open theists deny this implication. Their standard response to this argument is to regard all unconditional predictive prophecies as either

---

[15] Adding to the force of these biblical passages are the testimonies of some prominent persons of faith in the Old Testament who frankly affirm God's sovereignty. See Hannah's prayer (1 Samuel 2:6-7), the song of Moses (Deut. 32:39), and Job's reflections on his own agony (2:10). Each frankly affirms God's sovereignty.

[16] Divine governance over all things is communicated in a variety of ways in Scripture, as we have seen. But perhaps the most descriptive metaphor is that of the potter and the clay. It is an image used by the Old Testament prophets (Isa. 29:16 and Jer. 18:6) and Paul in the New Testament (Rom. 9:20-21).

"the announcement ahead of time of that which God intends to ensure will occur . . . or predictions based on God's exhaustive knowledge of the past and present."[17] Now notice that the former explanation admits divine *determination* of the foretold events, which is not an alternative explanation from the classical position. In order to maintain their view, then, open theists must rely on the latter explanation of unconditional predictive prophecies. William Hasker describes such prophecies as "predictions based on foresight drawn from existing trends and tendencies."[18] Just as we humans make forecasts based on our knowledge of the past and present, God makes his forecasts but can "do it much better" than we can.

The obvious problem with this approach is that it implies God's predictive prophecies are fallible. While his predictions are vastly more reliable than ours, on the open theist view, God still could be mistaken in some of his predictions. This conclusion contradicts the biblical portrait of God as absolutely trustworthy. Furthermore, this view is not even philosophically plausible, given the open theists' assumptions about human freedom. If, as they claim, God cannot certainly know in advance any particular free choice a person makes, then even perfect knowledge of the past and present would not enable him to reliably predict events in the distant future. Even a partially accurate prediction about an event a century from now presupposes the ability to accurately predict millions of other free choices (which themselves arise due to millions of other preceding free choices). These include decisions leading to human procreation, a single mistake about which would ramify so significantly throughout a few generations—let alone thousands of years—that reliable long-term prediction would be impossible. It seems, therefore, that exhaustive divine foreknowledge is the only reasonable explanation of predictive prophecy about the distant future, particularly as regards the sorts of detailed events foretold in the Old Testament.

---

[17] David Basinger, "Can an Evangelical Christian Justifiably Deny God's Exhaustive Knowledge of the Future?" *Christian Scholar's Review* 25:2 (December 1995): 141. See also William Hasker, *God, Time, and Knowledge* (Ithaca, N.Y.: Cornell University Press, 1989), 194-196; Richard Rice, *God's Foreknowledge and Man's Free Will* (Minneapolis: Bethany House, 1980), 77-79; and Clark Pinnock, "God Limits His Knowledge," in *Predestination and Free Will*, 157-158. Precisely the same account of predictive prophecy is given by each of these scholars.

[18] William Hasker, *God, Time, and Knowledge*, 194.

A Few Hermeneutical Guidelines

This is merely an overview of the major categories of biblical evidence for the Augustinian view of providence. For more detailed defenses of the Augustinian view, I refer the reader to relevant works by D. A. Carson,[19] Paul Helm,[20] Bruce Ware,[21] and R. K. McGregor Wright.[22] Now we must not forget the passages discussed earlier that emphasize God's relational nature, passages that open theists use to defend the low view of providence. Obviously, I have interpreted the biblical data about God's relational nature in light of his sovereignty. But, one may ask, why interpret these expressions to make them fit with the biblical teaching about sovereignty rather than vice versa? My approach (like that of all proponents of the Augustinian view) is based upon a basic hermeneutical guideline. When doing systematic theology, doctrine is more reliably built upon didactic passages (those whose primary purpose is to doctrinally instruct) than upon historical narrative. And the didactic biblical passages heavily favor the Augustinian perspective, while the low view of openness theology rests predominantly upon historical narrative. This is not to say that biblical narrative does not contain considerable evidence for meticulous providence, for it does, particularly in the area of predictive prophecy.

It is also useful here to distinguish between biblical teaching on the *phenomenology* and the *metaphysics* of divine action. The former regards the way God's activity *appears* to human beings, while the latter has to do with the way God *actually* works within and behind the world. Both are real and important aspects of scriptural teaching about God, and we must affirm both fully without allowing our focus on the one to blind us to the other. Open theists have made this mistake, allowing their focus on the phenomenology of divine action (especially as manifested in human choices and actions) to blind them to the metaphysics of divine providence. Thus, they are guilty of the polar opposite mistake of hyper-Calvinists who allow their insights into the meta-

---

[19] D. A. Carson, *Divine Sovereignty and Human Responsibility* (Eugene, Ore.: Wipf and Stock, 2002).
[20] Paul Helm, *The Providence of God* (Downers Grove, Ill.: InterVarsity Press, 1993).
[21] Bruce A. Ware, *God's Lesser Glory: The Diminished God of Open Theism* (Wheaton, Ill.: Crossway Books, 2000); idem, *God's Greater Glory: The Exalted God of Scripture and the Christian Faith* (Wheaton, Ill.: Crossway Books, 2004).
[22] R. K. McGregor Wright, *No Place for Sovereignty: What's Wrong with Freewill Theism* (Downers Grove, Ill.: InterVarsity Press, 1996).

physics of divine providence to blind them to the reality of human freedom and responsibility. Of course, in each instance the mistake is somewhat understandable, as there is much scriptural reflection upon both the metaphysics and phenomenology of divine providence. Open theists have mined the latter passages extensively and have discussed them at length, but they fail to properly interpret the former passages. They commit the egregious mistake of using biblical phenomenological data as evidence for metaphysical claims about God. Consequently, their doctrine of providence is fundamentally unbiblical, and their portrait of God is woefully incomplete.

WHERE THE OPEN THEISTS WENT WRONG

The open theists' concern to preserve and even heighten our recognition of God's relational nature is laudable. The biblical evidence for a high view of providence ought not to blind us to the truth in their view. God is genuinely relational, personally engaged with human beings both individually and corporately. He is caring, loving, and intimately concerned with every detail of our lives. It is crucial that all Christians affirm these essential truths. However, in their zeal to emphasize God's relational nature, open theists have abandoned the classical attributes of divine omniscience, immutability, and atemporality. As we will see, there is no reason to think that divine relationality precludes such attributes. But first let us look more closely at the philosophical and theological concerns motivating the open theists' disavowal of these elements of the doctrine of God.

Toward an Historical Explanation for Openness Theology

In our survey of the theological precursors of openness theology—process theology, liberation theology, and feminist theology—some recurrent themes emerged. Many of them are echoed by the open theists. Positively, open theists affirm God's dynamic relationship with the world, his overriding concern to respect and extend human freedom, and his capacity to suffer and experience real emotion. And negatively, like these alternative theologies, open theists deny divine immutability, exhaustive divine foreknowledge, and God's purposeful use of all suffering.

Of course, no theology develops in an historical vacuum; so we should not be surprised if open theists have taken their cue from these other theological models. But such scholarly influences alone do not explain the twentieth-century drift from the classical doctrine of God and its affirmation of meticulous providence. Could there be some common causes that have independently influenced all of these theologies and help to account for this theological shift? I think there are and would suggest the following as possibilities:

(1) *The contemporary association of sovereignty with tyranny.* The use of the metaphors of royalty to describe God (e.g., "king," "ruler," "sovereign") has become unfashionable. This might be due to the predominance of democratic thinking in the West, or it might just be due to the fact that the last few generations have had too few positive examples of kingship to encourage a healthy use of such descriptions of God. Thomas Boogaart notes that his seminary students "associate kingship with tyranny." To their minds, "the decrees of a sovereign do not bring justice and righteousness to the land, but exploitation and enslavement."[23] And Bernhard Anderson writes, "the word 'kingdom' is alien to the social experience of most people and is charged with objectionable hierarchical meanings. It connotes *superiority over*: one race over another, men over women, people over the environment."[24] If this is so, it is no wonder that theological reactions against the high view of providence have been so strong.

(2) *The retreat from a biblical cosmology.* In the twentieth century the church was prompted to focus heavily on the individual for various reasons. Many Christians perceived scientific discoveries, from biology to astronomy, to be a threat to the authority of Scripture and to biblical faith. Rather than explore the implications of these discoveries for their theological fruitfulness, however, the church retreated. As Boogaart explains, the church "effectively reduced God's activity to saving individual humans, and this privatizing predisposition has affected biblical interpretation and theological discourse."[25] This narrowing of theological focus, from a cosmic perspective to the evangelical focus on indi-

---

[23] Thomas Boogaart, "Deliberation and Decree: The Biblical Model of Sovereignty," *Perspectives* 12:3 (March 1997): 9.

[24] Bernhard Anderson, "The Kingdom, the Power, and the Glory: The Sovereignty of God in the Bible," *Theology Today* 53:1 (April 1996): 5 (emphasis his).

[25] Thomas Boogaart, *op. cit.*, 9.

vidual salvation, naturally influenced the doctrine of God. "Doctrines like sovereignty were cut off from their native theological environment, and they slowly expired in the hearts of believers like beached whales."[26]

(3) *The modern emphasis on individual rights and personal autonomy.* The Western rejection of monarchical forms of government was inspired by a particular moral anthropology that placed a strong emphasis on human rights and individual freedom. Modern political theorists, especially Locke and Rousseau, made human rights the foundation of their social contract theories, and the great Enlightenment philosopher Immanuel Kant saw human reason as autonomous and foundational to all moral duties. Such thinkers transformed Western thought about ethics and political philosophy, inspiring a more anthropocentric perspective to dominate these disciplines. Consequently, today scholars typically assume, rather than argue for, these beliefs: (a) that significant freedom is inconsistent with causal determination, (b) that humans naturally deserve to be happy or at least have a life that is, on the whole, satisfying, and (c) that suffering is susceptible only to an anthropocentric (usually utilitarian) justification, as opposed to a theocentric justification. Even the most perspicacious scholars are inclined to read these questionable philosophical assumptions into their theological meditations.

(4) *The commodification of Western culture.* The assumption of human autonomy, combined with the rise of Western capitalism, has had significant socioeconomic ramifications. Today much of human culture has become commodified, so much so that nearly every aspect of human life is readily viewed as a product or service to be bought, sold, or consumed. This includes American religious life, where even church services are now marketed like any other commodity. Regarding this point, Vincent Miller argues that Americans' cultural training to be consumers penetrates the core of our being. In our society, he observes, "the self is constructed as a chooser, not as one who is called and responds." He adds, "the idea that there might be something more fundamental than [our] choices, that the chooser . . . might need to be questioned . . . does not appear within this system."[27] Obviously, if this analysis is cor-

---

[26] Ibid.
[27] Vincent J. Miller, interview with Ken Myers, in *Mars Hill Audio Journal* 69 (July/August 2004). For Miller's complete analysis, see his *Consuming Religion: Christian Faith and Practice in a Consumer Culture* (New York: Continuum Publishing Group, 2003).

rect, our concept of personal choice will deeply impact our belief systems, including our theological predilections.

(5) *Twentieth-century violence and suffering*. It perhaps goes without saying that contemporary theology has been fundamentally affected by the massive suffering that occurred in the twentieth century, the most violent in history. Two world wars, the Nazi Holocaust, Stalin's purges, and Mao's brutality, as well as the continuing ravages of disease, crime, natural disasters, and social injustice have understandably provoked questions about God's power and goodness. The human need to make sense of such evils in a way that is consistent with one's religious faith is irrepressible. To some this seems to require a rejection of ultimate scriptural authority. Consequently, the emergence of theologies that depart from a truly biblical portrait of God is probably inevitable.

Cultural trends always threaten to seduce the unwary theologian. Open theism is a graphic symptom of the extent to which evangelical thinkers have succumbed to current thought forms. These have influenced other areas of church life as well, including worship, evangelism, and pastoral care. Openness theology, like so much evangelical thinking these days, is: (1) individual-oriented rather than cosmically-oriented, (2) consumer-driven rather than revelation-driven, and (3) historically myopic, ignoring the consensus of the best Christian thinkers over the past two thousand years. Regrettably, much of the church today does not recognize how problematic these trends are, precisely because Christians tend to read Scripture through contemporary cultural lenses.

Such are some possible *cultural-historical* explanations for openness theology, as well as for the other theologies that affirm divine risk.[28] Let us now examine the fundamental *philosophical* motivations for these departures from classical theism. As we have seen, they are: (1) the concern to reconcile God's goodness with human suffering and immorality and (2) the aim to preserve human freedom and moral responsibility in a world governed by God. These are perhaps the two most challenging philosophical puzzles for any theist. So the efforts of open theists to resolve these tensions are admirable in principle. Unfortunately, as we have seen, the model they propose is unbiblical. It would be some con-

---

[28] For a much more detailed discussion of cultural factors inspiring openness theology, see William C. Davis's insightful "Why Open Theism Is Flourishing Now," in *Beyond the Bounds*, eds. John Piper, et al. (Wheaton, Ill.: Crossway Books, 2003).

solation, however, if no adequate approaches to these problems were previously available to Christians. But there *are* other ways of reconciling the classical doctrine of God with human freedom and the presence of evil in the world. Helpful strategies for dealing with these problems already exist, which are philosophically coherent but do not compromise the classical divine attributes. Next I will look at some of these strategies.

Reconciling Evil with the Goodness of God

There are a variety of approaches to the problem of evil that don't require rejection of the orthodox doctrine of God.[29] One promising approach is to recognize the morally constructive effects of evil in many circumstances. John Hick proposes a "soul-making" theodicy that endorses this paradoxical perspective.[30] Human history is a phase in the ongoing divine creative process that will culminate in the full maturation of God's people. Evil is an unfortunate but crucial part of this process. Similarly, Richard Swinburne says, "various evils are logically necessary conditions for the occurrence of actions of certain especially good kinds."[31] For example, forgiveness, courage, and compassion are moral virtues, and it is better for a person to have these virtues than not to possess them. But one cannot forgive unless sinned against. One cannot be courageous except in a dangerous situation where there is a real possibility of harm. Nor can one have compassion without a suffering person toward whom one is compassionate. Hence, evil is necessary for the acquisition of some significant moral goods. And to purpose the development of these virtues entails the purposing of the requisite evils.

Some have taken the "aesthetic" approach to the problem of evil. They argue that suffering and moral wrongs ultimately contribute to the aesthetic value of the cosmos and are therefore desirable in an ultimate sense by the Creator. Augustine was among the first to see evil as enhancing the overall beauty of the cosmos. For example, he notes, "the ugliness of sin is never without the beauty of punishment."[32] Others have

---

[29] Several of these are examined in detail in Chapter 6.
[30] John Hick, *Evil and the God of Love* (New York: Harper and Row, 1978).
[31] Richard Swinburne, "The Problem of Evil," in *Reason and Responsibility*, ed. Joel Feinberg (Belmont, Calif.: Wadsworth, 1993), 87.
[32] Augustine, *On Free Choice of the Will*, trans. Anna S. Benjamin and L. H. Hackstaff (Indianapolis: Bobbs-Merrill, 1964), 123.

followed this line of thinking, including Leibniz, who argued that ours is, in fact, the best of all possible worlds.[33] Most recently, Marilyn McCord Adams has elaborated a personalized version of this perspective. She argues that aesthetic qualities of all kinds, including moral virtues, are essential ingredients in the good life. And evils of various kinds are crucial to the realization of many of those aesthetic valuables. Like Hick, Adams recognizes the ways in which suffering can morally strengthen the soul and help catalyze personal virtue. Even where one does not morally profit or mature as a result of the evils he or she suffers, Adams notes, there are other aesthetic gains to be appreciated, such as dramatically beautiful developments and reversals in one's life or personal relationships. Thus, she says her theodicy "offers a select package of aesthetic goods . . . *sufficient* to guarantee God's goodness even to participants in horrendous evils."[34]

As part of Adams's approach to the problem of evil, she has focused on the tremendous value of suffering for the person of faith. Since Jesus himself suffered terribly, suffering provides "a vision into the inner life of God."[35] John Edelman has gone so far as to suggest that suffering may be seen as the will of God. He demonstrates that major objections to this idea tend to beg the question. Furthermore, he shows the value of suffering for imparting wisdom, not the least aspect of which is recognizing the limits of human power. There is, he says, "a suffering that necessarily accompanies and often occasions this understanding, namely, the suffering—the pain—one feels in running up against those limits. So the understanding and the suffering cannot come one apart from the other."[36]

While this notion is shocking to some, it ought not to be, given that the divine purposefulness of suffering is a plain biblical teaching. James writes, "Consider it pure joy, my brothers, whenever you face trials of many kinds, because you know that the testing of your faith develops perseverance. Perseverance must finish its work so that you may be mature and complete, not lacking anything" (Jas. 1:2-4). And

---

[33] See Leibniz's *Monadology*, sections 54-55.

[34] Marilyn M. Adams, "Aesthetic Goodness as a Solution to the Problem of Evil" in *God, Truth and Reality*, ed. Arvind Sharma (New York: St. Martin's Press, 1993), 58, emphasis hers.

[35] Marilyn M. Adams, "Horrendous Evils and the Goodness of God," in *The Problem of Evil*, eds. Marilyn M. Adams and Robert M. Adams (New York: Oxford University Press, 1990), 219.

[36] John Edelman, "Suffering and the Will of God," *Faith and Philosophy* 10:3 (July 1993): 383.

Peter says that trials "come so that your faith—of greater worth than gold, which perishes even though refined by fire—may be proved genuine and may result in praise, glory, and honor when Jesus Christ is revealed" (1 Pet. 1:7). Such language indicates that suffering is not only consistent with God's will but is intended by him to accomplish his most significant work in his children.

A further argument may be made in support of the idea that God wills our suffering, specifically appealing to the passion of Christ. We begin with the assumption that God intended for Christ to suffer and die (e.g., Isa. 53:10; Acts 2:23). If the divine intention to cause Jesus to suffer does not undermine the goodness of God, then neither should any suffering of a mere human being. So the suffering of Christ provides *a fortiori* evidence that human suffering is not necessarily inconsistent with divine goodness. This is because (1) Jesus was morally perfect and deserved no such suffering, nor did he require it for moral improvement (though his suffering provided the occasion for displaying his virtuous character), and (2) human beings are fallen, and all of us deserve condemnation anyway.[37]

Of course, there are many biblical cases of divine causation of other kinds of suffering. In the Old Testament there are numerous instances in which God commanded the killing of masses of people, including children. For example, God commands King Saul, "Now go, attack the Amalekites and totally destroy everything that belongs to them. Do not spare them; put to death men and women, children and infants, cattle and sheep, camels and donkeys" (1 Sam. 15:3).[38] And in the Passover, God himself "struck down all the firstborn in Egypt" (Exod. 12:29). Such events no doubt caused unthinkable suffering to hundreds of thousands of people, including children. Yet God commanded or even directly executed these things. Clearly, these facts are at odds with the open theists' assumption that God would never ordain horrendous suffering. The fact that he would even countenance the killing of infants and children should especially cause us to reflect how his ways are not

---

[37] This points up an additional faulty assumption of some open theists, who do not take the doctrine of original sin seriously enough. The theologian who gives appropriate weight to the moral corruption of the human heart is always less likely to complain of divine injustice in the face of human suffering. For if we understand that all of us deserve God's condemnation, then we will recognize that anything short of immediate annihilation is grace.

[38] See also Deut. 13:15, 20:17, and Josh. 11:12.

our ways. In any case, we may conclude that God does sometimes will extreme human suffering; so it must somehow be consistent with his goodness. Even if we cannot explain *how* this is so, we must confess *that* it is so, if only because it is the plain teaching of Scripture. It is better to embrace difficult truths as mysterious than to deny them in the name of rational explicability.

I will have more to say about mystery in the next section, and I will discuss the problem of evil in much greater depth in Chapter 6. But the preceding survey is sufficient to demonstrate that openness theology ignores a potentially fruitful means of dealing with the problem of evil that does not involve rejecting aspects of orthodox Christian doctrine.

Reconciling Human Freedom and Divine Sovereignty

Two different models of human freedom have traditionally been used to reconcile the tension between divine foreknowledge and human freedom. They are libertarianism and compatibilism. As explained earlier, libertarians maintain that freedom is a characteristic of a human will. In order to be free a person must possess the power of contrary choice. That is, in the case of any choice a person has made, it must really have been possible for him to have chosen contrarily to what he actually chose, even given all the same preconditions. For instance, if he elected to turn right, his choice is genuinely free if and only if in precisely the same situation he could have turned left or not turned at all. Libertarians, therefore, demand that a free will not have any causal preconditions guaranteeing its choice. As J. P. Moreland explains, one's "desires, beliefs, etc. may influence his choice, but free acts are not caused by prior states in the agent."[39] The only causal determinant of the will is the will itself. One's will is, as Moreland says, an "unmoved mover."

If we possess libertarian freedom, then neither God nor anyone else can properly be said to be the determiner of the will. We determine our own wills. And although God knows the future in exhaustive detail, this does not change the fact that we are free. He simply foreknows our freedom. Therefore, God is in no way to blame for the sins we commit. He knows them in advance, but he does not ensure that they come about.

---

[39] J. P. Moreland, "Complementarity, Agency Theory, and the God-of-the-Gaps," *Perspectives on Science and Christian Faith* 49:1 (March 1997): 7.

Libertarians are naturally drawn to Molinism as an attempt to further safeguard God's goodness and sovereign governance of the world from objections based on evil. He creates the world knowing what each of us would do if placed in any possible circumstances. As I have already noted, Molinism has much to recommend it, as it preserves a strong conception of predestination and exhaustive divine foreknowledge.

However, the libertarian concept of freedom is fraught with problems. First, it suffers from an incoherent conception of causality of the will. If there is nothing in the agent that causes (i.e., provides sufficient conditions for) one's choice, then that choice is arbitrary. Moreover, if my own desires, beliefs, and motives do not cause my choice, then in what sense can it be said that the choice is really mine? And how, then, can I be responsible for that choice? Only by locating the causes of a choice in my own desires, beliefs, and motives can I properly be held accountable. Only in terms of such factors can we make sense of personal intentions, and unless an act is intentional, it is not free.

This problem can be explained another way. Suppose I freely do some action X, which in the libertarian view means that I had the power of contrary choice. That is, at the point of my decision to do X, it really was possible that I could choose not to do X, *given exactly the same circumstances.* The question arises, "Why did I in fact choose X?" The libertarian will answer, "because the will so moved." But this is not an adequate response, because the point of the question is *why* the will so moved. Here one must say either that (a) there is a sufficient reason (e.g., a prevailing motive or desire) for the will's movement or (b) there is no sufficient reason for the will's movement. The former route is unavailable to libertarians, by definition of their view. So they must affirm the latter—there is no sufficient reason for the will's choice. But this implies the choice is arbitrary, which, again, undercuts personal responsibility.

Here the libertarian will likely insist that the will simply chooses. However, a bare choice is not a responsible choice but a blind and random choice. Furthermore, the question arises why our choices are so often explicable and predictable. Typically, when we ask others to explain their choices, they readily do so by appealing to their purposes, beliefs, motives, etc. And many times we are able to predict the choices of those whom we know well. For example, I can often predict how my wife will respond to various aspects of a film she has not seen. This is because I understand her character, the sum of her psychological and moral attributes that condition the way she views and acts in the world. Whether I explain my own behavior or predict my wife's, I do so in terms of the conditions that cause it. Libertarianism fails to account for these basic facts of human experience.

The other traditional model of human freedom is compatibilism. Compatibilists, too, believe that humans are free but insist that freedom is consistent with universal causation. They reject the notion that the will is undetermined, for the reasons noted above. The human will, they maintain, *is* causally determined just as is every other aspect of the world. It is caused to choose as it does by such things as beliefs, intentions, motives, and a person's general character. Such factors both *explain* our choices and enable others to sometimes *predict* what we will choose. And by grounding choices within the agent, compatibilism accounts for personal responsibility. Thus, compatibilists maintain that freedom is a characteristic of persons, not wills. A person is free if he is able to act according to his nature. An agent's will is determined, but so long as he can carry out what his will chooses, he is free. Hence, this view is sometimes called the doctrine of *free agency*.[40]

Compatibilists offer as evidence for their model situations from everyday life. For example, consider the choice someone might give you to eat either apple pie or grub worm pie. Which would you choose? Presumably, you would select the former. Was your choice determined? Of course, this is apparent from the predictability of your choice. And what determined your choice was such causal influences as your desire to eat something you like and your natural aversion to eating worms. But, now, was your choice free? Again, the answer is yes. You were free because you were not externally, compelled to give a pro-apple-pie response. However, had something so compelled you, such as the threat of physical violence or manipulation of your vocal cords, then you would not have acted freely. So even ordinary situations such as this suggest that freedom is not a property of wills but rather pertains to agents and their capacity to act upon their choices.[41]

Some biblical considerations also support a compatibilist conception

---

[40] Philosophers who have advanced varying forms of compatibilism include Thomas Hobbes, John Locke, David Hume, John Stuart Mill, P. F. Strawson, W. T. Stace, Harry Frankfurt, and Daniel Dennett.
[41] For this vivid illustration I am indebted to my mentor, Dr. Wynn Kenyon at Belhaven College.

of freedom. Consider, for instance, Peter's denial of Jesus in Matthew 26. Was Peter's action guaranteed to happen? Yes; Jesus' prior knowledge of his disciple's threefold denial shows that it was. This follows from the fact that to certainly know X implies that X itself is certain. Surely Jesus knew with *certainty* that Peter would deny him three times.[42] And, as Jonathan Edwards notes, "there must be a certainty in things themselves, before they are certainly known, or which is the same thing, known to be certain. For certainty of knowledge is nothing else but knowing or discerning the certainty there is in the things themselves, which are known."[43] So Peter's denial of Christ was sure to happen. But we may also assume that Peter was free, for his action was blameworthy. So the compatibilist account must be correct. Peter's freedom consisted in the fact that he was not externally compelled (though the circumstances presumably made faithful action more difficult). Peter's choice was determined by his own cowardly nature and his desire to avoid harm. Moreover, his resolve to act rightly was no doubt weakened by a lack of sleep and emotional fatigue. All these factors led to Peter's denial of Christ. But it was freely performed, for he acted according to his choice.

Paul's discussion of divine sovereignty in Romans 9 also suggests a compatibilist model of human freedom. In fact, in verses 19-22 he anticipates a main concern of the open theists. After underscoring God's meticulous control of human hearts, he says, "One of you will say to me: 'Then why does God still blame us? For who resists his will?'" His answer is, "Who are you, O man, to talk back to God?" And he quotes the prophet Isaiah, who likens our relation to God to that of clay in the potter's hands. We have no right to question God about his choices. It is his prerogative to use whomever he wants for whatever purposes he chooses.

Note that two problems are raised in this passage. One is the metaphysical problem of reconciling divine sovereignty and human freedom. The other, which rests upon the first, is the moral question as to whether we are in fact responsible in spite of God's sovereignty. Paul's approach is to address the moral issue and seemingly ignore the metaphysical ques-

---

[42] Incredible as it might seem, some open theists would challenge this claim, insisting that Jesus' prediction was merely highly probable. Of course, this introduces the distinct possibility that Jesus could be wrong, which leads to the sorts of problems discussed earlier. The subject of predictive prophecy will be discussed at length below.

[43] Jonathan Edwards, *On the Freedom of the Will*, in *The Works of Jonathan Edwards* (Edinburgh: Banner of Truth, 1974), 1:38.

tion, a strategy some find frustrating. But Paul's silence here might be the most salient feature of this passage for our purposes. Perhaps his refusal to give a metaphysical explanation suggests that we cannot comprehend the true answer. Or perhaps Paul intends to remind us that such disputes ought not distract us from our first order of business, which is right living. In any case, I believe this passage constitutes strong scriptural support for a compatibilist approach. For although Paul does not metaphysically explain *how* divine predestination and human moral responsibility are logically compatible, he does tacitly affirm their compatibility. He does this by answering the moral question alone. If there is no moral problem, Paul seems to be telling us, then there must be no metaphysical problem (or, at least, not one that we can reasonably hope to solve), for moral responsibility implies human freedom. To be assured of our responsibility is to know that we are free.

But now, we may ask, how is Paul's answer even a legitimate response to the moral question? His response reminds us that we do not have, nor can we ever have, a "case" against God, because we have no moral leverage. Our essential moral status before God as creatures is defined not by rights but by the most basic and extensive duties toward him. Simply put, we are morally indebted to God because he is our creator and sustainer, as he is of the rest of the universe.[44] The psalmist writes, "the earth is the LORD's, and everything in it, the world and all who live in it" (Ps. 24:1). And God says to Job, "Who has a claim against me that I must pay? Everything under heaven belongs to me" (Job 41:11). God exercises absolute ownership over every one of his creatures. So, as Paul notes, he may do as he pleases with any of us.

What I have tried to show is that there are good biblical reasons for believing in the compatibility of divine sovereignty and human freedom. But we need not limit ourselves to particular passages that imply the reality of both. The biblical argument for compatibilism derives from

---

[44] Several philosophers of religion have argued this way. Richard Swinburne notes that we are naturally obligated to our parents because they have raised us and provided for us. Thus, we are that much more obligated to God, for "if God is our creator and sustainer, our dependence as the children of God on God is so much greater than the dependence of the children of men on men" (from *The Coherence of Theism* [Oxford: Oxford University Press, 1977], 212). Similarly, George Mavrodes notes, "the creator/creature relation is very special, unique. So maybe Paul is correct in holding that it generates special rights" ("Is There Anything Which God Does Not Do?" *Christian Scholar's Review* 16:4 [July 1987]: 389). I regard this as a colossal understatement.

copious biblical assertions of divine sovereignty *and* equally plentiful passages assuming human responsibility, the latter implying significant human freedom.[45] Scripture clearly tells us *that,* though it never explains *how,* these facts are logically compatible. So while the Bible doesn't provide for us a positive account of divine sovereignty and human freedom, it does affirm the truth of both. What this does implicitly provide is basic parameters for philosophical inquiry into this issue. Specifically, whatever explanations we devise to solve or dissolve this problem, we must not embrace one of these truths at the expense of the other. Theories of human freedom must not deny the complete sovereignty of God, nor may our pronouncements of strong providence deny real human freedom and responsibility. They must be affirmed together, however much rational tension or psychological discomfort this might cause us. This, it seems to me, is the basic rule of engagement when it comes to philosophical proposals about divine sovereignty and human freedom. And, as we have seen, open theists and other proponents of the low view of providence flout this biblical guideline, for they affirm human freedom at the expense of divine sovereignty.

Some will complain that the compatibilist view is incomprehensible, that it is impossible to conceive how God could be utterly sovereign while at the same time human beings are free and morally responsible. To this I say that the mere fact that we do not understand something is not grounds for rejecting it. Otherwise put, human inability to rationally comprehend how X could be true is not sufficient grounds for concluding that X is false. Notice that this does not deny that lack of rational comprehensibility may provide *some* warrant for rejecting a belief. The inability to conceive or make sense of a claim is certainly no mark in its favor. The point is just that this quality does not by itself prove the belief false. Still, the question naturally arises, why believe in the truth of a proposition if one cannot comprehend how it could be true? One possibility—which is also most relevant to our present discussion—is the

---

[45] D. A. Carson has shown that the Old Testament and Johannine New Testament materials strongly affirm both divine sovereignty and human responsibility. See his *Divine Sovereignty and Human Responsibility, op cit.* Both truths are repeatedly asserted throughout these biblical materials, suggesting that the writers themselves sensed little tension between the doctrines. Thus, the biblical writers' refusal to rationally reconcile these doctrines for us is instructive in itself. And their example is certainly worth emulating. We may affirm both human responsibility and the sovereignty of God even in the absence of a rational explanation of their compatibility.

force of authority. We may affirm a proposition if it is communicated to us by a sufficiently reliable authority. Given the right authoritative source, a belief might be altogether rational even if it is counterintuitive or utterly incomprehensible. For instance, I believe that light appears in various experimental conditions to be both a particle and a wave. Like most laypersons to the science of physics, this leaves me nonplussed. Yet I accept this idea, albeit with a wince. Why? Because I have been assured of its truth by competent authorities, some of whom share my perplexity in the face of this paradoxical claim. Similarly, may we not accept what Scripture tells us about God's sovereignty, even though this teaching defies our rational capacity to comprehend it (at least in conjunction with our belief in human freedom)?

Christians properly believe that God is all-wise and transcendent while humans are fallen and foolish. These considerations alone should prompt us to defer to the plain affirmations of Scripture, however mysterious these might turn out to be. With some notorious exceptions, the church has done a good job of taking this approach regarding the doctrines of the Trinity and the divine incarnation. And, until comparatively recently, the same has been true of the doctrine of providence. But the church and its theologians have slipped in this area. And the explanation in each case is the same. We have succumbed to the temptation to rationally explain theological mysteries. J. I. Packer notes, "we ought not . . . to be surprised when we find mysteries . . . in God's Word. For the Creator is incomprehensible to His creatures."[46] But to appeal to mystery is not to admit a real logical inconsistency. Rather, Packer says, such tensions are better termed "antinomies," merely apparent contradictions that "all find their reconciliation in the mind and counsel of God, and we may hope that in heaven we shall understand them ourselves."[47]

The appeal to mystery, therefore, does have biblical grounds. Still, it should be emphasized, Christian theologians and philosophers of religion do properly strive to work out theological problems pertaining to the Christian faith in a way that is rationally consistent. Though sometimes speculative in nature, such work is immensely important. But the

---

[46] J. I. Packer, *Evangelism and the Sovereignty of God* (Leicester: InterVarsity Press, 1961), 24.
[47] Ibid.

aim of finding rationally satisfactory solutions to philosophical-theological problems must not eclipse faithfulness to the biblical witness. Ignoring or warping the plain teaching of Scripture, however counterintuitive or unpleasant a particular teaching might be, is not a legitimate avenue for resolving theological tension.

THE PROBLEMS AND INSIGHTS OF OPENNESS THEOLOGY

Open theists offer their perspective as an improvement upon the classical Christian doctrine of providence. It should be clear by now that this is not the case. In fact, openness theology creates many more problems—theologically and philosophically—than it solves. But like all false doctrines, there are elements of truth within open theism that must be acknowledged. In closing this chapter I will summarize some of the major problems as well as some insights of openness theology.

A Summary of the Main Problems with Openness Theology

With regard to the doctrine of providence, the alleged advantages of open theism over classical theism are moral, metaphysical, and practical. In fact, each of these claims is mistaken.

(1) *Open theism is not a moral improvement on classical theism.* Open theism does not shield God against culpability for evil (assuming, for the sake of argument, that he is culpable in the classical view). According to openness theology, God allowed evil to occur in the world. Also, he has been immediately aware of it and able to prevent it. So how is he, in this view, any less responsible for evil than he would be if he ordained evil? In other words, since in the open view God is at least the indirect cause of evil, how does the insertion of an intermediate causal step (human beings and their free will) exonerate God? To do X with advance knowledge that X will lead to evil consequences is tantamount to willing the evil itself. So openness theology does not provide the moral buffer that it was designed to provide.

Here some open theists would likely propose the unorthodox notion that God could not anticipate the fall of humanity, that he did not foresee the sin of Adam and Eve. However, this only leads to a further inconsistency in their view. If God can, as the open theists say, "predict what individuals will freely decide to do in the future in many cases"[48] or even "anticipate perfectly the course of creaturely events,"[49] then why was God unable to predict that human beings would sin and that evil would enter the world? Here we find a basic incoherence in the open theists' model. They affirm that God has enough foresight to make reliable predictive prophecies, but they deny that God had the foresight to reliably anticipate the human fall into sin.

(2) *Open theism is not a metaphysical improvement on classical theism.* Open theists assume a libertarian view of freedom. But this is necessary only if compatibilism is a demonstrable failure. However, as we have seen, Scripture implicitly affirms the compatibility of divine sovereignty and the moral responsibility of human beings. In fact, open theists have made no conclusive argument against the compatibilist position. Typically, they don't even attempt to critique this model of human freedom.

The absurdity of the open theists' position becomes more obvious when we consider the following. The open theists essentially say that human freedom (as they understand it) is so important that God created a world in which (a) he knew evil was likely to occur, (b) he watched evil in fact occur, but (c) he did not intervene, even to prevent holocausts. All of this, they imply, was a reasonable price for the sake of human freedom. But they deny the Augustinian view of providence because of the existence of such evils, even though according to this view God governs all these things to bring about the best world and to maximize his own glory. Thus, the open theists maintain that it is worth the price of evil to bring about human freedom, but it is *not* worth the price of evil for God to bring about his own glory. At bottom, then, open theism gives greater consideration to human freedom than to the glory of God.

(3) *Open theism is not a practical improvement on classical theism.* Open theists maintain that their perspective provides practical benefits, such as making better sense of petitionary prayer from a psychological standpoint. But the negative practical fallout of their model is severe. For one thing, they cannot account for ultimate meaning in all human suffering. Since God does not control all things, there must be evil "that

---

[48] David Basinger, *op. cit.*, 134.
[49] Richard Rice, *op. cit.*, 65. William Hasker, too, admits that God can make reliable predictions "based on foresight drawn from existing trends and tendencies" (*God, Time, and Knowledge*, 194).

serves no higher end"[50] and "involves permanent loss."[51] This is a profoundly discouraging teaching and quite at odds with the Christian belief "that in all things God works for the good of those who love him" (Rom. 8:28).

Moreover, open theists cannot reasonably thank God for all the good things we receive from other people. If human wills possess libertarian freedom, and God neither predestines nor foreknows all their good deeds, then he is not properly praised for them. In this sense open theism dilutes the glory due to God and violates the spirit of Scripture, such as when James says that "every good and perfect gift is from above, coming down from the Father of the heavenly lights" (1:17). Surely James does not mean this in the trivial sense that everything comes from God, since he is Creator. He must mean it in a more intimate, immediate sense. But open theism cannot account for this.

Lessons to Be Learned From Openness Theology

In spite of the besetting problems with openness theology, proponents of the high view of providence must grant that we have something to learn from their perspective, both philosophically and theologically. First, classical theists need to take the problem of evil more seriously. We must develop creative theodicies that are philosophically rigorous, theologically informed, and personally sensitive. Second, we need to do more work on our models of human freedom. Compatibilists must identify philosophical considerations recommending a free-agency view of freedom (e.g., appealing to common sense, ordinary language, and the approach of the biblical writers). Molinist libertarians must continue to develop their model, but with a view to addressing some of the open theists' concerns more directly.

From a theological standpoint, classical theists must affirm the relationality of God. He genuinely loves and cares for his creation, and he is personally involved with our lives. He really hears and answers our prayers. He really does commune with us in our fellowship. And he really is compassionate with us in our suffering. Open theists are correct in emphasizing this crucial aspect of the biblical portrait of God, too

---

[50] Gregory Boyd, *God at War: The Bible and Spiritual Conflict* (Downers Grove, Ill.: InterVarsity Press, 1997), 20.
[51] Richard Rice, *op. cit.*, 73.

often forgotten in the history of Christian theology, especially by proponents of the high view of providence. Finally, we must reevaluate the doctrine of divine impassibility. While openness theology goes too far in ascribing changing emotions to God, perhaps the classical tradition veers too far to the opposite extreme of denying that God has genuine emotions.

CONCLUSION

The foregoing discussion has featured standard theological and philosophical arguments in favor of the high view of providence generally and the Augustinian doctrine of meticulous providence in particular. God is not a risk-taker, notwithstanding the claims of open theists and other proponents of the low view. The remainder of this book aims at unpacking some overlooked applications of the Augustinian view that serve as additional recommendations of this perspective. The following chapters also serve as a constructive response to some of the critical insights of openness theology. In the next chapter I will discuss the doctrine of divine conservation of the world and develop an aesthetic model that has many edifying applications to Christian thought and practice. In Chapter 4 I will explore some implications of this model for scientific theory and methodology. In Chapter 5 I will propose a doctrine of divine emotion that overcomes the problems inherent in the standard views on the issue. In Chapter 6 I will discuss the problem of evil in greater depth. And in the final chapter I will make numerous applications of the Augustinian view of providence to the Christian moral life. I wish to stress that not all of the theoretical and practical applications that follow are the exclusive privilege of proponents of the Augustinian view of providence or even the high view generally. However, I do believe that they are most at home with the high view and are best fitted to a specifically Augustinian version of the high view.

3

THE WORLD
AS DIVINE ART

Having reviewed some of the philosophical and theological difficulties with the low view of providence, it is time to look at the benefits of the high view of providence. As will become evident, what I call "benefits" of the high view are both theoretical and practical in nature. The theoretical virtues of the high view pertain to issues in philosophy of science, the philosophical problem of evil, and some issues in philosophical theology, particularly regarding the divine attributes. The practical benefits pertain to scientific methodology, the problem of evil at the existential level, the Christian devotional life, and various implications related to art, education, and ethics.

Whatever original things I have to say in this book will be found in the remaining chapters. And any originality I manage is really only a unique presentation of many old ideas. We stand on the shoulders of giants, as the old adage goes. In fact, one of the main points of this book is that the greatest theologians of the Christian tradition endorse the high view of providence, specifically the Augustinian version, and for this reason we ought to especially revere and carefully explore it. What has been lacking in the Augustinian tradition of late, however, is innovative application of this view of providence to many potentially fruitful areas of thought and practice. What follows is an attempt to help rectify this problem.

DIVINE CONSERVATION OF THE COSMOS

I want to begin by drawing attention to a significant but often over-looked feature of classical theism. It has not been overlooked altogether, but its relevance for the issue of divine providence has not been adequately appreciated, although its implications for this issue are immense. The feature to which I refer is the doctrine of divine conservation of the cosmos. All orthodox theists, Christians included, affirm that God sustains the universe. From moment to moment the cosmos is dependent upon him, and were God to suddenly withhold his active sustaining power, the world would immediately disappear. This doctrine is grounded in biblical texts affirming that God "sustain[s] all things by his powerful word" (Heb. 1:3) and that "He is before all things, and in him all things hold together" (Col. 1:17). Thus, Christian theologians down through the ages have affirmed the doctrine of divine conservation (*creatio continuans*) in conjunction with divine creation (*creatio originans*). Of course, many have denied this claim, including naturalists and deists. Naturalists reject divine conservation because they reject all things supernatural. Deists (who occupy a halfway house between naturalism and theism) affirm the existence of an eternal creator but deny this being to be personal (or at least deny it is personally *involved* with creation). But any theist deserving of that title affirms divine conservation of the cosmos.

But exactly what form does this divine conservation take? Many Christian theologians take the view known as "constant creation," which affirms that God's ongoing conservation of the cosmos is essentially no different from his original creation. His producing and preserving the world are really one and the same.[1] For example, Aquinas writes, "the preservation of things by God is a continuation of that action whereby He gives existence, which action is without either motion or time; so also the preservation of light in the air is by the continual influence of the sun."[2] And Jonathan Edwards writes:

---

[1] For philosophical defenses of this idea, see Augustine, *De Genesi ad litteram*, 4:12; Thomas Aquinas *Summa Theologica*, trans. English Dominican Fathers (New York: Benziger Brothers, 1947), 1:511-513; Rene Descartes, *The Principles of Philosophy*, in *The Philosophical Works of Descartes*, trans. Elizabeth S. Haldane and G. R. T. Ross (New York: Dover Publications, 1955), 1:227-228; G. W. Leibniz, *Discourse on Metaphysics*, section 14; and Jonathan Edwards, *On Original Sin*, in *The Works of Jonathan Edwards* (Edinburgh: The Banner of Truth Trust, 1974), 1:223-224.

[2] Thomas Aquinas, *op. cit.*, 1:512.

God's *preserving* created things in being is perfectly equivalent to a *continued creation*, or to his creating those things out of nothing at *each moment* of their existence. If the continued existence of created things be wholly dependent on God's preservation, then those things would drop into nothing, upon the ceasing of the present moment, without a new exertion of the divine power to cause them to exist in the following moment.[3]

Now there is disagreement within this camp as to the precise role of secondary causes. Still, all of those who affirm the doctrine of constant creation agree that God actively preserves all other beings and that were it not for his continuous sustaining activity they would cease to exist.

Clearly this conception of divine conservation implies a high view of providence and fits best with the Augustinian view in particular. What alternatives might proponents of the low view pose? In a superb analysis of the doctrine of divine conservation, Jonathan Kvanvig and Hugh McCann discuss the natural alternative to the constant creation position—namely, the notion that God endows created beings with the power of "self-sustenance."[4] But how is such cosmic self-sustenance to be conceived? One cannot appeal to the laws of nature (e.g., the law of gravity, the laws of thermodynamics, etc.). Such laws are features *of* the physical world and thus presuppose its persistence. So they cannot be appealed to as causal explanations of the continued existence of the cosmos. Another option considered by Kvanvig and McCann is the appeal to a metaphysical law, a principle of cosmic conservation. But this, too, is inadequate, for the simple reason that laws of any kind, whether natural or metaphysical, merely describe regularities. They are not entities or agents such that they could operate upon or causally influence anything. They are, rather, summations of regularities.[5] (This point will be discussed in greater detail later in this chapter.)

Yet another route for making sense of self-sustenance is to appeal to the inherent nature of substances. Of course, medium-sized sub-

---

[3] Jonathan Edwards, *op. cit.*, 1:223 (emphasis his).
[4] Jonathan L. Kvanvig and Hugh J. McCann, "Divine Conservation and the Persistence of the World," in *Divine and Human Action: Essays in the Metaphysics of Theism*, ed. Thomas V. Morris (Ithaca, N.Y.: Cornell University Press, 1988), 13-49. At several points in the following discussion I am indebted to their analysis.
[5] Ibid., 31-34.

stances such as human bodies, trees, and bears won't do, for their existence is obviously ephemeral. That such substances decay and cease to be is at odds with the notion that they are self-sustaining. So one might consider instead the possibility that the ultimate physical constituents of material objects—atoms and their component parts—are immune to this problem. As it turns out, however, even subatomic particles such as protons and neutrons are subject to decay and destruction. In fact, no subatomic entities have been discovered that are indestructible.

It seems, then, that whatever capacity for self-sustenance physical objects might have, it cannot be located in the physical world. The only remaining option, then, is to account for self-sustenance by appealing to something metaphysical. One approach would be to regard self-sustenance as a metaphysical *quality* of physical objects. Thus, for instance, to say a physical object is self-sustaining just means that it needs no active support in order to endure from one moment to the next. On this view, God simply endowed all physical objects with this quality. Now this looks promising. But let's look more closely. This basic quality of self-sustenance (call it *ss*) is either an essential or accidental quality of physical objects. If *ss* is an essential quality of objects, this implies that it is the very nature of physical objects to exist. However, this has some unsavory implications for the Christian theist. First, it means that physical objects are absolutely indestructible, even by God. Furthermore, this implies that all physical objects are necessary beings and could not have been created (by God or anyone else) in the first place. Clearly, this is unacceptable. So, then, let's suppose that *ss* is an accidental (i.e., nonessential) quality of physical objects. Now an accidental quality, such as hair color, is one that may or may not persist in a thing and that demands a causal explanation for as long as it does persist in an object. It appears, then, that *ss* cannot be an accidental quality of physical objects, for this begs the question *why* *ss* persists in physical objects. Thus, since *ss* can be neither an essential nor accidental quality, it cannot be a metaphysical quality of objects at all.

A final alternative is to appeal to a metaphysical *medium* in order to explain *ss*. Presumably, this would be a non-physical substance of some kind that explains the self-sustenance of physical objects. However, to appeal to a medium violates Ockham's razor (i.e., do not multiply entities without good and sufficient reason), as it may be asked why God would use a medium when he could simply support physical objects directly without the use of an instrument. Indeed, this applies as well to any appeals to God to save the above appeal to *ss*, for at any point where the defender of the self-sustenance view calls upon God to guarantee *ss* so that objects can sustain themselves, the question may be asked why we need to appeal to *ss*, when God could sustain objects immediately.

Thus, it appears that the doctrine of constant creation is not only theologically justified but is also philosophically reasonable. Now this doctrine has several significant implications. For one thing, it follows that the physical world is mind-dependent. After all, God is essentially a mind, where a mind is defined as a conscious subject with ultimate capacities for cognition, will, and emotion. Thus, the doctrine of divine conservation functions as evidence for the view sometimes known as "metaphysical idealism" or "immaterialist realism." Espoused by prominent Christian thinkers such as George Berkeley and Jonathan Edwards, this view says that when it comes to the reality of the physical world, "to be is to be perceived." There is no reality that is independent of God's mind and the power of his thought. The whole of the cosmos was dreamed up by him, thought into existence, and is ever sustained by his thinking.[6]

Secondly, given the complete and constant dependence of the physical world upon the divine mind, it follows that God controls all of cosmic history, including every event in our lives. Indeed, if God actively sustains each and every molecule from one moment to the next, it is hard to imagine how he could not also control the major events of our lives and world history. Comprehensive micromanagement of the universe suggests an equally comprehensive cosmic macromanagement.

THE LAWS OF NATURE

The doctrine of divine conservation, understood as "constant creation," has a variety of significant implications. Among these is the way that we view the laws of nature. For example, the inverse square law of gravitation refers to a particular constancy observable in nature. This law

---

[6] For a thorough defense of the theological orthodoxy of this brand of idealism, see my essay "The Theological Orthodoxy of Berkeley's Immaterialism," *Faith and Philosophy* 13:2 (April 1996): 216-235.

says that every object is attracted to other objects proportional to their size and inversely proportional to the square of the distance between them. So gravitational attraction will increase with size and decrease with distance. This is a regularity in nature. Many other lawlike constants are observable in the world, including the laws of thermodynamics, Boyle's law, the Meissner effect, Faraday's law, Avagadro's constant, Ampere's law, the ideal gas law, and scores of others. That nature displays an astonishing consistency in its operations is empirically obvious. What is a matter of dispute is just how we are to understand these regularities. Three basic perspectives have been taken on this issue: the regularity view, instrumentalism, and the necessitarian approach.

Proponents of the regularity view regard laws as summary descriptions of how things have happened and will continue to happen. On this view, the laws of nature are simply generalized statements about nature's workings, and the question *why* these regularities occur is either ignored or seen as illegitimate. Thus, regularity theorists are concerned only with the fact of nature's regularity and refuse to venture causal explanations for this fact. Regularity theorists' hesitance to offer such accounts traces back to David Hume's critique of causality, to be reviewed shortly.[7] Instrumentalists take a pragmatic tack when it comes to the scientific enterprise generally, and this includes their view of the laws of nature. They say that the apparent universality of certain phenomena is not what is of first scientific importance. Rather, it is the practical value of the general statements that matters. Thus, for the instrumentalist, the laws of nature are useful fictions. They do not have a truth-value but are essentially conceptual tools that scientists use to make inferences and solve problems.[8]

Note that regularity theorists and instrumentalists refrain from making metaphysical claims about the laws of nature. Rather, in these

---

[7] Proponents of the regularity view include A. J. Ayer, "What Is a Law of Nature?" *Revue Internationale de Philosophie* 36 (1956): 144-165; Carl Hempel, "Provisos: A Problem Concerning the Inferential Function of Scientific Theories," in *The Limitations of Deductivism*, eds. A. Grunbaum and W. C. Salmon (Berkeley, Calif.: University of California Press, 1988); and Ernest Nagel, *The Structure of Science* (Indianapolis: Hackett Press, 1979), Chapter 4.

[8] For examples of instrumentalist theories, see Nicholas Rescher, *The Limits of Science* (Berkeley, Calif.: University of California Press, 1984); Stephen Toulmin, *Foresight and Understanding: An Inquiry into the Aims of Science* (New York: Harper Torchbooks, 1980); and Larry Lauden, *Progress and Its Problems* (Berkeley, Calif.: University of California Press, 1977) and *idem, Science and Values: An Essay on the Aims of Science and Their Role in Scientific Debate* (Berkeley, Calif.: University of California Press, 1984).

views, the laws of nature are only descriptions of phenomena or mere conceptual tools that serve practical scientific ends. Proponents of the third approach, however, do venture to make metaphysical claims. Necessitarians maintain that nature's regularities reflect not just how the world in fact behaves but how it *must* behave. An especially strong brand of necessitarianism sees the laws of nature as logically necessary.[9] Proponents of this view often describe the laws of nature as instances of universal truths, exceptions to which are logically impossible. This view is commonly rejected because it is possible to conceive of a world in which our current physical laws do not hold (which should be impossible, given the logical necessitarian position). Moreover, if the laws of nature were logically necessary truths, then we would not need to rely upon empirical inquiry to discover them but could arrive at the laws of nature through simple reflection. Thus, since most such laws are not discoverable in such an *a priori* manner, this proves that they are not logically necessary.

More typically, necessitarians ground their conception of natural laws in what they regard as active powers inherent in physical systems. Thus, A. F. Chalmers writes, "The inverse square law of gravitation describes quantitatively the power to attract possessed by massive bodies, and the laws of classical electromagnetic theory describe, among other things, the capacity of charged bodies to attract and radiate. It is the active powers at work in nature that makes laws true when they are true."[10] This analysis accounts for lawlike behavior by appealing to efficient causation, which in turn is explained by the natural dispositions of material objects. Chalmers takes this view to be implicit in the intuition that "the material world is active. Things happen in the world of their own accord, and they happen because entities in the world possess the capacity or power or disposition or tendency to act or behave in the way that they do."[11] One advantage of such a view is that the many laws of nature may accordingly be seen as so many expressions of the more fundamental law of causality. And appeals to the laws of

---

[9] For various versions of this view, see E. Fales, *Causation and Universals* (London: Routledge Press, 1990); C. Swoyer, "The Nature of Natural Laws," *Australasian Journal of Philosophy*, 60 (1982): 203-223; J. Bigelow, B. Ellis, and C. Lierse, "The World as One of a Kind: Natural Necessity and Laws of Nature," *British Journal for the Philosophy of Science*, 43 (1992): 371-388.
[10] A. F. Chalmers, *What Is This Thing Called Science?* third edition (Indianapolis: Hackett, 1999), 219.
[11] Ibid., 218.

nature hold the promise of providing genuine causal explanations for phenomena.[12]

But causal necessitarianism has some serious problems that date all the way back to David Hume's famous analysis of causality. Hume inquired into the notion that there is a necessary connection between a cause and its effect. As a thoroughgoing empiricist, he asked what empirical evidence we have for the idea. To be precise, what we experience when observing a causal relation (such as in a game of billiards) is one event (the moving of the cue ball) occurring just prior to another (the moving of the eight ball). We also observe contiguity (the two balls touching), and we observe the same sorts of events occurring repeatedly, what Hume calls a "constant conjunction" of similar events. However, says Hume, "we are never able, in a single instance, to discover any power or necessary connection; any quality, which binds the effect to the cause, and renders the one an infallible consequence of the other. We only find that the one does actually, in fact, follow from the other."[13] Moreover, according to Hume, the temporal priority, contiguity, and constant conjunction do not justify our inferring a power or necessary connection between a cause and its effect. Hume's critique thus undermines the causal necessitarian view of the laws of nature, founded as it is upon the notion that there are active powers inherent in material objects.

Still, philosophers like Chalmers persist in their commitment to the notion that the laws of nature are causally necessary. This is understandable, given the naturalism of such philosophers. But for the Christian theist, this view is untenable because it implies a self-sustenance view of divine conservation, which as we saw above is indefensible. To affirm the doctrine of constant creation, on the other hand, renders necessitarianism (in any form) unnecessary, even foolish. If the omnipotent Mind sustains the universe from moment to moment, then what other explanation for nature's regularities is possible? To interpose such things as "dispositions," "powers," "forces," or any other sort of

---

[12] For an extended defense of this account, see R. Harré and E. H. Madden, *Causal Powers: A Theory of Natural Necessity* (Oxford: Blackwell Press, 1975). For other versions of this approach see Fred Dretske, "Laws of Nature," *Philosophy of Science* 44 (1977): 248-268; and Michael Tooley, "The Nature of Laws," *Canadian Journal of Philosophy* 74 (1977): 667-698.

[13] David Hume, *An Enquiry Concerning Human Understanding*, in *The Essential Works of Hume*, ed. Ralph Cohen (New York: Bantam Books, 1965), 90.

active agent to explain the laws of nature is irrationally redundant. God himself is sufficiently powerful to explain all of nature's regularities (as well as the occasional *irregular* phenomena, as I shall explain in the next section).[14]

Let me spell out how by an Augustinian[15] view of providence (which I will henceforth assume includes the doctrine of constant creation) we are properly to conceive of the laws of nature and, more fundamentally, the law of causality. Essentially, we should see the law of causality as referring to the regular coordination of observable events, rather than as signifying some intrinsic necessity in the natural world. Physical events, by this conception, are not really productive of one another but are systematically correlated by God. And, of course, neither are the laws of nature causally or logically necessary; they are simply the result of the regular governance of the world by the Mind who runs things.

So how does this affect the way we do science? I will address some particular methodological and substantive scientific implications of the Augustinian view of providence in the next chapter, but generally speaking the scientific method may be applied without change. In spite of the metaphysical commitments entailed in the Augustinian view, the basic elements of scientific research, from testing and experimentation to theory formation and selection, are unaffected by the concept of constant creation. Of course, since even natural scientists often cannot resist thinking metaphysically, the scientist who affirms this view will adjust accordingly. For example, he or she will resist the temptation to regard the phenomenal world as somehow self-sustaining or as in any respect a purposeless mechanism. While assuming universal causation and the uniformity of nature, the scientist will attribute these facts about the natural world to the immediate governance of the Mind behind the world. But the practice of science itself should look very much the same for the

---

[14] As Richard Swinburne writes, "the theist holds that any natural laws only operate because God brings it about that they do. That things have the effects in accord with natural laws which they do is, for the theist, itself an act of God" (from *The Coherence of Theism* [Oxford: Oxford University Press, 1993], 143).

[15] I hope that it is obvious that I am using the term "Augustinian" in a very technical sense—basically as shorthand for the doctrine of meticulous divine providence as opposed to the literal doctrines of St. Augustine. So, lest there be any confusion, I do not intend to suggest that every idea developed in this book under the rubric "Augustinian" was actually espoused by Augustine himself. Rather, I conceive many of them to be embellishments that flow naturally from the view of divine providence affirmed by him and his theological descendants.

person who affirms an Augustinian view of providence as it does for those who do not, including metaphysical naturalists. Having said that, I do believe there are some important methodological advantages and additional theoretical options for those who take the Augustinian view, which go beyond the general scientific method. These will be explored in the next chapter.

MIRACLES

We have seen the benefits of the Augustinian view of providence as applied to nature's regularities. This perspective provides a philosophically and personally satisfying explanation: God is the regulator of nature. Significantly, the Augustinian perspective affords similar conceptual benefits regarding nature's occasional beneficial irregularities, known as miracles. To take this view is to see all of nature's operations as divine handiwork, whether the laws of nature hold or, as in the case of miraculous events, they do not.

Of course, conceptions of the miraculous vary. One popular view, held by some Christians as well as by agnostics and atheists, regards miracles as essentially violations of nature's laws. For just this reason many religious skeptics conclude that miracles are impossible or at least that reports of miracles are not credible. David Hume took such an approach, noting, "a miracle is a violation of the laws of nature; and as a firm and unalterable experience has established these laws, the proof against a miracle, from the very nature of the fact, is as entire as any argument from experience can possibly be imagined."[16] So Hume roundly rejects the possibility of miracles, even after his earlier critique of the notion of necessity in nature. (This is indeed an embarrassing inconsistency in his thinking, widely recognized by philosophers of religion.) But what of the conception of a miracle as a "violation" of the laws of nature? Why should we accept this definition, seeing as it suggests some sort of inherent necessity in nature? Only a necessitarian would affirm the inviolability of the laws of nature. If, as is more reasonable, the laws are understood as simple regularities, then *violation* is much too strong a term. Something like *exception* or *anomaly* would be far more appropriate.

---

[16] David Hume, *op. cit.*, 128.

In the Augustinian view, God's conservation of the world is tantamount to constant creation; so a miracle differs from an ordinary event only insofar as it is an exception to divine routine. Its cause and purpose are no different than those of nature's usual operations. God is the cause, and his purpose is to convince humankind of his power and goodness and ultimately to draw people to himself. As George Berkeley writes:

> It may indeed on some occasions be necessary that the Author of Nature display overruling power in producing some appearance out of the ordinary series of things. Such exceptions from the general rules of nature are proper to surprise and awe men into an acknowledgment of the Divine Being. . . .[17]

This perspective serves as a corrective to the misleading language of divine "intervention" in the world. It is true that God might alert us to some danger or introduce some obstacle to prevent us from doing something foolish, which may be loosely described as intervention. But often God is thought to intervene in the sense that his activity in our lives is somehow only intermittent or exceptional. Some people regard miracles in this way, as instances of exceptional divine activity in the world. This not only flouts the orthodox Christian doctrine of divine conservation—it amounts to a view that could be characterized as "deism plus miracles."

Even more common is the view that miracles demonstrate God's presence and power beyond what is proven in nature's regularities. But making an exception to nature's ordinary operations is no more difficult for God than maintaining regularity. Doing something different to help someone in need (or to punish the wicked) involves no additional exertion of divine effort. Thus, the Augustinian view of providence discourages seeing miracles as inherently greater demonstrations of God's power and goodness than nature's regularities. In fact, one might say that the laws of nature should be *more* impressive to us than miracles, because such extensive providential consistency benefits the whole human race,

---

[17] George Berkeley, *A Treatise Concerning the Principles of Human Knowledge* (New York: Bobbs-Merrill, 1957), 53-54. C. S. Lewis takes a similar approach: "A miracle is emphatically not an event without a cause or without results. Its cause is the activity of God. . . . The great complex event called Nature, and the new particular event introduced into it by the miracle, are related by their common origin in God" (*Miracles: A Preliminary Study* [New York: Macmillan, 1960], 60).

as opposed to the relatively few people who benefit from miracles. However, since we are accustomed to nature's regularities, it is miraculous events that turn our thoughts toward God much more readily. Ironically, because the majority of people take for granted God's faithful governance, his occasional deviations from cosmic routine are necessary to shake them out of their doldrums. Miracles, then, are uniquely impressive to us more because of the peculiarities of human psychology than because of any additional divine power they display (which is objectively no greater than when things run as usual). We are wowed by the miraculous only because we have been spoiled by God's awesome regular providence (which, I should add, is our fault, not his). Montaigne sums up this point as follows: "What a man frequently sees never produces wonder in him, even though he does not know how it happens. But if something occurs which he has never seen before, he takes it as a portent."[18]

Now someone might object as follows. In accounting for both the laws of nature and their miraculous exceptions by appealing to the immediate governance of God, aren't we trying to have our cake and eat it too? To this I answer: Absolutely! But not without very good reason. As we have seen, the doctrine of constant creation enjoys strong support, philosophically and theologically. Once we recognize that the cosmos is a constant divine creation, nature's operations, regular or not and pleasant or not, must also be recognized as following from the activity of the wise and omnipotent God. Concepts such as "law of nature" and "miracle" may thus be seen for what they are—categories devised for the purpose of making sense of God's ordering of the cosmos.

The popular notion that the laws of nature are absolutely exceptionless is grounded in the idea of a deep metaphysical necessity underlying these regularities. A proper doctrine of providence displaces this

---

[18] Michel de Montaigne, "On a Monster-child," in *The Complete Essays*, trans. M. A. Screech (London: Penguin Books, 1987), 808. Montaigne continues: "Whatever happens against custom we say is against Nature, yet there is nothing whatsoever which is not in harmony with her. May Nature's universal reason chase away that deluded ecstatic amazement which novelty brings to us" (ibid.). Montaigne discusses this point specifically in regard to severe congenital deformities, which originally gave rise to the term *monster*. Derived from the Latin *monstrum*, meaning "portent" or "warning," this appellation first referred to the way such deformities *demonstrate* divine providence. (Today, of course, these are thought by many to prove quite the opposite.) Montaigne's high view of providence enabled him to conclude, "What we call monsters are not so for God who sees the infinite number of forms which he has included in the immensity of his creation: it is to be believed that the figure which astonishes us relates to, and derives from, some other figure of the same genus unknown to Man. God is all-wise; nothing comes from him which is not good, general and regular: but we cannot see the disposition and relationship" (ibid.).

notion of mechanistic causal necessity with purposeful divine direction. Consequently, both nature's regularities and miraculous events are seen to be equally divinely intended. This is not a self-serving apologetic ploy calculated to make all events confirm belief in the classical theistic God. Rather, it follows simply from the Augustinian view of providence, for which there is much independent evidence.

Thus, we see that the Augustinian perspective provides some significant philosophical-theological benefits when it comes to the doctrine of miracles. But there are some salutary applications of the doctrine that are even more practical in nature, pertaining to the life of faith. The conception of miracles in this view of providence wards off doubts with which Christians sometimes struggle when it comes to such doctrines as the resurrection of Christ, the virgin birth, the inerrancy of Scripture, and the miracles of Jesus. Persons who struggle with believing these events to be historical often do so because of their low view of providence. This perspective, of course, encourages us to think that the world essentially runs on its own, while God occasionally intervenes to answer prayers and direct events in certain ways. To them the performance of a miracle is a special event in a deep metaphysical sense. God does not usually act directly in the world, so a miracle event is fundamentally different from regular, natural occurrences in terms of their causal origins. A much simpler perspective, of course, would be to view all events as having the same sorts of causes. Now since the low view regards the great majority of events as naturalistic, the attraction to a simpler view of the matter obviously invites a thoroughly naturalistic (or deistic) perspective and, concomitantly, doubt about the historicity of the central miracles of our faith. It is no wonder that some Christians struggle with doubt about the resurrection or scriptural inerrancy when they nurse the view that divine activity in the world is episodic and unusual.

The situation is completely different from the standpoint of the Augustinian view of providence. God is always working directly in the world in the most fundamental metaphysical sense, actively sustaining it, in the sense of constant creation, from moment to moment. Therefore, a miracle claim does not disturb belief about the underlying cause of nature's uniformity. God is no more or less at work in the world when turning water into wine than when grapes ferment during the normal process of making wine. What makes the former sorts of events special and deserving of the term *miracle* is, of course, the absence (or rear-rangement) of certain secondary causes. But the supernatural cause behind it all remains constant in the Augustinian view, and consequently the strain to believe is significantly less than in the low view.

The pull to abide by Ockham's razor—which prefers parsimony to complexity, other things being equal—is strong at an intuitive level, even among laypersons who have no scholarly inclinations. We all want our belief systems to be unified and coherent. Regarding this point, I have tried to show that the historic Christian belief in miracles creates much less rational difficulty for the believer in the Augustinian view than for the one holding the low view, because the uniqueness of such events is not metaphysical but only psychological. Admittedly, miraculous events are odd, but only relative to human expectations regarding the ordering of secondary causes. Abiding by Ockham's razor rewards belief in miracles in the Augustinian view of providence, while it militates against such belief in the low view. Accordingly, the Augustinian view preempts doubts commonly associated with Christian doctrines pertaining to miraculous events.

AESTHETIC IMPLICATIONS

We have seen that the Augustinian view of providence makes the best sense of the doctrine of divine conservation and effectively accounts for the lawlike regularities in nature. Likewise, we have noted a beneficial application of this perspective as regards personal belief in miracles. These points add to the case in favor of the Augustinian perspective (and the high view generally) that has already been built in previous chapters. But there are many more benefits yet to be explored. In the remainder of this chapter I will show how the Augustinian view of providence inspires the recognition of beauty as a central category for Christian thought. I will conclude by noting how this insight should affect our view of education.

Traditionally, Christian aestheticians have formulated their models for the arts in light of several important biblical facts.[19] First, human

---

[19] See, for example, Leland Ryken, *The Liberated Imagination: Thinking Christianly About the Arts* (Wheaton, Ill.: Harold Shaw, 1989), Chapters 2-3; Nicholas Wolterstorff, *Art in Action: Towards a Christian Aesthetic* (Grand Rapids, Mich.: Eerdmans, 1980), part 3, Chapter 1; Francis Schaeffer, *Art and the Bible*, in *The Complete Works of Francis Schaeffer: A Christian Worldview* (Wheaton, Ill.: Crossway Books, 1982), Vol. 1; and Dorothy Sayers, "Toward a Christian Aesthetic," in *The Whimsical Christian* (New York: Macmillan, 1969).

beings are made in the image of God, and in reflecting his nature we, too, act creatively. Also, Scripture sanctions creativity in the arts, though more by example than direct injunction. The Bible is full of poetry, songs, and beautiful tales that tantalize the imagination as powerfully as they challenge the mind and convict the heart. Third, Scripture gives us models of artistry in such figures as David, for his musicianship and songwriting, Solomon, for his poetic skills, and Bezalel and Oholiab for their craftsmanship. From such models we learn that art and artistic ability are gifts from God.[20]

In addition to these important rudiments of a biblical conception of the arts, some scholars have grappled fruitfully with some of the harder questions in Christian aesthetics. Frank Burch Brown and Leland Ryken, for example, illuminatingly address the question "What is Christian Art?"[21] Nicholas Wolterstorff has done some outstanding work on the ontology of art and the nature of the artistic process.[22] And several recent scholars, including Patrick Sherry, Edward Farley, and David Bentley Hart, have demonstrated the significance of aesthetic concepts for Christian theology.[23] Yet there remains something sorely needed in the field of Christian aesthetics that no one, not even the above-noted scholars, have provided. We need a model that not only recognizes the significant relevance of aesthetics for Christian thought but that also demonstrates the *centrality* of aesthetics in a Christian worldview. It is just this that the Augustinian view of providence properly delivers.

The World as an Aesthetic Phenomenon

I want to use Friedrich Nietzsche as my point of departure. This is ironic, of course, since Nietzsche was an outspoken critic of Christianity and

---

[20] We learn of Bezalel and Oholiab in Exodus 31:1-11, where Moses relays instructions to the Israelites regarding the construction of the tabernacle. These two individuals are identified as gifted artists, endowed by the Holy Spirit with special creative abilities to beautifully adorn the tabernacle. See Gene Veith's *State of the Arts: From Bezalel to Mapplethorpe* (Wheaton, Ill.: Crossway Books, 1991), Chapters 6-7 for an extended discussion of this passage and its implications for Christian aesthetics.
[21] Frank Burch Brown, *Good Taste, Bad Taste, and Christian Taste: Aesthetics in Religious Life* (Oxford: Oxford University Press, 2000), Chapters 6-9; Leland Ryken, *op. cit.*, Chapter 7.
[22] Nicholas Wolterstorff, *op. cit.*, Part 3, Chapters 2-3.
[23] Patrick Sherry, *Spirit and Beauty: An Introduction to Theological Aesthetics* (Oxford: Clarendon Press, 1992); Edward Farley, *Faith and Beauty: A Theological Aesthetic* (Burlington, Ver.: Ashgate, 2001; and David Bentley Hart, *The Beauty of the Infinite: The Aesthetics of Christian Truth* (Grand Rapids, Mich.: Eerdmans, 2003).

certainly no friend of the doctrine of providence.[24] Remarking on one of his early works on art,[25] he asserts that "art, and *not* morality is . . . the truly *metaphysical* activity of man."[26] In fact, he continues, "the existence of the world is *justified* only as an aesthetic phenomenon."[27] Indeed, Nietzsche finds

> only an artistic meaning and crypto-meaning behind all events—a 'god,' if you please, but certainly only an entirely reckless and amoral artist-god who wants to experience, whether he is building or destroying, in the good and in the bad, his own joy and glory—one who, creating worlds, frees himself from the *distress* of fullness and *overfullness*, and from the *affliction* of the contradictions compressed in his soul.[28]

Further on, we find Nietzsche's anti-Christian sentiments percolating, as he boldly proclaims,

> nothing could be more opposed to the purely aesthetic interpretation and justification of the world which are taught in this book than the Christian teaching, which is, and wants to be, *only* moral and which relegates art, *every* art, to the realm of *lies*; with its absolute standards, beginning with the truthfulness of God, it negates, judges and damns art.[29]

Now, the question these passages beg to be asked is this: Are Nietzsche's claims here correct? As I have reflected upon his words in light of the Christian worldview and its historical development, I have arrived at two key conclusions. The first is that Nietzsche certainly is on target when he regards the world as "an aesthetic phenomenon." And secondly, while it clearly is the case that historically many

---

[24] The crux of Nietzsche's critique lay in his contention that Christian theism enshrines the attributes of the weak (e.g., humility, meekness, self-denial, etc.) as moral virtues, while it opposes characteristics of the strong (e.g., pride, self-reliance, etc.) as morally vicious. This value system, he maintains, essentially represents a denial of life, as it works against the "will to power," an urge that is both natural and necessary for human growth and survival. See Nietzsche's two principal works in this connection: *Beyond Good and Evil* (1886) and *The Genealogy of Morals* (1887).

[25] *The Birth of Tragedy* (1871).

[26] *The Birth of Tragedy and The Case of Wagner*, trans. Walter Kaufmann (New York: Random House, 1967), 23 (emphasis his).

[27] Ibid. Emphasis his.

[28] Ibid. Emphasis his.

[29] Ibid., 24 (emphasis his).

Christians have for one reason or another "damned," shunned, or otherwise devalued artistic endeavor, it is not true that *Christianity* does so. On the contrary, I am convinced that a truly Christian perspective highly values the arts precisely *because* the world is, as Nietzsche suggests, "an aesthetic phenomenon." To recognize this is at once to commend the great German scholar for his first claim and to reject the latter.

That an aesthetic emphasis is properly biblical is clear from such facts as those noted above, namely: (1) the Genesis account of God's creation of the world, (2) his fashioning human beings in his own image, and (3) the examples of David, Solomon, and Bezalel and Oholiab. However, several important Christian thinkers have gone beyond a bare recognition of the legitimacy of the arts to intimate the centrality of aesthetic concerns for the Christian. Building upon their ideas, I want to suggest that a Nietzschean "aesthetic interpretation" of the world provides a fruitful model for the Christian. And, as I shall demonstrate, this model is most naturally suggested by an Augustinian view of providence.

Consider G. W. Leibniz, an early modern thinker who employed the comparison of the world to an artwork for apologetic ends. Like some of his contemporaries, Leibniz regarded every living organism as

> a sort of divine machine or natural automaton, which infinitely surpasses all artificial automata. For a machine made by human art is not a machine in all its parts. . . . The machines of nature . . . are, on the contrary, machines even in their smallest parts without any limit. Herein lies the difference between nature and art, that is, between divine and human art.[30]

Thus, in Leibniz's conception, God is like a craftsman, and the cosmos is his art. It is on the basis of this model that Leibniz addresses the problem of evil raised by skeptics. He offers what has been called an aesthetic theodicy,[31] where he reasons that just as in a painting darker shades are necessary to complement and accentuate the brighter colors

---

[30] G. W. Leibniz, *Monadology and Other Essays* (Indianapolis: Bobbs-Merrill, 1965), 158-159. Similar analogies are abundant in the writings of other early modern philosophers and scientists, such as René Descartes, Isaac Newton, Robert Boyle, and William Paley.

[31] A theodicy is any attempt to explain God's permission of evil in the world.

in order to bring about the beauty of the whole, so must evil serve the purpose of contributing to the good of the whole cosmos.[32]

A more elaborate aesthetic conception of the world comes from the philosopher George Berkeley. Probably influenced by Leibniz, Berkeley employed an aesthetic theodicy much like that of his elder contemporary.[33] But the Irish bishop extended the metaphor by comparing the cosmos to a work of literary art.[34] The visible world, he suggested, may be conceived as a sort of language for the eyes. Consider first the written word. When we read a text, what we literally see are sequences of symbols. We only indirectly encounter meaning as we make associations and inferences from the symbols we perceive. It was Berkeley's point that this goes for visual perception generally. As we look around us, what we see directly is a multitude of shapes and colors, none of which carry any significance by themselves. When seen repeatedly in certain combinations and sequences, however, meaning emerges much as in written language. For instance, just as particular words (e.g., *cat*, *apple*, etc.) are complexes of simple components or universals (e.g., *c*, *a*, *t*, etc.) in a text, so are particular objects in the visible world (e.g., a cat, an apple, etc.) analyzable into universals of color (e.g., black, orange, etc.) and shape (e.g., oval, rectangular, etc.). Furthermore, the rules of syntax that govern the "linguistic world" are analogous to the laws of nature in the physical world, meanings being possible in each case if and only if there is sufficient consistency in the way the symbols are grouped and sequenced.[35]

Thus, given an ordinary understanding of language, nature is properly considered such, for it is constituted by

---

[32] At this point in the argument Leibniz appeals to two key principles: the principle of sufficient reason and the principle of perfection. The former states that for any positive fact whatsoever there must be some sufficient cause. The latter dictates that given God's perfection, he will always make the most rational choice in any situation. Combining these two principles, Leibniz infers, first, that there must be some rational explanation for the world's being exactly as it is and, second, that since God chose to make this world the explanation must be that it is the *best* choice. Hence the conclusion for which Leibniz is most famous, that this is the "best of all possible worlds."

[33] See, for example, Berkeley's essay "Minute Philosophers," in *The Works of George Berkeley*, eds. A. A. Luce and T. E. Jessop (London: Thomas Nelson and Sons, 1955), 7:206-209.

[34] It is true that many early modern thinkers, including scientists such as Galileo, saw the world as analogous to a text, the "book of nature" as it was sometimes called. But no one spells out this metaphor in such detail as Berkeley.

[35] See Colin Turbayne's "Berkeley's Metaphysical Grammar," in *Berkeley: Principles of Human Knowledge*, ed. Colin Turbayne (Indianapolis: Bobbs-Merrill, 1970), 3-36, for a fine elucidation of Berkeley's notion of the world as a divine visual language. Turbayne draws out several further analogies between written text and the language of the eyes.

sensible signs which have no similitude or necessary connexion with the things signified; so as by the apposite management of them to suggest and exhibit to [our] mind[s] an endless variety of things, differing in nature, time, and place; thereby informing . . . entertaining . . . and directing [us] how to act, not only with regard to things near and present, but also with regard to things distant and future.[36]

The implications of this view that were of most interest to Berkeley were apologetic in nature. For if this conception is a proper one, the natural inference to draw is that, just as in any discourse, there is some intelligent mind behind nature that aims to communicate with us. "This visual language proves," Berkeley concludes,

a provident Governor, actually and intimately present, and attentive to all our interests and motions, who watches over our conduct, and takes care of our minutest actions and designs throughout the whole course of our lives, informing, admonishing, and directing incessantly, in a most evident and sensible manner.[37]

Though they conceive of the cosmos under different media, both Berkeley and Leibniz understand the Creator as a cosmic artist. Whether figuratively interpreted as architect, painter, or author, God is engaged in crafting something beautiful.[38]

Turning now to another eighteenth-century scholar, Jonathan Edwards, we find an aesthetic emphasis applied not to the physical world but to the moral realm. In *The Nature of True Virtue* Edwards offers an ethical theory that runs against the grain of traditional philosophical categories. Instead of distinguishing virtue and beauty as distinct qualities, he identifies the former as a species of the latter. Virtue, says Edwards, is a kind of beauty of the mind, pertaining to those choices and acts that are of a moral nature. Otherwise put, "virtue is the beauty of the qualities and exercises of the heart, or those actions which proceed from them."[39] To be more specific, virtuous acts are essentially

---

[36] George Berkeley, *Alciphron*, in *The Works of George Berkeley*, 3:149.

[37] Ibid., 3:160.

[38] A twentieth-century thinker who prefers the literary metaphor is Dorothy Sayers. See her "Creative Mind," in *The Whimsical Christian* (New York: Macmillan, 1969). Her provocative comparison of God to a playwright, though undeveloped, served in part as inspiration for the central claims of this chapter.

[39] Jonathan Edwards, *The Nature of True Virtue*, op. cit., 1:122.

manifestations of the love of being, and any person who acts in a consistently benevolent way is a virtuous person.[40] To this Edwards adds that God, being the most excellent being, is also most beautiful. Being the source of all things, he is also the source of all beauty. And since he is most beautiful, the loving of God or striving after him is another way of conceiving the essence of beauty.[41]

Applications of the Aesthetic Model

The theoretical and practical implications of this Christian aesthetic interpretation of the world are significant, as we shall see shortly. But why, as I suggested above, is this model most naturally suggested by an Augustinian view of providence? Before arguing for this point I should note that each of the modern philosophers just discussed—Leibniz, Berkeley, and Edwards—did in fact affirm such a view. While the case can be made that each of their emphases on beauty derived ultimately from their perspective on providence, doing so here would demand an extensive exposition of their writings. In any case, the weightier matter is why an Augustinian view would inspire *anyone* to see the world in fundamentally aesthetic terms (as I believe it did for each of these thinkers). This is the larger claim that I wish to make and for which the ideas of Leibniz, Berkeley, and Edwards will have to serve as useful illustrations.

An Augustinian view of providence inspires the aesthetic interpretation of the world as follows. According to this perspective, everything in the world, including both the phenomena of inanimate nature and the free actions of human beings, is the result of divine design. God's conservation of the world is utterly teleological, actively aiming all things and events toward the end of expressing his glory. Now since God is maximally beautiful, and his glory is tantamount to beauty itself, the aim of creation is principally aesthetic in nature. The purpose of all creation is the glory of God—the shining forth of his beauty for all minds to adore and enjoy. The story of the cosmos, and more locally human history, is thus beautiful in its totality. And we have good reason to see the world through the lens of beauty. All things are rich with aesthetic value, both inherently and in the sense that God is using them ultimately to magnify his own beauty.

---

[40] Ibid., 1:124.
[41] Ibid., 1:125.

Now it is true that those who espouse a low view of providence might insist that their view, too, allows for divine responsibility for all the beauty of creation. But this is true only in a derivative sense. Free human actions that result in beautiful works of art, such as Vivaldi's *Four Seasons* or Da Vinci's *Mona Lisa*, are not necessarily even foreseen by God in the low view of providence; so God is responsible for these things only in the remote causal sense that he endowed these artists with the talents to produce them. (Or, to be more precise, in the low view God endowed the original human beings with creative capacities that could be procreatively passed on to their progeny in such a way that beautiful works of art could be produced.) Thus, whereas the Augustinian view sees such works of art as first conceived by God and secondarily caused by human minds, the low view must regard all works of human art as primarily caused by human beings and only remotely caused by God. The former view warrants greater praise for God as it inspires us to see all beauty in the world, human-made as well as "natural," as coming first and foremost from him.

In the Augustinian view all human-made beauty is primarily of God and only secondarily from us. In the low view, the situation is reversed. The beauty resulting from our creative acts is, due to our libertarian freedom, primarily ours and only secondarily God's. In the Augustinian view, all that is beautiful, whether physical or moral, is a divine creation, not the fortunate consequence of the work of one of God's creatures. God ordained it; so ultimately he and he alone deserves the praise for it and recognition as its creative source. In the low view, human artists deserve exclusive praise for some of the things they create.

Art as Expression and Communication

Thus far I have only presented and applied the aesthetic model in its most general form. In the Augustinian view of providence, the world is fundamentally an aesthetic phenomenon, because it is an artistic creation, intentionally fashioned in every detail by the cosmic Artist for the purpose of publicly expressing and communicating his own beauty. But more needs to be said about the elements of expression and communication, since these seem to be essential to art and the creative process. So I will give a closer look, with the help of a few aestheticians whose theories duly emphasize these key features of art and the artistic process.[42]

Let us begin with Leo Tolstoy. Tolstoy is most renowned for his literary achievements, but his contribution to the philosophy of art is noteworthy in its own right. Tolstoy maintains that the artistic process is essentially an activity whereby feelings are shared between persons. The artist creatively translates certain feelings into objective forms with the intention of replicating these in the audience when they receive the work. Thus, Tolstoy defines the artistic process as follows: "to evoke in oneself a feeling one has once experienced and, having evoked it in oneself by means of movements, lines, colors, sounds, or forms expressed in words, so to transmit that feeling that others experience the same feeling—this is the activity of art."[43] And he defines art itself as "a human

---

[42] The expression and communication theories discussed here are two of several major perspectives on the nature of art. Other major theories include representationalism, formalism, subjectivism, and institutionalism. The representationalist or imitation theory was championed by Aristotle, who regarded *mimesis* as the essential purpose of art. According to him, this is epitomized in tragedy, where the misfortunes of a noble hero are imitated, thus replicating fear and pity in the audience. The ultimate aim is catharsis, the purging of these negative emotions. (See Aristotle's *Poetics* in *The Basic Works of Aristotle*, ed. Richard McKeon [New York: Random House, 1941].) The besetting problem with the imitation view is its overly narrow conception of art. Surely imaginative and other nonrepresentational forms of creativity should be considered art as well.

Among formalists, Clive Bell's version has been most influential, defining the essence of art as "significant form," such as lines, colors, and other formal elements in a painting or sculpture. Interestingly, Bell identifies significant form as essential because of its capacity to produce what he calls the peculiar "aesthetic emotion." (See Bell's *Art* [London: Chatto and Windus, 1914].) His view differs from expressionism in locating the focus for aesthetics in the formal features of the artwork rather than in the artist and the artistic process. Formalist theories are most appealing as applied to the visual arts, but they are less workable and even counterintuitive when applied to music and the literary arts.

The aesthetics of David Hume represented a subjectivist turn in the history of philosophy of art. Like many of his contemporaries, he focused on the concept of audience taste rather than artists or artworks themselves. He maintained that "Beauty is no quality in things themselves: It exists merely in the mind which contemplates them; and each mind perceives a different beauty" (from "Of the Standard of Taste," in *Essays Moral, Political and Literary*, ed. Eugene F. Miller [Indianapolis: Liberty Classics, 1985], 230). At the same time, he insisted that the faculty of aesthetic judgment, or "delicacy of taste," could be developed and refined. The problematic upshot of such a subjectivist approach is its implication that any work of art may be rationally judged good (or bad).

Finally, institutionalist theories, such as those of Arthur Danto and George Dickie, regard institutional context as definitive for art. In short, art is whatever is *presented* as art in an "artworld," which is defined as a social system that includes museums, curators, artists, etc. (See Arthur Danto, "The Artworld," *Journal of Philosophy* 61 (1964): 571-584 and George Dickie, *Art and Aesthetics: An Institutional Analysis* [Ithaca, N.Y.: Cornell University Press, 1974].) Not surprisingly, the institutionalist theory has been roundly criticized both for its circularity (defining art in reference to an artworld, which must in turn be defined in terms of art) and its counterintuitive implications (as it entails that a urinal or a piece of driftwood are no less art and potentially aesthetically appreciable than a Rembrandt painting or Michelangelo sculpture).

[43] Leo Tolstoy, *What Is Art?*, trans. Almyer Maude (Indianapolis: Bobbs-Merrill, 1960), 51. Tolstoy converted to Christianity in the middle of his literary career, after he had written *War and Peace* but prior to publication of *Anna Karenina* and *The Death of Ivan Ilyich*. *What Is Art?* appeared toward the end of his career, when Tolstoy was in his late sixties. Thus, it represents the mature aesthetic reflections of one of Western civilization's finest literary artists.

activity consisting in this, that one man consciously, by means of certain external signs, hands on to others feelings he has lived through, and that other people are infected by these feelings and also experience them."[44]

So for Tolstoy, art is essentially social, a community affair. And it may be evaluated accordingly, the criteria for assessment being implicit in the very nature of art. Since the sharing and evocation of feeling is the purpose of art, the quality of a work depends upon how well, if at all, it succeeds in this. Thus, "the degree of infectiousness is . . . the sole measure of excellence in art. The stronger the infection, the better is the art as art."[45] Tolstoy identifies three conditions that determine the degree of contagiousness of feeling in art: (1) the individuality of the feeling transmitted, (2) the clarity with which the feeling is transmitted, and (3) the sincerity of the artist. The last of these is the most important, as the artist's sincerity will inspire clarity and individuality of feeling in an artwork. To create sincerely is to draw from the depths of one's nature to produce an artwork. "The artist," says Tolstoy, is "compelled by an inner need to express his feeling."[46]

R. G. Collingwood takes an approach quite similar to Tolstoy's, agreeing that the essence of the artistic process is the expression of emotion. But in Collingwood's view, artists do not address their art primarily to an audience. Rather, a work of art is intended first to clarify the artist's emotions to himself or herself. The creative process is an act of exploring emotions. An artist does not know precisely what they are until the artwork is complete. Thus, "the artist proper is a person who, grappling with the problem of expressing a certain emotion, says, 'I want to get this clear.'"[47] Artistic creation, then, is not only an act of expression but also an act of self-disclosure. This, in turn, explains how art arouses emotion in others. By witnessing the artist's emotional self-disclosure through the creative process, the audience is prompted to do the same. So the successful artist really accomplishes two things simultaneously, both expressing his or her own emotion and evoking the same in others. In Collingwood's words, "Art is emotional: that is, it is a life of pleasure and pain, desire and aversion, intertwined, as these opposite

---

[44] Ibid.
[45] Ibid., 140.
[46] Ibid., 141.
[47] R. G. Collingwood, *The Principles of Art* (New York: Oxford University Press, 1958), 114.

feelings always are, in such a way that each is conditioned by the felt or implied presence of the other."[48]

Collingwood stresses the difference between emotional expression and description of emotion: "To describe a thing is to call it a thing of such and such a kind: to bring it under a conception, to classify it. Expression, on the contrary, individualizes."[49] The artist, then, must be "absolutely candid" in the creative process if the emotions expressed are to be personally authentic. This does not preclude systematic deliberation, planning, and careful execution. It does mean, however, that the creative process is not governed by a fixed technique. The exploration of emotion in artistry forbids this.

Another theme of central importance in Collingwood's theory is his emphasis on imagination. While it might be a truism that artists use imagination, he goes much farther in claiming that a work of art is essentially an imaginary object. Collingwood declares, "the work of art proper is something not seen or heard, but something imagined."[50] The real work of the artist occurs in his or her mind. The actual construction of an artifact is incidental. Collingwood uses music composition to illustrate this thesis, noting that when a composer comes up with a melody, it already exists, though still "in his head." Thus, "if the making of a tune is an instance of imaginative creation, a tune is an imaginary thing. And the same applies to a poem or a painting or any other work of art."[51] True artistry occurs in the artist's mind, and the consequent work of art is but a public expression of that mental reality.

A work of art is indivisible in a crucial way, according to Collingwood. It has an irreducible wholeness, which the audience perceives when experiencing the object aesthetically. The object is experienced as beautiful when there is "imaginative coherence," which pertains not only to the quantitative unity of the art object itself but also to the qualitative experience of the object, which is essentially emotional

---

[48] R. G. Collingwood, *Essays in the Philosophy of Art* (Bloomington, Ind.: Indiana University Press, 1964), 51.

[49] R. G. Collingwood, *The Principles of Art*, 112. This insight accounts for the wisdom in the well-known literary adage "show, don't tell." William Wordsworth famously extends this caution to our attitude toward natural beauty: "Sweet is the lore which Nature brings / Our meddling intellect / Misshapes the beauteous forms of things / We murder to dissect." ("The Tables Turned," in *Wordsworth and His Poetry*, ed. William H. Hudson [London: George Harrap & Co., 1914], p. 86).

[50] R. G. Collingwood, *The Principles of Art*, 142.

[51] Ibid., 139.

in nature. Imaginative coherence, or beauty, is not apprehended discursively but intuitively; it is felt rather than simply thought. And the experience is not always pleasurable:

> Beauty is present to the mind simply in the form of an emotion. This emotion is bipolar; it is not merely pleasant, but pleasant and painful; and whereas those people who never go very deep into art regard it as a pleasant experience, but one whose pleasure is somewhat trivial and unimportant, those who exert their imaginative powers to the utmost find in that exertion not only a higher and more valuable pleasure but frequent and intense pain. This pain is caused not only by the spectacle of bad art, but equally, though in a different way, by all acute awareness of beauty; so much so that one constantly finds oneself afraid to go to a concert, to read a poem, to look at a very beautiful scene, not from fear of possible ugliness but from fear of too great beauty; and it is this fear that prompts the hatred and suspicion which a respectable mediocrity feels towards the highest art and the greatest splendors of nature.[52]

A closely related approach to art focuses on the capacity of artworks to communicate ideas. Arthur Schopenhauer was a leading proponent of such a view. Most fields of knowledge seek truth via causal reasoning, as is epitomized in empirical science. The scientist studies particulars and works toward ends that are practical in nature. Schopenhauer contrasts this with the work of the artist, whose subject matter is universal truths and whose work is an end in itself. Art, he says, "repeats the eternal Ideas apprehended through pure contemplation, the essential and abiding element in all the phenomena of the world."[53] In this way, art provides the most direct avenue to the fundamental truths of reality. Through science and other forms of causal reasoning, the best we can do is make generalizations about the physical world and solve temporal problems. The scientist cannot access universals, or Ideas as Schopenhauer calls them (in a roughly Platonic sense of the term), the key to finding ultimate meaning. But art transcends the physical world, enabling us to access such Ideas. Science merely deals with natural phenomena. Art informs us of the eternal realities behind nature, and "its

---

[52] R. G. Collingwood, *Essays in the Philosophy of Art*, 72.
[53] Arthur Schopenhauer, *The World as Will and Representation*, trans. E. F. J. Payne (New York: Dover Publications, 1969), 1:184.

sole aim is communication of this knowledge." Science "can never find an ultimate goal or complete satisfaction, any more than by running we can reach the point where the clouds touch the horizon; art, on the contrary, is everywhere at its goal."[54]

Artists are endowed with *genius*, the skill of pure contemplation that enables them to perceive universals in particular objects. Capable of ignoring personal aims and interests, the artistic genius is thus endowed with the ability to perceive the world with "complete objectivity." Genius is not distracted by the scientific impulse to solve problems nor the hardships of life that give rise to this impulse. Rather, "the objects of genius as such are the eternal Ideas, the persistent, essential forms of the world and all its phenomena."[55] Artists also have a talent for making the Ideas known to others through the creative process. An object's beauty is "that quality of it which facilitates knowledge of its Idea," and artists have the unique ability to make beautiful objects.[56] Thus good art enables the audience to transcend the limits of their own rational comprehension and access universal truth. To properly appreciate beauty is essentially to acquire knowledge of the eternal.

Divine Art as Expression and Communication

The above aesthetic theories are, I believe, profoundly insightful accounts of art and the creative process. There are, in fact, many considerations to recommend both the Tolstoy-Collingwood focus on the emotional expressiveness of artworks and Schopenhauer's stress on art's capacity to communicate ideas. However, I see no reason why the expressionist and communication theories can't both be correct as far as they go. Neither perspective need be pressed to the exclusion of the other. They can be merged into a single theory that affirms the functions of art to express emotion and communicate ideas. Indeed, this is the theoretical approach I affirm and will incorporate into my aesthetic model. As divine art, the world is both an expression of divine emotion and a divine communication of eternal truths.

Applying the major elements of the expressionist and communica-

[54] Ibid., 1:185.
[55] Ibid., 1:186.
[56] Ibid., 1:202.

tion theories to my aesthetic model will give it a certain distinctive character. But before I do so I want to make two caveats. First, the specific version (i.e., expression-communication) of the aesthetic model I am developing is admittedly tentative and exploratory. Here I am pursuing just one potentially fruitful paradigm inspired by the Augustinian view of providence. Similar models could be developed by applying any among several aesthetic theories. I happen to find the expression and communication approaches the most compelling. This is not to say that this model is purely speculative or somehow unwarranted. On the contrary, as I have tried to show, there are biblical and philosophical considerations that point in this direction. But like any theoretical proposal, the expression-communication (hereafter E-C) model is underdetermined by the evidence. This leads us to my second caveat. As with any philosophical-theological model, the adequacy of the E-C model must be evaluated in terms of its fit with Scripture, internal coherence, existential viability, and conceptual explanatory power. Such assessment is hardly a simple and straightforward matter but necessitates careful and sympathetic (though, of course, not gullible) review of the main elements of the model. If some of my applications seem contrived or ponderous, I ask the reader to ignore them in the interest of assessing the overall merits of the model.

The essence of the E-C aesthetic model is that the cosmos is an expression of divine emotion and a communication of God's eternal ideas. And the beauty of the world is attributable to just this fact. Otherwise put, nature's beauty is a doorway to the divine mind. In creation God makes known his thoughts and transmits his feelings. With regard to the former, the world is imbued with truth and meaning, which we access in diverse ways. As we study the tangible, visible, and audible manifestations of divine ideas, we learn, in the words of Johann Kepler, to "think God's thoughts after him." The world is also rich with emotive content. The cosmos is a clear, unique, and sincere expression of divine feelings. God conveys his internal emotions through external signs, and we experience these, sometimes sharing God's feelings—his pleasure, pain, humor, sorrow, and joy. Accordingly, we learn *to feel God's emotions after him.* Thus, in thinking and feeling with God we are mysteriously privileged to "participate in the divine nature" (2 Pet. 1:4).

As a manifestation of God's ideas and emotions, the cosmos is fundamentally an act of divine self-disclosure. God communicates and expresses to his audience, which includes persons outside the cosmos (angels and the rest of the heavenly host) and within the cosmos (human beings). The self-manifestation of God's noetic and emotive life is his glory or splendor. These are aesthetic terms, of course, referring in one way or another to divine beauty. Tolstoy speaks of the fact that artists are compelled by an inner need to express. On the E-C model, this may simply be seen as an aspect of the *imago Dei*, reflecting God's own basic disposition to express himself. Jonathan Edwards suggests as much when he writes, "we may suppose, that a disposition in God, as an original property of his nature, to an emanation of his own infinite fullness, was what excited him to create the world."[57] The world "emanates" God's nature, as any artwork reflects the nature of the artist. The Creator's personality is imprinted on all that he has made. As the psalmist says, "the heavens declare the glory of God; the skies proclaim the work of his hands" (Ps. 19:1).

God has, in Schopenhauer's words, a "pure perception" of the eternal ideas, his own thoughts, according to which he has fashioned the universe. He has made known universals in each of the particulars that we observe in nature and human history. That we are able to identify the "essences" of things, from apples and dogs to love and justice, owes to God's gracious act of embodying his eternal ideas in the various phenomena of the world. Every object and event is replete with eternal meaning, because its reality traces to some divine idea. Also, God is the ultimate artistic genius, in Schopenhauer's sense, privileged with a truly "complete objectivity." God's work in the world is not problem-solving in some local sense, as if his will were just an especially powerful one among many, struggling to overcome forces that oppose him. On the contrary, his omnipotence guarantees that all things unfold according to his eternal will. He uses the whole of his creation, including its rebel elements, to achieve his own glorious purposes. His ideas are continuously made known to the other minds he has made, and the facilitation of this knowledge is beautiful.

The contagiousness of feeling in the cosmic artwork is evidenced by the endless aesthetic inspirations that artists draw from nature. The

---

[57] Jonathan Edwards, "The End for Which God Created the World," *op. cit.*, 1:100.

transmission of the divine emotions in creation (*originans* and *continuans*) is entirely adequate to the divine aesthetic purpose of transmitting the divine emotions (as revealed in the Genesis 1 refrain, "it is good"). In making his imaginations publicly accessible, God is "absolutely candid," to use Collingwood's phrase. Creation is a perfectly authentic divine self-expression. Even though creation is tainted by sin, the divine personality is evident everywhere. As Paul notes, "since the creation of the world God's invisible qualities—his eternal power and divine nature—have been clearly seen, being understood from what has been made" (Rom. 1:20). It is nature's awesome beauty that prods us toward transcendence of the world, to find our way back to our eternal source, who is himself the consummation of all beauty. He has placed eternity in our hearts (Eccl. 3:11), and the sublime loveliness of creation properly causes us to ache for our heavenly home where we will be united with our Maker.

According to the E-C model, among the aspects of the divine nature evident in creation are God's emotive attributes. God is emotional just as he is both rational and volitional. But, then, what is the nature of his emotions? Specifically, if God is eternal and immutable, then does he have the same emotions for all eternity? Do the divine emotions run the gamut even as do those of human beings? These questions introduce a tangle of issues that warrant extended treatment, which will occupy us in Chapter 5. In sum, I will answer the latter two questions affirmatively and will propose a model of divine emotion that avoids the inadequate extremes of the standard views on this issue. I will propose that God is *omnipathic*, experiencing all emotions, though not in a way that implies he is mutable or temporally bound. According to this view, the world is a contingent, temporal manifestation of eternal divine emotions, just as the world contingently and temporally manifests eternal divine ideas.

So, then, does divine omnipathos imply that God experiences pain? After all, some emotions, such as grief and sorrow, are unpleasant. As I shall argue later, there are some good theological reasons to think so, especially considering the doctrines of divine omniscience and the divine incarnation. But the E-C aesthetic model suggests the same as well. As Collingwood notes, both the exertion of imaginative powers and the acute apprehension of beauty can be intensely painful, perhaps in the sense of deep sorrow. And, of course, God both creates and apprehends beauty in the most extreme way. Does it follow, then, that God is sorrowful, that he suffers because of the intensity of his own beauty? This might seem to go too far, as human sorrow associated with experience of exquisite beauty might be attributable to our finitude rather than the essential painfulness of extreme beauty. However, God's personal entry into his artwork, as its central character, Jesus of Nazareth, the "hero" in the drama of world history, is excruciatingly painful. In Jesus "all the fullness of the Deity lives in bodily form" (Col. 2:9), and at the same time he was a "man of sorrows, and familiar with suffering" (Isa. 53:3). Indeed, the God-man suffered violently. And why? To redeem the world, his cosmic artwork. But God was not simply redeeming a world gone wrong beyond his control. The fall, after all, was part of his plan, a painful but definitive component of his art. So God's sovereign governance of human rebellion and gracious redemption is essentially painful. And, of course, it is most beautiful. So it would seem that even for God the making of extreme beauty is intensely painful, a source of both deep sorrow and exceedingly great joy.

Some further theological considerations point in the same direction, such as the biblical concept of the fellowship of suffering as a means of entering into the divine life. This theme is captured in the Catholic concept of "beatific vision." As we suffer in diverse ways we find union with the suffering Savior, who was afflicted beyond what we can possibly imagine. We enter into his exquisite sorrow and in so doing glimpse the beauty of his nature in ways too deep and profound to otherwise grasp. This theme will be explored in more detail in Chapter 6.

These are the basic contours of the E-C aesthetic model. The cosmos is a divine artwork, an "aesthetic phenomenon" of the highest order, through which: (1) God communicates eternal ideas and universal truths, including many facts about his own nature and essential moral truths, and (2) God expresses a range of emotions, from sorrow to joy, in which we participate and through which we find deeper union with him. The sheer beauty of creation exalts human minds to contemplate eternal truths in ways that transcend our ability to think about them discursively. And nature's beauty arouses emotional longings for the eternal in the human heart, prompting us to seek the divine Artist when we otherwise would remain apathetic.

Some Final Applications

The aesthetic model has a number of salutary implications in the fields of art and education. It prompts us to take more seriously the natural human impulse to create, as we are made in the image of a creative God and are ourselves players in his cosmic drama. Also, the aesthetic emphasis helps to explain why art is so therapeutic, since in the act of creating we mirror God. To create is to actively reflect his image, which is satisfying even for the most godless artist. Furthermore, to understand this is to better appreciate the strength of the temptation to engage in idolatry of graven images, for like our Maker, we are prone to admire and appreciate the fruits of our artistic endeavor. Hence, it should not surprise us when we encounter cases of art worship, the deification of artists, and other characteristics of religiosity within the art community.[58]

As for the educational applications of this aesthetic model, there are several. First, we Christian educators can be encouraged in the confirmation that we are engaged in an educational task that is unified. Since the aesthetic interpretation conceives of any subject matter as either the study of God or his artwork, discoveries about any aspect of one domain become crucially relevant to inquiry about all aspects of the other. We may, then, reconceive the disciplines accordingly, with the following threefold division:

1. The pure and applied studies of God's handiwork (e.g., the empirical sciences of physics, chemistry, and biology; engineering, history, psychology, sociology, anthropology, archaeology, linguistics, comparative religious studies, etc.).

2. The pure and applied studies of the ways in which God's creativity is humanly mirrored (e.g., literature, music, theater, painting, sculpture, architecture, pottery, the culinary arts, etc.).

---

[58] Gene Veith describes this phenomenon in illuminating detail: "The vocabulary of aesthetic criticism is now replete with language borrowed from religion: 'inspiration,' 'vision,' 'transcendence,' 'myth,' 'epiphany,' 'revelation.' Artists are described as special people, above the humdrum limits of ordinary society, endowed with mystical powers, a sacred aura, and authority. The artist, in effect, is treated as a seer, a prophet, or, more precisely, a shaman. The work of art is treated as an oracular utterance of inexpressible depth, an authoritative guide to life. Often the arts are presented as esoteric mysteries. The 'art world' becomes a privileged inner circle, possessing secret knowledge from which the nonelect are excluded. As in the mystery religions of old, membership in the inner circle requires initiation. The priests of the art world would be the teachers and critics who introduce their congregations to the arcane language and secret knowledge of the elect. These clergy also preserve the relics of the departed saints and construct elaborate theologies of the arts, which they defend with sectarian zeal and enforce with inquisitorial rigor" (*State of the Arts* [Wheaton, Ill.: Crossway Books, 1991], 137).

3. The study of the cosmic Artist himself (i.e., revealed theology and natural theology).

This catalogue of the disciplines, though incomplete, provides a rough idea of how the subject matter of the various academic fields may be reconceived within the aesthetic model. Among unlisted disciplines, some fields, such as business, economics, and philosophy, fall into two or more categories, while placement of the *a priori* sciences of mathematics and geometry depends upon one's philosophy of mathematics.[59]

Another application regards the firm conceptual foundation for the integration of faith and learning that the aesthetic model provides. However different may be the methodologies among Christian scholars' various fields, our goals at bottom are one: we all are engaged in the process of learning about either the cosmic Artist or his artwork. The aesthetic model not only makes the integration of Christian theistic commitment with academic inquiry more natural—it reveals the lunacy of the believer who neglects to do so. Such failure is comparable to engaging in an in-depth study of a work of literature while refusing to make any reference to the author, though the author's identity is known.

For this reason the natural scientist should never feel uneasy about making direct reference to God either in the classroom or in the context of research, for it is always appropriate to speak of the artist when analyzing the art object. In fact, to do so is necessary from an epistemological standpoint, for adequate knowledge of the effect always implies at least some knowledge of the cause. The shame of contemporary natural science is the predominance of methodological naturalism, which idealizes empirical inquiry that makes no explicit reference to a supernatural, intelligent cause of the world. Not only is this restric-

---

[59] Just where the *a priori* sciences of mathematics and geometry fit into this schema is a point of contention that will not soon be settled. There are three positions on the issue of the ontological status of mathematical truths. Mathematical realism (or "Platonism") is the view that such truths pertain to the real world. Intuitionism says that truths of mathematics and geometry regard only the way humans think. And the nominalist denies even this, suggesting that math and geometry are simply artificial formal languages that have no existential import whatsoever. Now if mathematical realism is true, the *a priori* sciences perhaps tell us about God's artwork as well as the divine mind itself, in which case they fall into the last category in the schema. If mathematical intuitionism is correct, then math and geometry tell us about concepts in the human mind, in which case these disciplines fall into the second category. Finally, if the mathematical nominalist is correct, then math and geometry fall into the first or second category. In any case, the *a priori* sciences fall into one of these three categories, depending upon which philosophy of mathematics is true. For a helpful discussion of philosophy of mathematics, see J. P. Moreland's *Scaling the Secular City* (Grand Rapids, Mich.: Baker, 1987), 24-26.

tion epistemologically problematic and historically aberrant,[60] but it reveals a tragic irony in the history of natural science. Nearly four centuries of modern science and two and a half millennia of systematic inquiry about the natural world have converged in pointing toward an intelligent world-designer; yet it is precisely at this point in history that methodological naturalism dominates. The good news is that this methodology is currently under serious and sustained attack. However, I am convinced that the eradication of this academic disease would occur all the more swiftly should the model I am proposing be largely embraced. I will further discuss methodological naturalism in the next chapter.

Finally, and most significantly, with the aesthetic model we have much more reason to place a special accent on the fine arts than we might have had before. The dearth of quality Christian art these days is scandalous. This problem will be rectified only if centers of Christian higher learning take initiative to recapture the territory lost in the last century or more (which, interestingly, has coincided with the growing prevalence of the low view of providence). I would submit that the proper inspiration for this endeavor is the realization that all artistic endeavor is theological in nature. The question is not *if* this poem, painting, or film is relevant to one's faith, but *how* it is relevant. Not *whether* a particular stage play or musical composition relates to some theological truth, but *in what way* it relates.

There is no greater challenge to the Christian college than to preserve a genuine commitment both to the liberal arts and to an orthodox theological orientation. A more expansive aesthetic vision is called for to maintain this commitment in full vitality. The model I have presented here can serve to buttress such a vision, as it will ensure that, in the words of Abraham Kuyper, we "keep [our] eyes fixed upon the Beautiful and the Sublime in its eternal significance and upon art as one of the richest gifts of God to mankind."[61]

---

[60] Historically, from Aristotle to the nineteenth century, theists engaged in the study of nature have freely referred to God in the context of their research. The view that renders illicit such references is a relatively new and unique phenomenon in the history of thought. Two informative works on this topic are Stanley Jaki, *The Road of Science and the Ways to God* (Chicago: University of Chicago Press, 1978) and Nancy Pearcey and Charles Thaxton, *The Soul of Science: Christian Faith and Natural Philosophy* (Wheaton, Ill.: Crossway Books, 1994).

[61] Abraham Kuyper, *Lectures on Calvinism* (Grand Rapids, Mich.: Eerdmans, 1931), 143.

CONCLUSION

I began this chapter by noting the implications of the orthodox doctrine of divine conservation for the doctrine of providence. Specifically, I showed how the "constant creation" view is the most reasonable interpretation of this basic doctrine. Based on this approach, I explicated the aesthetic model and applied it in diverse ways, both generally and as specifically conceived in terms of the expressionist and communication aesthetic theories. I offer this as just one potentially fruitful model of the Augustinian view of providence. The remainder of this book can be seen as an application of the aesthetic model broadly construed. More specifically, Chapter 5 is a detailed exploration of the expressionist component, and portions of Chapters 4, 6, and 7 can be seen as applications of the communication component.

4

THE PRACTICE OF SCIENCE

In the previous chapter we saw that the doctrine of divine conservation suggests an Augustinian view of providence. We also noted how an Augustinian perspective inspires an aesthetic interpretation of the world. In this chapter I want to demonstrate just how deep and far-reaching are the ramifications of the Augustinian view for scientific practice. To this end, I will discuss two methodological issues and two substantive issues in science. One of the methodological issues concerns induction, which is the use of inferences from observed phenomena to what is unobserved. This mode of inference is foundational to scientific inquiry and apparently a matter of common sense. But with his famous critique of induction, David Hume showed that this commonsense belief was problematic, thus shaking the foundations of science. Consequently, the very rationality of scientific enterprise was eventually called into question in many quarters.[1] The Augustinian view of providence, as I will claim, dissolves the notorious Humean problem of induction and thus—excuse the scholarly melodrama—saves science as a rational enterprise.

The other methodological concern to be discussed is of special concern to theists (and Christians in particular)—namely, the question whether scientific study should be conducted as if only the physical

---

[1] The reverberations of Hume's critique were not fully felt in the philosophy of science until the middle of the twentieth century, when within the analytic philosophical tradition formal theories of scientific inference began to reach maturity. The explosion of anti-realist philosophies of science in the last few decades can be seen, in part, as a long-term ramification of Hume's skeptical arguments.

world exists. Those who believe so subscribe to what is called "methodological naturalism," because to do so is to proceed in science *as if* naturalism were true (i.e., as if only the physical world were real). Those who reject this approach endorse what is sometimes called "theistic science," as they favor integrating our scientific study with our theistic convictions, when appropriate. Debate over this issue has been sharpest in biological science, as the implications of this methodological issue for the substantive issue of origins are significant. Accordingly, methodological naturalists prefer an evolutionary perspective, while practitioners of theistic science tend to opt for a creationist or intelligent-design perspective on the question of the origin of species. I will show that the Augustinian view of providence undermines methodological naturalism and, in turn, reduces the epistemic justification for subscribing to a theistic evolutionary paradigm.

The other substantive issue to be addressed pertains to the central question of contemporary consciousness studies: Just what *is* consciousness, and how does it arise? Currently, physicalism is the reigning research paradigm in the mainstream study of the human mind, with only a few dissenting theories receiving serious attention. Thus, according to most scholars, consciousness must ultimately be explained in terms of some more basic physical facts. The pressing question is just what those facts are. Among theists with whom methodological naturalism holds sway, this basic approach is regarded as reasonable. But in this context methodological naturalism seems less compelling to many because of the apparently strong evidence for the immateriality of the human mind. A number of Christian scholars still affirm various forms of mind-body dualism, despite the problems accompanying this traditional approach. We will see that some version of this view is to be preferred, all things considered, notwithstanding the audacious claims made by its critics. Also, we will see how the Augustinian view of providence opens the door to a unique brand of dualism that overcomes the standard problems with this view and goes further toward solving the riddle of consciousness.

Obviously this is a dauntingly broad range of territory to canvass. But I must do so in order to demonstrate how extensive are the constructive applications of the Augustinian view of providence. A proper treatment of the subject would warrant a book-length study, but this is true of each of the chapter topics in this book. Other scholars can provide more detailed and rigorous explorations within these subject areas (indeed, some already have). The purpose of this book is to provide an overview of the many benefits of the Augustinian view of providence for Christian belief and practice. And I hope this overview will inspire more such efforts, especially as they pertain to the scientific issues discussed in this chapter.

THE PROBLEM OF INDUCTION

The inductive method is crucial to science. It involves reasoning from the observed to the unobserved, or inferring from what we have experienced to what lies beyond experience, such as future events. For example, based on past sunrises one concludes that the sun will rise tomorrow. Science involves the basic assumption that the laws of nature remain constant, that the future will resemble the past. Without this assumption no experimental procedures are possible, as the constancy of nature's basic operations is always assumed. Of course, it is not only scientists who make this assumption. It is a matter of common sense.

Hume's Critique of Induction

However, in his *A Treatise of Human Nature* David Hume makes the following shockingly bold claim:

> [T]here is nothing in any object considered in itself which can afford us a reason for drawing a conclusion beyond it; and, even after the observation of the frequent or constant conjunction of objects, we have no reason to draw any inference concerning any object beyond those of which we have had experience.[2]

Hume's argument for this thesis, which is set in the context of a discussion of the relation of cause and effect, is two-pronged. If our belief in causal laws is to be justified, this must be done either via reason or experience. He attacks the first approach on the following grounds. Since I can conceive the occurrence of any cause without its being accompanied by its usual effect, it follows that it is not impossible that

---

2 David Hume, *A Treatise of Human Nature*, second edition., ed. L. A. Selby-Bigge (Oxford: Oxford University Press, 1978), 139.

any effect could follow from any cause. For "whatever is intelligible, and can be distinctly conceived, implies no contradiction, and can never be proved false by any demonstrative argument or abstract reasoning *a priori*."[3]

Hume's critique of the justification of our belief in causal laws via experience goes as follows. In appealing to experience to justify causal laws one can appeal to past and present experiences only. However, in doing so we inevitably beg the question, since it is our belief that the future will resemble the past that we are trying to justify. Hume concludes, "It is impossible, therefore, that any arguments from experience can prove this resemblance of the past to the future; since all these arguments are founded on the supposition of that resemblance."[4] The notion that the future will resemble the past is known as the uniformity of nature. Hume's argument basically undermines this belief and may be rephrased as follows. In order to justify our belief that nature is uniform, our only possible philosophical recourse is to appeal to the fact that in the past nature has been uniform. Obviously, in arguing this way we presuppose that nature is uniform, the very belief we are attempting to justify. Hence we are arguing in a circle. The upshot in Hume's view, as we see in the passage quoted above, is that our belief in the uniformity of nature is philosophically unjustified. In view of this predicament, Alfred North Whitehead declared, "The theory of induction is the despair of philosophy—and yet all our activities are based upon it."[5]

Hume's own response to the problem was to take a pragmatic tack. While acknowledging what he considers to be a lack of rational grounds for believing that the future resembles the past, he grants that this belief is irresistible, and although entirely a product of instinct and custom, it is in fact very practical. If we are to get along in life, we must assume, if not in word, at least in deed, that nature is uniform. It is a sort of "animal faith" that abides with us for our own good.[6] This approach, however, is widely regarded as deficient, as it is basically a concession to

---

[3] David Hume, *An Enquiry Concerning Human Understanding*, in *The Essential Works of David Hume*, ed. David Cohen (New York: Bantam Books, 1965), 69.

[4] Ibid., 71.

[5] Alfred North Whitehead, *Science and the Modern World* (New York: The Free Press, 1967), 23.

[6] See Hume's *Enquiry*, XII, 1. This notion, exploited by, among others, George Santayana in his *Skepticism and Animal Faith*, is not a pejorative one for Hume, as it is simply descriptive of the fact that despite our exalted status as *rational* animals, at the end of the day we actually have good reasons for relatively few of our beliefs.

skepticism. Consequently, philosophers have developed a variety of strategies to solve the problem.

A Kantian strategy appeals to certain truths of fact known independently of experience that when combined with particular facts known from experience can justify an inference from empirical data to unobserved phenomena. This is a sort of attempt to make a deductive reconstruction of inductive arguments. Examples of candidates for such *a priori* principles include the principle of sufficient reason, the principle of causality, and the *ex nihilo nihil fit* ("out of nothing, nothing comes") principle. The main difficulty with this strategy lies in the controversial nature of such *a priori* propositions. Efforts to demonstrate that principles like those listed above qualify have been tenuous at best.

An alternative approach was advanced by the nineteenth-century philosopher William Whewell. He proposed that a scientific theory is not built through simple enumeration of observable phenomena but is only indirectly suggested by them. Through a special inferential process he calls "colligation," a scientist arrives at a theoretical account that unites and clarifies all of the observations. Whewell compares particular facts to individual pearls. A theory must unite the facts as a string unites pearls. This creates a "true bond of unity by which the phenomena are held together."[7] Further empirical data then serve to confirm the theory, though not to prove it, and from this general theory specific propositions about matters of fact may be explored. Unfortunately, Whewell's schema represents no real advance from ordinary inductive arguments. The initial generalization from empirical data to a scientific hypothesis, or colligation, involves precisely the sort of reasoning that Hume's critique undermines, viz. inference from the observed to the unobserved.

Karl Popper attempted to avoid the problem by insisting that inductive reasoning, strictly speaking, has no use in science. "There is," he says, "no need even to mention induction."[8] The *verification* of theories, he argues, is not the business of science. Rather, *falsification* is its purpose. Scientific theories are hypotheses dreamed up (rather than inferred or demonstrated) to explain natural phenomena and that are then sub-

---

[7] William Whewell, *The Philosophy of the Inductive Sciences* (London: John W. Parker, 1847), 2:46. See also Whewell's *On the Philosophy of Discovery* (London: John W. Parker, 1860).
[8] Karl Popper, *The Logic of Scientific Discovery* (New York: Harper and Row, 1959), 315.

jected to repeated tests aimed at impugning them. If an experiment succeeds in falsifying the theory, then it is rejected, but if it survives it is
retained and tested again. An hypothesis is never verified or confirmed,
though it does achieve what Popper calls "corroboration" through successful testing. A well-corroborated theory is one that is a bold conjecture that has endured numerous tests without falsification. The problem
with the Popperian approach is that it is difficult to distinguish his
notion of corroboration from the role of confirmation in the method of
Whewell. Moreover, his claim that science does not involve theory verification seems to fly in the face of the plain facts of scientific enterprise.
Most scientists, it seems, *are* interested in showing not only that some
hypotheses are false but also that others are at least likely to be true.

Perhaps what is regarded today as the most viable response to the
problem of induction is Hans Reichenbach's pragmatic justification.[9] He
acknowledges the force of Hume's arguments and concedes the impossibility of giving a rational justification of induction. Still, he counsels
against casting the method entirely out of hand, for vindication of induction is possible on the grounds that it will succeed if anything succeeds.
If there is uniformity in nature, then induction is a viable method, for so
long as some method of predicting the future works, induction will also
succeed. And if nature is not uniform, induction will fail, as will every
alternative method.

Suppose, for example, that the practice of crystal gazing has been
effective for predicting the future. If this were so, then an inductive argument for the continued success of crystal gazing could be made from its
prior efficacy. Therefore, as long as crystal gazing or any other method
enjoyed success, so would the method of induction. Reichenbach's conclusion, then, is that there is nothing to lose and much to gain by
employing the inductive method. The obvious limitation in this pragmatic approach is that it is less a solution than a wager, a variation of
Hume's response to his own arguments, largely concessionary to them.
Reichenbach provides us only with practical recommendations for
assuming the uniformity of nature, as opposed to *rational grounds for
believing* in the uniformity of nature.

These are some of the standard attempts at salvaging induction

---

[9] See Reichenbach's *Experience and Prediction* (Chicago: University of Chicago Press, 1938), Chapter 5.

from Hume's critique. I have paused to provide this brief survey both to give a sense of the range of proposals that have been offered and to show how woefully inadequate even the best attempts have been. Given that the scientific enterprise pivots on the inductive method, it is no wonder that many scientists and philosophers of science have turned to pragmatic and skeptical philosophies of science.

Induction According to the Augustinian View of Providence

In the previous chapter we noted the proper way to understand the laws of nature, according to the Augustinian view of providence. Natural "laws" are simply summations of God's regular providential governance of the physical order. The universe does not run on its own. Rather, God upholds and directs it from moment to moment. And the regularities in nature provide for us many benefits, not the least of which is the recognition of God's goodness. Indeed, here lies the key to solving the problem of induction from an Augustinian perspective (and other versions of the high view of providence).

We may begin by noting that we observe certain regularities in nature—for example that unsupported objects fall, fire burns, and a day is twenty-four hours long. Now it is also the case that as we observe that given certain qualifications these regularities are without exception and have in the past obtained universally (or nearly so, given the rare occurrence of miracles), we are able to exploit this knowledge to our own benefit. We learn to get out of the way of falling objects, to keep a safe distance from hot objects, and to refrain from leaping from great heights. We also learn when to sow and when to reap and how to warm ourselves when the cold season comes. In short, regularities in nature help us to survive and even to prosper in the world. These are mundane examples, but, of course, through sophisticated scientific technology we have discovered more subtle laws of nature and have been able to secure more substantial and impressive benefits. Discoveries of Boyle's law, the ideal gas law, the laws of thermodynamics, the laws of electricity, light and radio waves, etc. have brought us such goods as the air conditioner, electric heat, the telephone, television, radio, and the internal combustion engine. In these and countless other ways regularities in nature prove useful for the general welfare of humankind and thus indirectly testify to the existence of a purposeful, intelligent, and powerful mind at work behind the cosmic scene who seeks to benefit his creatures. That is, the laws of nature display the deity's power, intelligence, and benevolence, among other attributes.

Now since God is benevolent, we can trust that the regularities in nature will indeed remain constant as they have in the past, that they are in fact lawful. That is, we can trust that the future will resemble the past. Why? Because if, after observing the constancy of nature and employing this knowledge for our own benefit, this regularity ceased, the results would be catastrophic for us. We might cite as a simple example the chemistry of water. If the freezing point of water suddenly rose a few degrees, the consequences for the human race, as well as for other life on this planet, would be devastating. Ice would sink instead of floating; so oceans and lakes would freeze from top to bottom, thus killing all marine life and making life as we know it impossible. In short, we all would be destroyed if there occurred such slight deviations from the normal course of nature's basic operations, and this would be inconsistent with the benevolence of God and his love for his creatures. Therefore, we can and should believe that the future will resemble the past, since a loving God rules the world. Providence assures us that there are indeed "laws" of nature; so our belief that nature is uniform is not mere instinct or custom but is justified and hence rational.[10]

The following schema, then, represents the justification of induction according to the Augustinian view of providence:

Regularities in nature	→	The existence of an almighty and benevolent God	→	The uniformity of nature

The arrows in the diagram indicate inferences and may be interpreted as meaning "strongly suggests" or "provides good reasons for believing." From the regularities of nature and the benefits derived from exploiting them we conclude that an almighty and benevolent God

---

[10] My general approach is an adaptation of that implicit in the philosophy of George Berkeley. See my essay, "A Berkeleyan Approach to the Problem of Induction," *Science and Christian Belief* 10:1 (April 1998): 73-84.

exists. And given our knowledge of these attributes of God we are justified in believing that nature is uniform.

Now I want to draw attention to some interesting corollaries to this account of induction. First, let me note a significant implication of this view for the general practice of science. Since the laws of nature are some of the most basic tools of empirical science, it follows from this model that scientific enterprise as a whole is girded on the foundation of trust in divine providence. Rational scientific investigation critically presupposes reliance upon God to continue governing the cosmos as he has in the past. And every empirical scientist who embarks on gaining insight about the natural world at least implicitly demonstrates this faith.

Faith might be defined as an active trust in something or someone. So when it comes to the basic principle that nature is uniform, the scientist, whether or not he or she believes in the supernatural, exercises faith, precisely because no empirical evidence sufficient to justify this belief can be provided. Here we see the sense in Dallas Willard's claim that "faith is not restricted to religious people."[11] And William James writes, "the only escape from faith is mental nullity."[12] The question is not *whether* the scientist exhibits faith, but *what kind* of faith he or she exhibits.

Secondly, this approach has implications about scientific explanation, which Richard Swinburne sums up succinctly as follows:

> [I]f a very powerful non-embodied rational agent is responsible for the operation of the laws of nature, then normal scientific explanation would prove to be personal explanation. That is, explanation of some phenomenon in terms of the operation of a natural law would ultimately be an explanation in terms of the operation of an agent.[13]

Such an understanding of scientific explanation is clearly distinct from traditional views. The "covering law" model of Carl Hempel[14] and Ernest Nagel,[15] for example, conceives of scientific explanation

---

[11] Dallas Willard, "The Three-Stage Argument for the Existence of God," *Contemporary Perspectives on Religious Epistemology*, eds. R. Douglas Geivett and Brendan Sweetman (Oxford: Oxford University Press, 1992), 222.

[12] William James, "The Sentiment of Rationality," in *The Will to Believe and Other Essays* (New York: Dover Publications, 1956), 93.

[13] Richard Swinburne, "The Argument from Design," *Contemporary Perspectives on Religious Epistemology*, 206.

[14] Carl Hempel, *Aspects of Scientific Explanation* (New York: Macmillan, 1965), 331-425.

[15] Ernest Nagel, *The Structure of Science* (Indianapolis: Hackett Press, 1979), 15-78.

as the subsuming of particular events under general laws and would resist references to causes. Advocates of the Augustinian view of providence would properly reject this model for just this reason, maintaining that it serves merely to describe or categorize events rather than provide a relevant answer to the causal "why" question about them.[16]

THE ORIGINS DEBATE

Having applied the Augustinian view of providence to a crucial presupposition of science, let us apply this perspective to a substantive issue—the question of biological origins. In doing so, we will also have occasion to discuss another dimension of scientific methodology. The current origins debate among theists focuses largely upon the issue of methodological naturalism. Specifically, the question is whether it is proper for a person's belief commitments pertaining to the supernatural (principally, the theistic God) to influence his or her scientific inquiry.[17] The theistic evolutionist answers negatively, maintaining that from a methodological standpoint all scientific inquiry must proceed *as if* only the physical world exists. If research into the natural world is to be fairly done, they say, one's belief commitments regarding the supernatural must not impinge upon that process. It is a simple matter of maintaining research objectivity in science.[18] On the other hand, special creationists and intelligent design theorists object to this approach as an unnecessary restriction of the integration of

---

[16] The Augustinian approach to induction will be found unsatisfactory to some because in an essential respect this solution marks no genuine advance on Hume's response to his own criticisms, that our sole means of philosophical redress in the wake of such a critique is to appeal to faith. The only noteworthy difference in the Augustinian model, the critic might lament, is that the sort of faith it endorses is religious faith rather than Hume's "animal faith," and this is hardly a significant amendment. In response I would note that there is an appreciable difference between Hume's animal faith and trust in a sovereign God. The former refers to a mere human instinct or custom, in Hume's words, a natural proclivity to believe that the future will resemble the past. The latter has a transcendent object, God, who is omnipotently capable of ensuring that the future resemble the past. Thus, the Augustinian approach to induction calls us to trust in a being who actually *explains why* nature is uniform. Humean animal faith does no such thing and is more like a synonym for "blind faith" or acceptance of induction for no good reason.

[17] Such influence may occur on the "front" or "back" end of inquiry. For instance, in the former case, one's scientific inquiry (e.g., the experiments one conducts, the way results are gathered, what inferences about the results are made, etc.) may be determined in part by one's theological commitments. In the latter case, one's theological commitments may simply affect a researcher's inclination to consider an hypothesis or conclude its truth in light of the experimental data.

[18] See, for example, Robert O'Connor, "Science on Trial: Exploring the Rationality of Methodological Naturalism," *Perspectives on Science and Christian Faith* 49:1 (March 1997): 15-30.

beliefs across the disciplines.[19] Such a truncated view, they say, will skew research results, as a *methodological* naturalism inevitably inclines one toward a *metaphysical* naturalism.[20] That is, theistic evolutionists are more likely to ignore the theoretical import of some empirical data that actually do suggest intelligent design in the origin and history of biological forms.

What I want to address is not the merit or plausibility of methodological naturalism (or MN) per se for the Christian empirical scientist.[21] Rather, I intend to inquire into the relationship between the doctrine of providence and MN. In turn, of course, this will have implications for the substantive issue of theistic evolution.

Theistic Evolution and Intelligent Design

Let me begin by defining "theistic evolution."[22] There appear to be three core beliefs essential to the theistic evolutionary model in the sense that they are individually necessary and jointly sufficient to constitute theistic evolutionism. And it is the person who is rationally committed to all of these propositions whom I call a theistic evolutionist:

1. *Theism*: The theistic God exists. That is, there is an all-powerful, all-knowing, eternal, personal, morally perfect Spirit who created and sustains the cosmos. Although theistic evolutionists represent a broad spectrum of theistic theological commitments, these tenets seem to be the rudiments of any brand of theism.

2. *Natural selection*: The principle of natural selection, directly observable in the natural world, is a viable explanation for speciation in both the plant and animal kingdoms. This is the macroevolutionary thesis, as opposed to the merely microevolutionary claim that within par-

---

[19] Alvin Plantinga, for example, defends this position by arguing from the principle that "the rational thing is to use all that you know in trying to understand a given phenomenon" ("Methodological Naturalism?" *Perspectives on Science and Christian Faith* 49:3 [September 1997]: 144).

[20] See, for example, Phillip E. Johnson's *Reason in the Balance: The Case Against Naturalism in Science* (Downers Grove, Ill.: InterVarsity Press, 1995), 205-218.

[21] For some good recent critiques of MN, see Robert A. Larmer, "Is Methodological Naturalism Question-Begging?" *Philosophia Christi* 5:1 (2003): 113-130; Stephen Meyer, "The Methodological Equivalence of Design and Descent," in *The Creation Hypothesis*, ed. J. P. Moreland (Downers Grove, Ill.: InterVarsity Press, 1994); J. P. Moreland, "Theistic Science and Methodological Naturalism," also in *The Creation Hypothesis*; and Alvin Plantinga, "Methodological Naturalism," *Origins & Design* 18:1 (Winter 1997): 18-27 and *idem*, "Methodological Naturalism, Part 2," *Origins & Design* 18:2 (Fall 1997): 22-33.

[22] Some theistic evolutionists prefer "evolutionary creationism" as a tag for their perspective. However, for the sake of terminological familiarity I have chosen to use "theistic evolution."

ticular populations of species the more biologically fit tend to survive to reproductive maturity and thereby perpetuate their genes in the gene pool. (For ease of reference, however, I shall continue to refer to the macroevolutionary thesis as "evolution," except where context calls for explicit specification.)

3. *Common biological ancestry*: All living organisms have a common genealogical ancestry. This is the thesis that through entirely natural processes (i.e., natural selection, random variation, genetic mutations and drifts, environmental factors, etc.) all living things descended from a single living organism. (Or, if not descended from a single organism, every living thing is a descendant of some single original organism within its phylum.)[23]

The theistic evolutionist, I presume, believes each of these theses to be true. Now one might affirm any one or two of these theses without affirming the other(s), though of course the latter two claims naturally go together. And for those who are non-theists, the latter two claims will consequently be attractive as theoretical accounts of the origin and proliferation of species. But the question of interest here is internal to theism. Given the existence of a sovereign God, what grounds do we have to accept the evolutionary paradigm? As we shall see, much hangs on *which view* of providence the theist subscribes to.

Intelligent design (ID) theorists, too, affirm both theism and natural selection at the level of microevolution. They demur, however, at the thesis of common biological ancestry, because of the occurrence of *irreducible complexity* and *specified complexity* in living organisms. An irreducibly complex system is *complex* in the sense that it is composed of many interactive parts that combine to serve a particular function. Its complexity is *irreducible* in the sense that removal of any one of its components would render the overall system completely nonfunctional. For example, consider a mousetrap, which without the spring, catch, holding bar, or hammer is useless. Thus, Michael Behe notes, "an irreducibly complex system cannot be produced directly (that is, by continuously improving the initial function, which continues to work by the same mechanism) by slight, successive modifications of a precursor system,

---

[23] For a superb discussion of philosophical issues in evolutionary biology, see Elliott Sober, *The Nature of Selection: Evolutionary Theory in Philosophical Focus* (Cambridge: MIT Press, 1984).

because any precursor to an irreducibly complex system that is missing a part is by definition nonfunctional."[24] Behe describes numerous biochemical systems, from structures such as bacterial flagella to processes such as blood coagulation, noting how their irreducible complexity cannot be accounted for in Darwinian terms.

What ID theorists call "specified complexity" simply refers to the match between an event and a pattern that are both complex and independent of one another. Thus, the event of an arrow hitting a bull's-eye is a case of such specification in ordinary experience, as the event (the arrow shot) and the pattern (the bull's-eye) are independently given. If the bull's-eye is drawn around an already shot arrow, then there is no such independence, and hence no specificity. Examples of biological specificity include the amino acids sequencing in complex proteins and nucleotide base sequencing in DNA molecules.[25]

The prevalence of specified complexity and irreducible complexity in living organisms strongly suggests special theistic design, according to ID theorists. William Dembski, a leading light of ID theory, summarizes the essence of this paradigm as affirming the following propositions:

ID1: Specified complexity and irreducible complexity are reliable indicators or hallmarks of design.

ID2: Biological systems exhibit specified complexity and employ irreducibly complex subsystems.

ID3: Naturalistic mechanisms or undirected causes do not suffice to explain the origin of specified complexity or irreducible complexity.

ID4: Therefore, intelligent design constitutes the best explanation for the origin of specified complexity and irreducible complexity in biological systems.[26]

And, of course, this last claim directly contradicts the macroevolutionary thesis of common ancestry of all living organisms.

---

[24] Michael J. Behe, *Darwin's Black Box: The Biochemical Challenge to Evolution* (New York: The Free Press, 1996), 39.

[25] For a full explication of the concept of specified complexity, see William A. Dembski, *Intelligent Design: The Bridge Between Science and Theology* (Downers Grove, Ill.: InterVarsity Press, 1999), Chapter 5. And for biological examples, see Stephen C. Meyer, "Evidence for Design in Physics and Biology: From the Origin of the Universe to the Origin of Life," in *Science and Evidence for Design in the Universe* (San Francisco: Ignatius Press, 2000), esp. 68-71.

[26] William A. Dembski, *The Design Revolution* (Downers Grove, Ill.: InterVarsity Press, 2004), 42.

Functional Integrity and Theistic Evolution

It is now a truism that natural scientists do not merely make experimental observations and record their findings.[27] Scientists creatively devise theories that are underdetermined by the experimental data; they draw inferences and interpret data in light of theoretical frameworks; and they conduct experiments according to conceptual and theoretical needs. These and many other aspects of scientific research carried out by scientists take them outside the realm of pure experimentation, observation, and the recording of experimental results.[28] Most scientists readily admit their theoretical commitments, and many are prepared to explicitly identify other guiding principles and beliefs that lead them to make the inferences they do in light of the experimental data. I want, next, to identify a doctrine used as an auxiliary hypothesis by theistic evolutionists, whether explicitly or implicitly, in the context of theory justification.

Consider the concept of "functional integrity," so called by physicist and theistic evolutionist Howard J. Van Till. As explained by Van Till, this is the assumption that the cosmos "has been equipped by the Creator to do whatever the Creator calls upon it to do. It suffers no gaps or deficiencies in its economy that need to be bridged either by words of magic or by the Creator's direct manipulation."[29] For the biologist the notion of functional integrity (or FI) minimally implies that we need not look beyond the physical world itself for the causes of changes in living things, whether inquiring about the nature of existing species or the production of new species. It rules out supernatural causes for physical events. Theistic evolutionists sometimes appeal directly to FI in their defenses of MN, such as when John Stek asserts,

> Since the created realm is replete with its own economy that is neither incomplete . . . nor defective, in our understanding of the econ-

---

[27] What has been called simple (or "naive") inductivism represents a popular conception of science but is not defended by any serious philosophers of science these days. For a helpful exposition and critical analysis of inductivism, see A. F. Chalmers's *What Is This Thing Called Science?* third edition (Indianapolis: Hackett, 1999), Chapter 4.

[28] Of course, some philosophers of science maintain that even these aspects of the scientific method are not free from the influence of theoretical presuppositions. See, for example, Thomas Kuhn's seminal defense of the now widely accepted thesis that all observation is theory-laden in *The Structure of Scientific Revolutions*, second edition (Chicago: University of Chicago Press, 1970).

[29] Howard J. Van Till, "Is Special Creationism a Heresy?" *Christian Scholar's Review* 22:4 (June 1993): 385.

omy of that realm so as to exercise our stewardship over it . . . we must methodologically exclude all notions of immediate divine causality.[30]

Still other theistic evolutionists, such as Ernan McMullin, appeal implicitly to FI in suggesting that naturalistic explanations deserve preferred consideration because of their greater likelihood. Speaking of divine "special intervention in the cosmic process," McMullin writes, "from the theological and philosophical standpoints, such intervention is, if anything, antecedently *improbable*."[31] Diogenes Allen gives yet another affirmation of this approach and connects it to MN:

> God can never properly be used in scientific accounts, which are formulated in terms of the relations between the members of the universe, because that would reduce God to the status of a creature. According to a Christian conception of God as a creator of a universe that is rational through and through, there are no missing relations between the members of nature. If in our study of nature we run into what seems to be an instance of a connection missing between members of nature, the Christian doctrine of creation implies that we should keep looking for one.[32]

Thus, MN is for these (and I would say most) theistic evolutionists grounded in a substantive metaphysical assumption—namely, FI. Now it is noteworthy that FI implies a certain perspective on providence, specifically the notion that somehow the universe can run on its own without divine intervention. Occasionally these writers speak of divine governance, but they conceive the idea along deistic lines, as when Van Till refers to the universe being "endowed with the capacities to transform itself, in conformity with God's will, from unformed matter into a marvelous array of structures . . . and life forms."[33] Yet to reject "the Creator's direct manipulation" and "exclude all notions of immediate

---

[30] John Stek, "What Says the Scriptures?" in *Portraits of Creation: Biblical and Scientific Perspectives on the World's Formation*, eds. H. J. Van Till, R. E. Snow, J. H. Stek, and D. A. Young (Grand Rapids, Mich.: Eerdmans, 1990), 261.

[31] Ernan McMullin, "Plantinga's Defense of Special Creation," *Christian Scholar's Review* 21:1 (September 1991): 74.

[32] Diogenes Allen, *Christian Belief in a Postmodern World* (Louisville: Westminster/John Knox Press, 1989), 45.

[33] Howard J. Van Till, "Is Special Creationism a Heresy?" 390.

divine causality," as these writers do, clearly suggests a low view of providence.

Or, since some of these scholars do seem to endorse divine governance of the world, they could be interpreted as merely denying that God deviates from his routine method of ordering the cosmos. But such a view would plainly preclude the possibility of miracles, something that I suspect these scholars would loathe doing. Thus, in light of MN's denial of immediate divine activity in nature, it is difficult to make sense of their perspective as constituting anything but a low view of providence. Thus, to summarize so far: MN depends upon FI, and FI involves a low view of providence.

Justifying the Evolutionary Inference

But it remains to be seen just how MN justifies the evolutionary inference. Let's look at exactly how MN would lead us to conclude in favor of an evolutionary account of origins. Or we might approach it another way by asking if independently of MN any justification can be provided for this inference. From a logical standpoint how can the case be made for the evolutionary thesis without using this methodological assumption as a guiding principle?[34]

Let us look at the facts. What do we literally observe, in terms of the biological data? Generally speaking, what we see are the following:

1. *Tremendous diversity of living organisms*: There are about 1.5 million known species of organisms,[35] and biologists conjecture that hundreds of thousands of others (principally marine organisms) have yet to be discovered and classified, and hundreds of thousands more are already extinct. Among known plants and animals there is a staggering variety in terms of morphology (anatomical structure), physiology (organ systems and functions), and other basic biological features.

---

[34] Notwithstanding the common, though unwarranted, dogma that evolution is not a theory but a fact, the theses of natural speciation and common biological ancestry are theoretical claims. If we understand a scientific theory as essentially involving some inferential claims about unobserved phenomena, then clearly the evolutionary thesis is a theoretical one. However much confirmed by the experimental data this paradigm may be, it remains a scientific theory and will be so at least until clear cases of evolution of new animal species are directly observed *and* the process resulting in common biological ancestry of all living things can in some way be experimentally replicated. (And even at such time it is questionable whether this would exalt evolutionary theory from theory to fact.) Unfortunately for dogmatic evolutionists, the prospects for such a development in the foreseeable future, if ever, are poor.

[35] Reliable estimates range from 1.4 to 1.75 million.

2. Hierarchically classifiable organisms: The great variety of organisms can be organized morphologically in a hierarchical fashion, from simple to more complex life forms. The biological taxonomic system originated by Linnaeus in the eighteenth century is based on this fact and is still used today. For Linnaeus such classifiability of organisms was possible because of the "essences" shared by various groups of plants and animals. Today, however, such essentialism is a controversial, disfavored notion among biologists and philosophers of science. But the Linnaean system has remained in use because of its practicality as an organizational scheme for biology.

3. Homologies and resemblances between species: Although species are reproductively bounded, between many such groups of organisms there are relatively close resemblances, in terms of structure, function, and genetic material. For instance, my biologist colleague Paul Rothrock has named dozens of species of sedges whose structural differences are very slight.[36] And, to take a more familiar example, horses and donkeys bear a close resemblance and can even reproduce, though their offspring, usually mules, are not fertile. Of course, in each of these cases the organisms are members of the same genus. Such similarities are not found between all members of, say, the same order. For example, although gorillas and lemurs are both primates, the structural differences between them are vast.

4. Adaptivity and natural selection: Genes for environmentally favorable characteristics are "selected" naturally as organisms live to reproductive maturity. Genetic traits that are disadvantageous, on the other hand, are removed from the gene pool as organisms die before reproducing. Consequently, change and adaptation occur within populations of organisms. But this almost always occurs within species (microevolution) rather than across reproductively bounded populations. The natural production of a new animal species has never been observed.

From these observable facts the conclusion drawn by theistic evo-

---

[36] See P. E. Rothrock and A. A. Reznicek, "A New Species of *Carex* Section *Ovales* Occurring in the Ozark Mountain Region," *Brittonia* 48 (1996): 104-110; A. A. Reznicek and P. E. Rothrock, "*Carex molestiformis* (Cyperaceae), a New Species of Section *Ovales* from the Ozark Mountain Region," *Contributions from the University of Michigan Herbarium* 21 (1997): 299-308; and P. E. Rothrock and A. A. Reznicek, "The Taxonomy of the *Carex bicknellii* Group (Cyperaceae) and New Species for Central North America," *Novon* 11 (2001): 205-228.

lutionists is that evolution has occurred. Or, otherwise put, theistic evolution is judged the best explanatory hypothesis. But this is an unjustified inference based on the above broad categories of data alone. It is here that the theistic evolutionist must appeal to his or her other belief commitments, which pivotally include MN. For how do species diversity, natural selection (microevolution), homologies and resemblances between species, and their hierarchical classifiability suggest common ancestry (as opposed to specified complexity via intelligent design)? These facts alone are not sufficient to warrant extrapolation from the microevolutionary thesis to the macroevolutionary thesis. Of course, these are admittedly *psychologically* persuasive considerations to many people, but I suggest this is precisely because of their unwitting commitment to MN.

Now when the doctrine of functional integrity is added to the above general observations as an auxiliary hypothesis, the inference to the macroevolutionary thesis becomes *more* plausible than it would be otherwise (though this is not to say that given this assumption it is *proven* or *most plausible* among competing theories of origins). The implication here, then, is that theistic evolution is a reasonable and plausible theory just to the extent that it vitally draws upon MN and, in turn, FI.

Here is another way of making the same point. What would the biological world look like if some form of intelligent design of individual species took place? That is, how would the biological data be different, if at all, if speciation were the direct result of divine action rather than natural processes? Let us review again the general observations highlighted earlier. If intelligent design occurred, would there likely be tremendous diversity such as that which we observe in the world today and in the paleontological record? Absolutely. In fact, given the divine imagination, we should expect a wide array of flora and fauna. What of the close resemblances and homologies between many species? Should we expect this if they arose through intelligent design? I don't see why not. In fact, the sheer plentitude of life forms would make this more likely, since presumably a finite number of functional living systems (morphologically and physiologically speaking) are possible on this planet.

As regards the hierarchical classifiability of organisms, this too we would expect, for much the same reason. In any category of physical objects where there is a great number and variety of particulars there will always be organizationally distinguishable subgroups unified by common features. And because of this there will be classifiability from simple to more complex members. Some have compared the biological situation to that of automobiles. There is only so much variety possible in the structure and function of cars, and different makes and models are categorizable according to basic features that are shared by different kinds of cars. The same would be true of living organisms, whether or not macroevolution occurred. We should expect specific intelligent design of so many organisms to involve similar common patterns shared by different kinds of living things and according to which we could classify them, from simple to more complex.

Finally, what about natural selection? Would it be reasonable to expect that the Creator would make organisms such that the fittest tend to survive? While this question is perhaps premised upon the notion of a moral fall of humankind, precipitating the death of organisms, it is still reasonable to ask. Again I see no reason why ID theory would not predict natural selection and the adaptivity of organisms. Given a world in which plants and animals must compete against environmental forces and each other in order to survive, it seems that any biological system would involve survival of the fittest.

It appears that the empirical data considered alone confirms ID theory at least as much as it confirms the macroevolutionary hypothesis. And what serves to bolster both paradigms is really not evidentially favorable to either. Again, what this shows is that something other than the experimental data leads theistic biologists to conclude in favor of macroevolution. And just what that something is I have already made clear—namely, a commitment to MN, which, in turn, is grounded in FI.[37]

We are now ready to see the relevance of all of this for the doctrine of providence (or perhaps vice versa). As we have noted, the assumption of MN is crucial for the case for macroevolution. And for theists, FI is

---

[37] It is interesting to note the irony of the fact that theistic evolutionists often justify MN by appealing to FI, which is, as we saw, essentially a theological doctrine. Given that theistic evolution is reasonable just to the extent that it depends essentially upon this piece of philosophical theology, it is odd, to say the least, that these scientists should hold so tenaciously to MN. On the one hand, they claim that one must do scientific inquiry *as if* only the physical world exists, and on the other hand they justify this methodological mandate by appealing to a theological doctrine. I won't go so far as to suggest that this combination of views is incoherent, but there is surely a deep tension here. And the following question begs for an answer: If theology can legitimately inform choice of scientific methodology, then why can't it also inform scientific theory selection?

crucial to the support of MN. Thus, to undermine FI is to undermine MN and, in turn, the case for macroevolution. Now FI, as we have also seen, is allied with a low view of providence. Consequently, since the Augustinian view of providence contradicts FI, it thereby undermines MN and considerably weakens the overall case for macroevolution. This is not to say that it *contradicts* the evolutionary paradigm. The Augustinian perspective is quite consistent with theistic evolution. For all we know, God's governance of the cosmos and the history of earth in particular has included the formation of species through a long and gradual process of natural selection, genetic drift, and other factors.[38] But the point here is that given the Augustinian view of providence, one's evidential *justification* for subscribing to the evolutionary paradigm is reduced. Otherwise put, my point is simply epistemological. An Augustinian doctrine of providence *diminishes one's reasons for believing* in macroevolution.

From an Augustinian perspective, there is not a sharp distinction to be made between God's original creative activity and his present conservation of the cosmos. God created the world and sustains it from moment to moment. He instituted secondary causes for the benefit of human beings, but he sovereignly governs all of these secondary causes. The low view of providence makes a strong distinction between God's creative activity and his preservation of the world. In fact, his preserving the world is, for the most part, not active at all but a passive allowance of the cosmic structures he instituted to run on their own. Given this distinction, two important differences between theistic evolutionists and ID theorists emerge. First, according to theistic evolutionists God only indirectly caused speciation, while according to ID theorists God directly caused speciation. It is interesting to note that given the Augustinian view of providence, even the evolution of species through natural selection can properly be conceived as the result of

---

[38] My own provisional view on the matter is actually an essentially evolutionary position, though of a hybrid nature. The account with the most explanatory power, it seems to me, is that God created "representative" species within the various classes (i.e., amphibians, reptiles, birds, mammals, etc.), and a proliferation of kinds, including new species and even families and orders of organisms, occurred within these boundaries. Space does not permit my spelling out the details of this model or the evidential considerations in its favor. Suffice it to say, however, that to my mind this compromise best accommodates the considerable evidential grounds for both the creationist and macroevolutionist paradigms. Of course, such a model is likely to make few friends and many enemies in an intellectual climate in which warring paradigms are so firmly entrenched.

direct divine causality, though not as a result of "intervention" as some proponents of MN would see it, since the concept of divine intervention only makes sense if God is not always at work in the world. So given the Augustinian perspective, theists enjoy the freedom to inquire into the question of biological origins without the worry that somehow their findings will exclude God. On the contrary, if they decide in favor of macroevolution, their conclusion pertains only to *how*, not whether, God meticulously engineered the different species.

In the Augustinian view of providence, one need not worry about scientific discoveries, biological or otherwise, that lead us away from God. One may inquire into the causal nexus of nature with a joyful freedom, safeguarded from the temptation to foreclose prematurely on one paradigm or another. This observation leads us to another important difference between theistic evolutionists and ID theorists. Given his commitment to MN, the theistic evolutionist essentially insists that we conclude *in advance* of inquiry that speciation occurred through secondary causes, while the ID theorist contends that we should only make such conclusions *on the basis* of inquiry. Did speciation occur as a part of the original divine creative activity or afterwards? This question is the crux of the controversy over biological origins. The methodological naturalist is by definition foreclosed in favor of the latter option, while the ID theorist is properly open to either possibility, though he at least provisionally favors the former option. Of course, the theistic evolutionist will defend his foreclosure in view of the integrity of *scientific* inquiry. In contrast, the intelligent design theorist will defend his approach in terms of the integrity of inquiry *generally*.

Thus, it seems that the Augustinian view of providence motivates openness to the ID approach. Or, to put it more strongly, one might say that among the competing methodological paradigms, the Augustinian view is most at home with ID. I will summarize the reasons as follows. First, the Augustinian perspective sees the whole world as divinely orchestrated; so to appeal to divine causation as an explanation for speciation is not properly construed as "gap filling" or "giving up," as it is sometimes characterized by advocates of MN. Rather, speciation would simply be an instance in which God acts directly rather than through secondary causes. Second, MN is necessary to clinch the macroevolutionary case for the theist, and it is FI that justifies acceptance of MN. But

FI depends upon the low view of providence, as it eschews divine involvement with the world's normal phenomena. Thus, to take an Augustinian view of providence rules out FI, thus undermining MN. And ID methodology is the natural alternative to MN. Third, MN, via FI, assumes a hard dichotomy between where God is and is not actively involved in the world. And it defines science exclusively in terms of the latter realm, thus closing the door to possible explanations from the former domain (where God *does* actively work). ID theory insists upon no such hard distinction, nor, of course, does the Augustinian view of providence. This may be put another way. The Augustinian perspective rejects the hard dichotomy between where God is and is not actively involved in the world, thus affirming *metaphysical integrity* (i.e., God is equally active at creation and in the conservation of the cosmos), which warrants practicing science with *methodological integrity*, where God is seen as a viable causal hypothesis at any juncture of cosmic history, so long as all plausible secondary causal hypotheses prove inadequate. And this, of course, is the basic schema of ID theory.

In brief, the Augustinian view of providence opens up more theoretical options for the theistic scientist, not limiting him or her to appealing to natural explanations for all phenomena. This is not to say that anything goes when it comes to theorizing about explanations for hitherto unexplained phenomena. Rather, the theistic scientist will simply reserve the option to appeal to supernatural intelligent causes, such as God, angels, or human souls, when all reasonable natural explanations have been exhausted.

THE PROBLEM OF CONSCIOUSNESS

I would like to make a final application of the Augustinian view of providence to scientific practice. It concerns the most intractable problem in the history of science, if not all human inquiry—the problem of consciousness. What is consciousness? What are minds? Where did consciousness come from originally, and how does it develop within us individually? Here, as in the biological sciences, MN reigns. Physicalism—the view that the cosmos is exhaustively describable in terms of physics and chemistry—is the dominant view today. Whatever research program one subscribes to, it seems agreed in most circles that the task of solving the riddle of human consciousness is an essentially scientific one. Here much of the philosophical guild has followed the scientific community, largely foreclosing on non-physicalist accounts of the mind.

Among non-physicalist theories, substance dualism remains the most popular. Substance dualists affirm the human mind to be a non-material substance, ontologically distinct from the physical body. However, their contributions to consciousness studies have been largely critical, serving the valuable function of keeping physicalists theoretically honest. Their constructive contributions have been few. Moreover, the same old problems still plague substance dualism, the problem of interaction being the most recalcitrant. In short, how does one explain the causal interaction between a physical substance and a non-material soul? Substance dualists insist that souls are different from bodies in nearly every way, yet they affirm their causal connection. How is this possible? It is for lack of a satisfactory answer to this question that substance dualism is so widely rejected. What is needed is a version of dualism that overcomes this problem.

In what follows I will review the major physicalist theories of mind, showing why some form of dualism is a preferable theoretical option. After this, I will propose a particular version of dualism that is readily suggested by an Augustinian view of providence and that avoids the pitfalls of substance dualism.

The Recent History of Physicalist Theories of Mind

The "physicalist project" in consciousness studies began in earnest with the publication of Gilbert Ryle's *The Concept of Mind* in the middle of the twentieth century.[39] This monumental work not only mercilessly critiqued the "Cartesian myth" of substance dualism but also offered a defense of philosophical behaviorism, thus setting the agenda for reductionist theories of mind. Ryle proposed that the Cartesian view of the mind as essentially inner, private, and distinct from the body is fundamentally flawed. It is a "category mistake," he suggested, to regard certain features of our physical lives as belonging to an altogether different ontological category, the "mental." In fact, he argued, we are purely and

---

[39] Gilbert Ryle, *The Concept of Mind* (New York: Barnes and Noble), 1949.

simply physical beings, and those qualities normally regarded as belonging to the ghostly realm of the Cartesian mind, viz. beliefs, desires, emotions, pains, etc., may be analyzed wholly and exhaustively in terms of behavior and dispositions to behave. To have a desire to eat is just to act in a certain way, e.g., to say things like "I want to have lunch now" or to go to the kitchen and prepare a sandwich. To have a pain is just to wince, cry aloud, contort, or to be disposed to act in such ways. In any case, for Ryle, one's behavior is not a mere sign of a hidden, inward mental event. Rather, the mental is just the behavior or tendencies to behave in certain ways.

The advantages of such a view are plain. Like all forms of physicalism, Ryle's account is metaphysically parsimonious, potentially uniting all of the data of human experience into a single ontological category. Moreover, behaviorism dissolves two persistent problems in the Cartesian tradition: the problem of interaction and the problem of other minds. The problem of interaction, as just noted, regards the difficulty of accounting for how two substances as different as a material body and an immaterial mind could causally interact. The problem of other minds pertains to the difficulty of justifying one's belief that there *are* minds other than one's own. If I directly experience only my own thoughts and feelings, then how can I justify my belief that *every other human being* has similar thoughts and feelings? As an inductive inference, this amounts to reasoning from one case (mine) to billions of others (everyone else), which provides weak grounds, to say the least. Ryle's behaviorism avoids the problem of interaction by denying that humans are composed of two distinct substances. And as for the problem of other minds, the behaviorist account makes mind a public matter. One can directly experience another's mental life by simply observing his or her behavior. Nothing about the mind remains hidden from view, because its states are empirically verifiable. So no skeptical problem regarding minds other than one's own remains.

Philosophical behaviorism, therefore, has strengths as a theory of mind. It is metaphysically elegant, and it eliminates in one stroke two nagging problems in philosophy. These considerations and its promise as a scientifically respectable account of human nature are why behaviorism enjoyed such popularity, albeit briefly, in philosophical circles. But the problems with this approach proved too great. For one thing, the behaviorist model could not account for the fact that some thoughts, feelings, desires, etc. are never manifested in behavior. In fact, one may act directly contrary to one's private thoughts or feelings. Moreover, there are some beliefs, such as beliefs about high-level mathematics, that seem to have no possible behavioral expressions. On top of these formal problems, there is the intuitive implausibility of philosophical behaviorism. It does not account for the essential subjective nature of experience. It ignores the first-person quality of human experience that *is* private and, in a sense, inner and hidden. The root problem with behaviorism is that it confuses the *epistemological criterion* for mind with the *metaphysical reality* of the mental. Mental states are indeed expressed behaviorally, and there is much that we learn about a person's mind by observing his or her actions. But this is far from admitting that there is nothing more to mind than these publicly observable facts.

The next chapter in the history of physicalist theories of mind was strict identity theory. Its two leading proponents, U. T. Place[40] and J. J. C. Smart,[41] recognized the problems with the behaviorist approach and sought to adequately account for the inner, hidden nature of mind while at the same time salvaging scientific plausibility. Their compromise was to identify mental states with brain states. Sensations, beliefs, and general awareness are nothing more than processes in the brain. To say, "I have a pain in my elbow" is just another way of saying, "nerve bundle C-468 is firing." Like behaviorism, the identity theory is simple and elegant. Moreover, it accounts for the observed correlation between mental states and brain states. States of mind are directly and predictably alterable by neurological manipulation, through such means as manual stimulation and blood chemistry alteration.

Early critics of the identity thesis claimed that the theory was logically absurd. They pointed out that where two entities are claimed to be identical, anything that is true of one must also be true of the other. But this is manifestly not the case as regards mental states and brain states. Consider a mental state X and the brain state Y, with which X is putatively identical. One may be introspectively aware of X but not Y. That is, for example, I may be immediately aware of my elbow pain and yet

---

[40] U. T. Place, "Is Consciousness a Brain Process?" *British Journal of Psychology* 47 (1956): 44-50.
[41] J. J. C. Smart, "Sensations and Brain Processes," *Philosophical Review* 68 (1959): 141-156.

know absolutely nothing about my brain states. Hence, the two cannot be strictly identical. Furthermore, all brain states have physical characteristics, but mental states do not. Brain states occur in specific places, and the neurological structures that constitute them have determinate shapes and sizes. But none of these predicates can be meaningfully applied to mental states such as hunger, love, fear, or belief. Thus, critics argued, the notion that mental states are identical with brain processes is logically absurd.

To their credit, the identity theorists glimpsed the flaw in this criticism. The identity between brain states and mental states, they clarified, is that of *composition*, not *definition*. The "is" of definition (as in "a square *is* an equilateral rectangle") pertains to the meaning of a thing, and identity theorists readily admitted such identity does not obtain between brain processes and mental states. But the "is" of composition (as in "this table *is* an old packing case") is the sort of identity claimed between the two.[42] Unlike the "is" of definition, the "is" of composition does not assert a definitionally necessary truth. This is why, as in the case of mental states and brain processes, distinct and non-identical descriptions of compositionally identical entities are possible.

The criticism that identity theorists were not able to overcome pertained to the phenomenal qualities (or qualia) characterizing experience when, for example, one has a sensation of red or a loud noise. Intuitively, we recognize that such qualia are not identical, even compositionally, to brain processes. As Frank Jackson pointed out, no description of the neurological events correlated with them could possibly capture this aspect of perceptual experience.[43] Even a person with a complete comprehension of optics and the physiology of color perception would still have much to learn in the way of understanding the phenomenon if she had never herself had a perceptual experience of color. This is because, as Thomas Nagel correctly argued, it is first-person subjectivity that essentially characterizes consciousness.[44] Subjectivity necessarily eludes third-person descriptions of events, even the most thorough and physiologically rigorous description of brain processes. So the most exhaustive such description of, say, a bat's neurological sonar mechanisms

---

42 U. T. Place, *op. cit.*, 45.
43 See Frank Jackson's "Epiphenomenal Qualia," *Philosophical Quarterly* 32 (1982): 127-136.
44 Thomas Nagel, "What Is It Like to Be a Bat?" *The Philosophical Review* 83 (1974): 435-450.

would not bring me any closer to understanding what it is like to be a bat. This is because such descriptions are necessarily "third-person" in nature. But to ask "what is it like to be X?" is to inquire about a particular first-person experience. No third-person (or "objective") description could ever provide that.

In more recent years, functionalism has risen to prominence among philosophers of mind, due in large part to the tremendous success and influence of computer technology. The basic proposal of the functionalists is that mental states are reducible to the functional operations of the brain and the causal roles these play in the larger human system, such as their relations to the body's behavior and environment. Early functionalists, such as Jerry Fodor[45] and Hilary Putnam,[46] rejected the strict identity thesis because it asked the wrong question when analyzing the brain for its capacity to explain mental states—namely, "What does it *consist* of?" But such an approach is wrongheaded, they insisted. Rather, the proper question to be asked of the brain is: "What does it *do*?" The former question is that of microanalysis and is hopelessly local in its focus. Consciousness, the functionalists tell us, is not a localized feature of the brain such that particular thoughts can be linked or reduced to particular neural processes. Rather, consciousness is a broader feature of the brain, perhaps systemic in nature. Thus, a functional analysis that asks what causal roles various neurological mechanisms play in the overall brain system is necessary for getting at the heart of mind.

In focusing on the causal roles that brain processes play in the brain, or in a living system generally, functionalists note that there is nothing special about the particular form these take in human beings, that is, our carbon-based biological brain. Such mental attributes as beliefs, intentions, and intelligence may potentially be realized in any number of systems, from silicon chips to aluminum cans, so long as the right causal roles are realized. All that is necessary is functional equivalence. This thesis provides the premise of strong Artificial Intelligence (AI), the notion that the mind is essentially like a computer program. Of course, the implications of this claim are vast, as it holds out the promise of producing thinking, feeling, creative, and even moral and loving AIs. It is

---

[45] See Fodor's *Psychological Explanation* (New York: Random House, 1968), 90-120.
[46] Hillary Putnam, "The Nature of Mental States," in *Materialism and the Mind-Body Problem*, ed. David M. Rosenthal (Indianapolis: Hackett Press, 1987), 150-161.

the fond hope of some theorists, such as Daniel Dennett, that this research program will one day provide the key to personal immortality. All such would require (as if this were a small task) would be to reproduce all of the functional operations of your brain in, say, a high-powered computer, and the result would be . . . you, or at least a replica of your mind.[47]

The besetting problems with functionalism return us again to the matter of qualia. Critics have argued that the functionalist account of mental states as reducible to causal operations within our brain/body system does not sufficiently account for the qualitative facts of mental life, such as colors, flavors, smells, and so on. The force of this objection is made plain with a famous thought experiment known as the "inverted spectrum" argument.[48] It is conceivable that the color sensations you and I experience are totally reversed, such that what you see as red, I would call green, and vice versa. Now since we have no way of comparing our private visual sensations, there occur no practical, observable signs of our inverted spectra. When I say, for example, "Hand me that green book," you respond by meeting my request, and no discrepancies are ever suspected. So we are functionally identical. But this means, if the functionalist is correct, there is no difference whatsoever between our mental lives, for mind is entirely analyzable in functional terms. And yet, *ex hypothesi*, there *is* indeed a difference between our mental lives, as our visual experiences are not the same. Therefore, functionalism cannot provide an exhaustive physicalist reduction of mind to matter.

Functionalists typically respond to this objection in one of two ways. Some deny the reality of qualia, at least as essentially first-person facts about the mental life. Daniel Dennett takes such an approach, but he does so at the expense of theoretical plausibility.[49] The more reasonable alternative taken by others is to admit qualia but insist that the identity of two intelligent systems does not require a perfect match between them when it comes to such private experiences. The problem with this

---

[47] Dennett writes, "If what you are is that organization of information that has structured your body's control system (or, to put it in its more usual provocative form, if what you are is the program that runs on your brain's computer), then you could in principle survive the death of your body as intact as a program can survive the destruction of the computer on which it was created and first run." From *Consciousness Explained* (Boston: Little, Brown and Co., 1991), 430.

[48] This argument actually originated with John Locke in *An Essay Concerning Human Understanding* (1690), II.32.15.

[49] Daniel Dennett, *op. cit.*, Chapter 12.

approach, however, is that it grants the reality of the inner and subjective characteristics of mind that the physicalist project has been so concerned to eliminate. Realizing the unavoidability of this conclusion, some physicalists have turned to the metaphysical halfway house of property dualism.

John Searle is a proponent of property dualism, which regards mental states as properties of the brain. A militant critic of functionalism, Searle has focused on the inability of this model to account for a particular feature of the mind's subjective character: intentionality. He devised the now famous Chinese room argument to demonstrate this and, more specifically, to show that Strong AI is false. Imagine that you are locked in a room with a supply of Chinese language symbols and that it is your job to implement a sort of program for answering questions in Chinese. Various Chinese symbols are passed into the room, and your task is to respond by passing symbols back out of the room in a certain order, as stipulated by a rulebook that you diligently consult. The rules state things like "When these symbols appear in such and such order, then pass out those symbols in this order." Now although you neither understand a word of Chinese nor have any idea what any of the symbols represent, you are able to give answers to the questions that are quite meaningful to the Chinese speakers outside of the room.

Now the task you perform in this thought experiment is essentially that of a computer program, which is made to manipulate symbols in a way that is meaningful to a computer user but which is neither meaningful to nor in any way understood by the computer itself. Like the person in the Chinese room, computers and their programs deal only in syntax, not semantics. That is, they do not have intentionality, the capacity to grasp meanings. Therefore, no computer could ever really "think," because, as Searle notes, "thinking is more than just a matter of manipulating meaningless symbols."[50] Computers merely simulate thinking, but this is far from being conscious and having mental states such as beliefs, feelings, desires, and sensations.

So Searle's conclusion is that subjectivity is fundamental, a "rock bottom element" in a proper picture of the world.[51] He maintains that

---

[50] John Searle, *Minds, Brains and Science* (Cambridge: Harvard University Press, 1984), 36.
[51] John Searle, *The Rediscovery of Mind* (Cambridge: MIT Press, 1992), 95.

consciousness is ontologically irreducible, but he guards his physicalism by affirming that consciousness is *causally reducible* to neurological processes. Mind is a causally emergent system feature of the brain. However, contra functionalism, it is not the brain's functional operations that give rise to mind. Rather, it is the microbiological structures themselves. Thoughts, beliefs, and sensations are every bit as essentially biological as photosynthesis, mitosis, and digestion. Thus, notwithstanding his own adamant claims to the contrary, John Searle is a property dualist, as he affirms the irreducibility of consciousness *and* that "there is really nothing in the universe but physical particles and fields of forces acting on physical particles."[52] He prefers to label his view "biological naturalism."

Searle's view is strong where other physicalist theories of mind are woefully weak. He takes subjectivity seriously, even to the point of admitting it is irreducible. But he refuses to follow this point to its obvious conclusion—namely, that a thoroughgoing naturalism necessarily leaves something—the most important something—out of the picture. To affirm naturalism is to commit oneself to the notion that every fact in the world is a physical fact or else reducible to physical facts. But by Searle's own admission neither is true of the fact of first-person subjectivity, which he claims is a fundamental feature of reality. On this latter point, I believe Searle to be correct, but this claim simply cannot be squared with naturalism. Thus, Searle, like all property dualists, must choose between taking consciousness seriously enough to regard it as something ultimately non-physical in nature or opting for a thoroughgoing naturalism.[53]

In recent years, several Christian philosophers of mind have defended their own physicalist theories of mind, thus paying deference to MN. Prominent among these are the views of Lynn Rudder Baker,[54]

---

[52] Ibid., 30.

[53] If space allowed, I would review some recent hybrid theories in philosophy of mind, such as David Chalmers's non-reductive functionalism and Owen Flanagan's constructive naturalism, as well as some narrowly scientific attempts to understand consciousness, such as Gerald Edelman's purely biological account and the appeals to quantum physics made by the likes of Roger Penrose and Henry Stapp. Let it suffice to note that in the final analysis each of these views fails for many of the same reasons that the views just discussed fail to explain consciousness. The latter scientific attempts of Edelman, Stapp, and Penrose prove metaphysically problematic or naive at points, while the former hybrid accounts of Chalmers and Flanagan are no more successful when it comes to the matters of subjectivity, qualia, intentionality, and the unity of the self.

[54] Lynn Rudder Baker, *Persons and Bodies: A Constitution View* (Cambridge: Cambridge University Press, 2000).

Ian Barbour,[55] Kevin Corcoran,[56] Nancey Murphy,[57] and Arthur Peacocke.[58] Some, such as Murphy and Corcoran, espouse a "constitution view" of persons, according to which "persons are constituted by bodies but are not identical with the bodies that constitute them."[59] Others have opted for versions of property dualism. William Hasker, for example, has defended what he calls "emergent dualism," which sees the mind as generated by the brain but possessing qualitative differences from the neurological properties from which it arises.[60] Spatial constraints prevent me from discussing these views in detail, but suffice it to say that they suffer from the same sorts of problems that plague the other accounts just reviewed.[61] This is no surprise, since such theorists subject themselves to the same methodological constraints that restrict the metaphysical naturalists. If Christian philosophers of mind, as devotees of MN, are constrained to appeal to physical causes in explaining consciousness, then their theories of consciousness will look no different from those of metaphysical naturalists. Nor will the problems with their accounts be any different.

Turning the Problem of Consciousness Inside Out

To scan the history of the physicalist project is to see just how stubborn is the problem of consciousness. Curiously, the rise of this physicalist dogma has coincided with a general failure on the part of major naturalistic views of mind to bring us any closer to explaining the most important features of consciousness—namely, first-person subjectivity, intentionality, and phenomenal qualia. For the last half-century physicalists have done their best to eliminate, downplay, or entirely ignore

---

[55] Ian Barbour, *When Science Meets Religion* (San Francisco: Harper San Francisco, 2000), Chapter 5.
[56] Kevin J. Corcoran, "Persons and Bodies," *Faith and Philosophy* 15:3 (July 1998): 324-340; *idem*, "Soul or Body?" in *Soul, Body and Survival: Essays on the Metaphysics of Persons*, ed. Kevin Corcoran (Ithaca, N.Y.: Cornell University Press, 2001); and *idem*, "Material Persons, Immaterial Souls and an Ethic of Life," *Faith and Philosophy* 20:2 (April 2003): 218-228.
[57] Nancey Murphy, "Supervenience and the Downward Efficacy of the Mental: A Nonreductive Physicalist Account of Human Action," in *Neuroscience and the Person: Scientific Perspectives on Divine Action*, eds. R. J. Russell, et al. (Berkeley, Calif.: Center for Theology and the Natural Sciences, 1999).
[58] Arthur Peacocke, *Theology for a Scientific Age* (Oxford: Basil Blackwell, 1990), Chapter 4.
[59] Kevin J. Corcoran, "Persons and Bodies," 330.
[60] William Hasker, *The Emergent Self* (Ithaca, N.Y.: Cornell University Press, 2001).
[61] For a general critique of physicalist theories of mind, see David W. Aiken, "Why I Am Not a Physicalist: A Dialogue, a Meditation, and a Cumulative Critique," *Christian Scholar's Review* 33:2 (Winter 2004): 165-180. For a critical assessment of Hasker's view, see Frank B. Dilby, "A Critique of Emergent Dualism," *Faith and Philosophy* 20:1 (January 2003): 37-49.

these facts. What they have altogether failed to do is *explain* them. In fact, the whole enterprise was doomed from the start. This is because physicalism was founded on the notion that consciousness is just another phenomenon in nature to be explained by other phenomena. But the last half-century of consciousness studies suggests otherwise. I do not mean to imply that all the work done in service of the physicalist project has been an utter waste of time. On the contrary, some valuable lessons may follow from failure. The repeated failures to explain mind naturalistically are all chapters in the general lesson that consciousness is scientifically inexplicable.

But, alas, the physicalists press on in their quest for an ultimate reduction of mind to matter. And they will continue to fail in the same ways they have in the past, because their desperate efforts are premised on a mistaken pre-theoretical assumption. The culprit, of course, is naturalism in both of its forms: metaphysical and methodological. Physicalists, from Ryle to Dennett, foreclosed on dualism because they don't believe in the supernatural. And Christian physicalists reject dualism because of their commitment to theorize *as if* they didn't believe in the supernatural. In either case, dualism is rejected because of prior commitments rather than a failure to explain the relevant data. And both metaphysical and methodological naturalists founder because of their own failure to account for the most important facts about consciousness.

The dualist recognizes that mind and body are just very different sorts of things and that the latter simply cannot explain the former. However, as noted earlier, substance dualists have problems of their own that need to be overcome. But, fortunately, not all dualisms are alike. There is at least one version of dualism that avoids—or at lest greatly diminishes—the problem of interaction plaguing substance dualism. Furthermore, this theory of mind is particularly inspired by an Augustinian view of providence.

Let me unveil this theory by proposing that contemporary philosophy of mind be turned upon its head. What is needed today—what is long overdue, in fact—is a Copernican revolution in consciousness studies. We must abandon the course of trying to explain mind in terms of matter and take exactly the opposite approach *by explaining matter in terms of mind*. What I am suggesting is that consciousness is not a thing to be explained like anything else in the cosmos but is, as Searle observes, a (I would say *the*) fundamental feature of reality and for this reason *cannot* be explained in terms of anything else. Mind, we have seen, is not reducible to matter or anything else. My proposal is that the reverse is true, that mind is itself the key to understanding everything else. In a proper ontology, consciousness is not *explanandum* (the thing to be explained) but *explanans* (that which explains). This means the physicalists have it all wrong, totally backward in fact. But, as I remarked earlier, the failure of a half-century of concerted efforts to reduce consciousness to matter is not a total loss. No, this work indirectly confirms my thesis. For the persistent failure of those laboring on behalf of the physicalist project *is just what we should expect* if consciousness is most basic.

So what, precisely, am I suggesting about the physical world if consciousness is the ultimate reality not to be explained by anything else? Just this: the physical world is constituted by nothing but the publicly observable ideas (e.g., colors, shapes, textures, sounds, etc.) of an underlying, pervasive consciousness. The whole cosmos is mind-dependent. Every physical object, including our own bodies, is upheld in existence from moment to moment by the Mind behind the world who also has decreed secondary causes such as the use of our physical senses to perceive the world.[62] All of the experiences of human minds are immediately and comprehensively coordinated by the divine Mind. Now it should be apparent that this perspective, which I will call "immaterialism," is basically an application of the Augustinian view of providence. That the physical world is essentially the product of a pervasive, fundamental consciousness is precisely what the Augustinian view teaches, as I explained in the previous chapter. And my proposal to, as it were, turn the problem of consciousness "inside out" pivots upon recognition of this fact.

Does this mean that someone who takes a low view of providence could not embrace the same solution to the problem of consciousness? Not necessarily, though the combination of these two doctrines would

---

[62] To illustrate my thesis, consider the recent movie *The Matrix*. The premise of this film is that the entire world of human experience is actually a very sophisticated computer-generated *virtual* reality, into which millions of human brains have been artificially hooked up so that they deem this artificially concocted world as *real*. Simply substitute God for the central computer of *The Matrix* and you have something analogous to the thesis I am proposing. On this view, however, this world is no mere illusion just because it is mind-dependent. An illusion presupposes some deeper reality that is being hidden. If consciousness is most basic, then there is no deeper reality. This mind and its public thoughts just *are* reality.

be awkward, to say the least. Those who take a low view of providence will be naturally disinclined to opt for this approach, precisely because of the strong doctrine of divine sovereignty that it naturally suggests. Unfortunately, this reluctance will also incline them away from the most promising route to solving the problem of consciousness. On the other hand, those who do take an Augustinian view of providence will for this reason be most inclined to embrace my proposal. Indeed, it is surprising that an advocate of the Augustinian perspective has not already proposed such a "Copernican revolution" in consciousness studies.

Does this mean that those who take the Augustinian view of providence will readily accept my proposal? Again, not necessarily. There are plenty of metaphysical issues that divide those of us in the Augustinian camp, including issues related to causality, perception, substance, and essences (though such matters are philosophical trifles compared to the more significant question about the scope of God's providential control of the cosmos). And some such considerations, depending upon one's metaphysical commitments, could discourage acceptance of my proposal. But since the doctrine of providence is so pivotal within a person's theology and since the issue of consciousness is such a looming mystery, one might easily reconsider one's other metaphysical doctrines in the interest of accessing the explanatory power my proposal offers. The point here is that to take an Augustinian view of providence, other metaphysical considerations being equal, opens up and even encourages a promising theoretical option when it comes to the question of human consciousness. Thus, we see that the solution to the riddle of consciousness is yet another extraordinary benefit of the Augustinian perspective.

Now, before closing, let me make a few more clarifications about my proposal. First, just how does the immaterialist model incorporate the strengths of both physicalism and substance dualism and at the same time avoid the pitfalls of each? While I can only offer schematic remarks, I would summarize these merits as follows. First, the immaterialist model enjoys the major strengths of both substance dualism and physicalism. With the former, it takes subjectivity, qualia, and intentionality seriously, in fact emphasizing their place in the life of the mind. And with the latter, it boasts a tremendous theoretical simplicity. There are only minds and their ideas (paralleling the physicalist thesis that there is just matter and its many qualities). Second, the immaterialist model avoids the major problems plaguing substance dualism and physicalism. There remains no nagging problem of interaction for the immaterialist, since ideas are the natural product and possession of minds. And this model avoids all of the specific problems highlighted in our earlier tour through the recent history of physicalism.

One likely objection to this proposal is the following. Isn't the pursuit of a non-physicalist solution to the problem of consciousness, such as immaterialism, just a form of surrender, a giving up of the quest for a scientifically respectable theory of mind? Such is Dennett's complaint against substance dualism and, presumably, all non-physicalist theories of mind.[63] In response, I would say that if by "giving up" one means that immaterialism constitutes a rejection of physicalism, then the immaterialist pleads guilty. Such surrender is appropriate when one's paradigm is in deep crisis. It is fitting to give up on a model when it consistently fails to accomplish its aims in service of the research project for which it was designed. So in opting for immaterialism one indeed gives up in this *local* sense, but she need not give up in the more important, *global* sense of refusing to pursue a complete account of the mind.

Some philosophers of mind, such as Daniel Dennett, regard all non-physicalist theories as giving up in the global sense.[64] But they miss the point that dualists do offer a complete account of mind, though it is of a metaphysical nature. Dennett and other physicalists also overlook the fact that they are themselves guilty of giving up in a crucial local sense by practicing methodological naturalism. To do so is to rule out alternative accounts in advance of sufficient inquiry. And, as William James once wisely noted, "a rule of thinking which would absolutely prevent me from acknowledging certain kinds of truth if those kinds of truth were really there, would be an irrational rule."[65] So while Dennett and others are free to continue work on their physicalist project, it is hasty and philosophically foolish to close off all consideration of competing

---

[63] Daniel Dennett, *op. cit.*, 37.

[64] In *Consciousness Explained* Dennett confesses, "I adopt the apparently dogmatic rule that dualism is to be avoided *at all costs*. It is not that I think I can give a knock-down proof that dualism, in all its forms, is false or incoherent, but that, given the way dualism wallows in mystery, *accepting dualism is giving up*" (p. 37, emphasis his). Given his unwavering commitment to physicalism, Dennett would presumably say something similar about any non-physicalist theory, including the immaterialist model I am proposing here.

[65] William James, "The Will to Believe," in *The Will to Believe and Other Essays* (New York: Dover Publications, 1956), 28.

research programs. For to do so just might be to disqualify ourselves in the pursuit of understanding the world and our place in it, since the ultimate answer to the question "What is consciousness?" just *might* be a non-scientific one. Of course, I think this actually *is* the case.

So what difference does all this make in practical terms? First, philosophers of mind and cognitive science researchers can stop wasting precious time (and funding) trying to achieve the breakthrough to understanding how human consciousness reduces, supervenes, or otherwise depends upon our physical makeup. That time will be better spent focusing on the practical side of these disciplines, such as in AI and robotics, simulating various functions of human intelligence. Second, bringing an immaterialist perspective to research on human consciousness just might open doors to discoveries that we cannot presently anticipate, just because we have yet to seriously pursue this research program. Yes, immaterialism might appear to be a quirky, impractical theory. But the same can be said of quantum physics with all of its paradoxes and brain-teasing postulates, and yet the practical benefits of this paradigm have been considerable. Who knows what beneficial consequences might await committed research in cognitive science based upon immaterialism. We will never know unless we try.

My guess is that in spite of the problems with all of the major naturalistic theories of mind, the physicalist dogma will persist for many years. But I am just as confident that so long as this approach reigns in consciousness studies, no major theoretical breakthroughs will be forthcoming. In that case, all that awaits us is more frustration and failure, reinventions and recombinations of the same old bad ideas, and in-house bickering over whose broken wheels work best. Meanwhile, a truly fruitful research program awaits those philosophers of mind courageous enough to run against the prevailing methodology of our times.

Those of us who affirm the Augustinian view of providence are uniquely situated to resist the pressure of the physicalist dogma, for we are able to consider the question of consciousness from a completely different point of view, from the standpoint of those who see consciousness not just as one more aspect of the cosmos but as the most basic reality and the sustaining source of all that is. To recognize this is to realize that physicalists have been asking the wrong question all along.

CONCLUSION

We have covered considerable ground in this chapter, including discussion of two methodological issues—the inductive method and methodological naturalism—and two substantive issues—biological origins and the problem of consciousness. I have tried to show the relevance of the doctrine of providence to each of these issues. More than this, I have tried to demonstrate some of the significant benefits of the Augustinian perspective in connection with them. To hold the Augustinian view is to gain access to what might be the only adequate response to Hume's tenacious critique of induction: appeal to the power and goodness of God. The Augustinian view also offers the Christian empirical scientist a wider range of perspectives when it comes to the question of origins, as it embraces intelligent design as a theoretical option. This goes for the study of consciousness as well, where the best solution just might be to recognize that consciousness is not properly something that needs to be explained as it is the key to explaining everything else. And when it comes to how we inquire into these issues, those who take the Augustinian view will not be constrained by a naturalistic methodology any more than they would be constrained by a naturalistic metaphysics. Advocates of the Augustinian view of providence will see that for the theist such a methodological rule would be an irrational rule indeed.

5

DIVINE EMOTION

At several junctures in previous chapters we touched upon the issue of divine emotion. In this chapter I will give the topic the extensive treatment it deserves. My purpose for doing so is twofold. First, I want to demonstrate that one need not embrace the low view of providence in order to affirm that God has emotions and relates to us in a passionate way. The high view of providence, especially the Augustinian version, is sometimes associated with belief in an apathetic God, which is quite unfortunate. This chapter will serve as a corrective to this error by showing that the Augustinian perspective is not only consistent with an emotive God but actually strongly recommends this belief. A second, more constructive aim in this chapter is to further elaborate the E-C aesthetic model developed in Chapter 3. I have proposed that, as the cosmic Artist, God both communicates ideas and expresses his emotions in the world. However, just what it means to say that God has emotions is far from clear—hence the need for this discussion.

The question whether God has emotions is just one aspect of the broader issue of divine passibility. To say that God is passible is to say that he can be affected by some outside force.[1] To affirm divine impassibility is to hold that God cannot be so affected. Now emotion is just

---

[1] Here I follow Richard Creel's "core definition." See his full discussion of various definitions of impassibility in *Divine Impassibility: An Essay in Philosophical Theology* (Cambridge: Cambridge University Press, 1986), 3-11.

one kind of affect, a particular way in which persons are sometimes moved, such as to become angry or giddy. The focus of our discussion will be just this particular kind of affect, including both pleasant and painful emotions. So I am not concerned to settle the debate over divine passibility per se but to address one significant aspect of it. And yet, since the matter of divine emotion is such an important part of the broader debate over divine passibility, to develop a reasonable position on the former will go a long way toward resolution of the latter.

The classical doctrine of divine impassibility is now a minority position. Apart from a few notable defenses of the classical position, the prevailing view among scholars today is that God has genuine emotions and experiences real suffering. If there is an overriding reason for this change of philosophical-theological opinion, it is that the doctrine of divine impassibility seems to contradict belief in divine relationality. Proponents of the low view of providence often argue that an impassible God is cold and aloof, not immanent and loving. A God void of genuine emotion, they claim, cannot be personal, which is an implication no orthodox theist can tolerate. Thus, believers have increasingly rejected divine impassibility, in favor of a picture of God that accommodates divine emotions, including joy, sorrow, affection, anger, grief, and satisfaction.

Such reasoning is often persuasive among Christians, and many have opted for the low view of providence because of it, thinking that only this view can sanction divine emotion. And some have tried—I think mistakenly—to guard the high view by warding off claims of divine passibility. However, it is noteworthy that the debate has been cast in strictly binary terms, presupposing that either God has no emotions or has emotions essentially as we humans do. Scholars on both sides of the debate have assumed this dichotomy, but I propose that this is a fundamental error. There is an alternative position that affirms elements of both views, while denying elements of both as well. I shall develop this position using the concept of divine *omnipathos* as a way of mediating between the standard views. I aim to capture the strengths and to avoid the major problems encountered on either side of this conceptual divide. So my aim is not to defend one of the traditional views in this debate so much as to resolve it with a model that achieves a reasonable compromise. Thus, in addition to disarming critics of the high view of providence, this model could potentially resolve a long-standing theological dispute.

PRINCIPAL ARGUMENTS FOR THE STANDARD POSITIONS

Let us begin by reviewing the main arguments for each of the standard views on divine passibility. What follows are what I consider the strongest, if not also the most common, lines of argument used in defense of these positions.

Arguments for Divine Impassibility

Defenders of divine impassibility have often appealed to notions of divine perfection and immutability to justify their position. This tradition traces back to Plotinus who argued that the very concept of eternity implies changelessness:

> One sees eternity in seeing a life that abides in the same, and always has the all present to it, not now this, and then again that, but all things at once, and not now some things, and then again others, but a partless completion, as if they were all together in a point . . . it is something which abides in the same in itself and does not change at all but is always in the present, because nothing of it has passed away, nor again is there anything to come into being, but that which it is, it *is*.[2]

Aquinas affirmed such a conception of divine eternality, saying that "God . . . is without beginning and end, having his whole being at once."[3] And elsewhere: "God's understanding has no succession, as neither does His being. He is therefore an ever-abiding simultaneous whole."[4] Proceeding with this conception of changeless eternity as essential to the divine life, impassibilists have sometimes argued that feelings and emotions imply change and thus are not appropriate characteristics of God.

---

[2] Plotinus, *Enneads*, in *Plotinus*, trans. A. H. Armstrong (London: William Heinemann, Ltd., 1967), 3:304-305.

[3] Thomas Aquinas, *The Disputed Questions on Truth*, trans. Robert W. Mulligan (Chicago: Henry Regnery, 1952), 1:98.

[4] Ibid., 218. Aquinas affirms a version of the Boethian doctrine of divine atemporality, where "God sees all things in His eternal present" (*The Consolation of Philosophy*, trans. W. V. Cooper [New York: The Modern Library, 1943], 117).

Some have appealed to a classical conception of omniscience, arguing that since God knows all truths regarding all events, whether in our past, present, or future, God cannot feel genuine surprise, wonder, or disappointment about anything that happens. These and many other emotions presuppose a passage from ignorance to knowledge about aspects of the world; so they are impossible for an omniscient being. A variation of this argument from divine knowledge is offered by Paul Helm, who says, "one clear reason for not ascribing . . . emotion or passion to God is that it is incompatible with his rationality and wisdom. To act upon emotion or passion is to act when the judgment is in abeyance. Emotion clouds the judgment, or functions in place of the judgment."[5]

Many impassibilists have focused on the negative or painful emotions as particularly problematic. Richard Creel notes that "if God is . . . eternal and suffers, then, because he is immutable in all respects, he is eternally transfixed by suffering. As a consequence God could never be perfectly happy, nor could his creatures if their happiness comes from a veridical vision of him."[6] Creel considers the first point—regarding eternal divine suffering—to be by itself an intolerable implication of divine passibilism. He identifies several further purportedly absurd consequences of the notion that God suffers, including the confusion of worshiping with pitying God, as well as the possibility of taking revenge upon God by intentionally increasing his sorrow.[7]

The notion of divine suffering has even been claimed to threaten God's goodness. Creel asserts, "in itself suffering is an evil."[8] And Baron F. von Hugel even compared suffering to sin itself, noting that "suffering and sin are, indeed, not identical, yet they are sufficiently like to make the permanent treatment of sin as intrinsically evil exceedingly difficult where suffering is treated as not really evil at all."[9] In support of his position, he cites Jesus' curing of pain and disease "as though they could not be uti-

---

[5] Paul Helm, "The Impossibility of Divine Passibility," in *The Power and Weakness of God: Impassibility and Orthodoxy*, ed. Nigel M. de S. Cameron (Edinburgh: Rutherford House, 1990), 130-131.

[6] Richard Creel, *op. cit.*, 132.

[7] Creel's argument is an extension of that made earlier by Marshall Randles, who complained that the notion of divine suffering makes God "the most miserable object of our pity" (*The Blessed God: Impassibility* [London: Charles F. Kelly, 1900], 16).

[8] Richard Creel, *op. cit.*, 122.

[9] Baron F. von Hugel, "Suffering and God," in *Essays and Addresses on the Philosophy of Religion*, Second Series (London: J. M. Dent and Sons, 1926), 199-200.

lized."[10] It is God's will to bring an end to suffering, and, von Hugel insists, this fact cannot be reconciled with the concept of divine suffering.

Impassibilists do not restrict their arguments to *a priori* considera- tion of the divine nature, though this is their preferred approach. They also use scriptural arguments to support their commitment to divine immutability and atemporality. For example, such passages as Malachi 3:6 ("I the LORD do not change") and James 1:17 (God "does not change like shifting shadows") suggest that God cannot have passions, again assuming that passions involve change. And passages such as Isaiah 46:10 ("I make known the end from the beginning, from ancient times, what is still to come. I say: My purpose will stand, and I will do all that I please") and Colossians 1:17 ("He is before all things, and in him all things hold together") suggest a God for whom genuine responses to human events, emotional or otherwise, would be inappropriate.[11]

Arguments for Divine Passibility

The passibilists have their arguments as well. They maintain that emo- tion is essential to divine personhood, just as it is essential to human per- sonhood. Charles Hartshorne declares, "God must have a system of emotions, including suffering, if he is a person. . . . Personality is achieved through suffering no less than through joy."[12] Jurgen Moltmann applies this point specifically to the attribute of love, noting that

> a God who cannot suffer is poorer than any man. For a God who is incapable of suffering is a being who cannot be involved. Suffering and injustice do not affect him. And because he is so completely insen- sitive, he cannot be affected or shaken by anything. He cannot weep, for he has no tears. But the one who cannot suffer cannot love either. So he is also a loveless being.[13]

---

[10] Ibid., 200.

[11] If God does not have emotions, then how is the impassibilist to account for both biblical and commonsense notions of divine compassion? The Anselmian approach, a popular one among impassibilists, offers a behavioral rendering of this and other apparent divine emotions. God does not literally *feel* compassion, so much as God *acts* in a way that we describe as compassionate. Anselm writes, "O Lord, . . . thou art compassionate in terms of our experience, and not compassionate in terms of thy being. . . . When thou beholdest us in our wretchedness, we experience the effect of compassion, but thou dost not experience the feeling" (*Basic Writings*, 2nd ed., trans. S. N. Deane [La Salle, Ill.: Open Court, 1962], 59).

[12] Charles Hartshorne, *Philosophers Speak of God* (Chicago: University of Chicago Press, 1953), 160.

[13] Jurgen Moltmann, *The Crucified God* (New York: Harper and Row, 1974), 222.

Still others, such as Charles Taliaferro, have suggested that even the divine attribute of moral goodness presupposes passibility.[14] To make proper sense of the notion that God disapproves of human cruelty and malice, for example, we must assume that he feels real sorrow about such things. And without genuine disapproval of evil deeds (and approval of those who live just lives), the concept of divine goodness loses all meaning.

Some passibilists have appealed to divine omniscience in support of their view. Assume that God knows all truths and knows them fully. Not all truths can be fully known in a merely propositional way. Some can only be fully known experientially, such as knowledge of what it is like to feel pain. So God must have an experiential knowledge of such truths if he is to really know them. Hartshorne puts it baldly: "to be omniscient is to include in one's experience all that is, whatever it be."[15] Now emotions are a particular kind of experience. Therefore, God knows emotions in an experiential way. And, of course, to know an emotion experientially is to have that emotion.[16] This notion of divinely shared emotional experiences is not a merely formal point. Rather, as passibilists often point out, it has practical therapeutic value. "At the most basic level," Paul Fiddes asserts, "it is a consolation to those who suffer to know that God suffers too, and understands their situation from within."[17]

Many passibilists, particularly Christian theologians, approach the whole matter of divine feeling through the lens of sympathetic divine suffering. God must suffer, they argue, because the very means of Christian redemption is the suffering of a divinely incarnate person, where in the words of Moltmann, "God himself loves and suffers the death of Christ in his love."[18] That God ordained the suffering of Christ for atonement of sin thus demonstrates the pathos of God. Fiddes puts it this way: "If theology affirms that, in any sense, 'God was in Christ,' then it seems

---

[14] Charles Taliaferro, "The Passibility of God," *Religious Studies* 25:2 (1989): 220.

[15] Charles Hartshorne, *Man's Vision of God* (Hamden, Conn.: Archon Books, 1964), 321.

[16] As was discussed in the previous chapter, subjectivity is an essential feature of consciousness. Presumably, God knows what it is like to be humanly conscious (or rodently, caninely, or angelically, for that matter). Now human consciousness always (or nearly always) features various emotive characteristics. So if God knows what it is like to be humanly conscious, then God must know what it is like to feel emotions. But there is no way to know what it is like to feel emotions except actually to have emotions. So God must be emotive. And, specifically, there is no way to know what is like to feel pain but by feeling pain. And so it goes for all feelings and emotions.

[17] Paul Fiddes, *The Creative Suffering of God* (Oxford: Clarendon Press, 1988), 31.

[18] Jurgen Moltmann, *op. cit.*, 227.

an inescapable conclusion that God suffered 'in Christ' at the cross. If God was involved with the person and career of Jesus, then he was implicated in the experience of the crucified Christ."[19] So the central doctrine of Christian theology, the divine incarnation, provides evidence for divine passibilism, insofar as Christ suffered during his life. As the second person of the Trinity, his suffering was the suffering of God.[20]

As for the scriptural witness to this issue, passibilists maintain that we need to take seriously and at face value the numerous references to God as experiencing a range of emotions. Biblical writers attribute grief and sorrow to God such as in Genesis 6:6, which says that upon observing rampant human wickedness "The LORD was grieved that he had made man on the earth, and his heart was filled with pain." Other passages attribute further emotions to God, such as regret (1 Sam. 15:11, 35), anger (Exod. 4:14), love (Jer. 31:3; Mal. 1:2), hatred (Prov. 11:20; Mal. 1:3), and humor (Ps. 2:4). These are only some of the more direct references to divine passions. Numerous narratives that describe or refer to the wrath, mercy, judgments, blessings, or rewards God bestows upon people may be seen as indirect evidence for the passibilist position. Nicholas Wolterstorff comments on such passages: "The fact that the biblical writers speak of God as rejoicing and suffering over the state of the creation is not a superficial eliminable feature of their speech. It expresses themes deeply embedded in the biblical vision. God's love for his world is a rejoicing and suffering love."[21]

DIVINE OMNIPATHOS: THE BASIC CONCEPT

Passibilists and impassibilists alike appear to have strong arguments to recommend their positions. My purpose here, however, is not to decide a winner in this debate but to resolve it by proposing a view that embraces most of the basic claims made by defenders of each view. It seems to me that all of the arguments above appeal to attributes of God that must be affirmed in order to preserve a philosophically, theologically, and existentially adequate theism. Therefore, I want to explore the possibility of developing a perspective that affirms the impassibilist's

---

[19] Paul Fiddes, *op. cit.*, 26.
[20] See also Terence E. Fretheim, *The Suffering of God* (Philadelphia: Fortress Press, 1984), Chapters 8-9.
[21] Nicholas Wolterstorff, "Suffering Love," *Philosophy and the Christian Faith*, ed. Thomas Morris (Notre Dame, Ind.: University of Notre Dame Press, 1988), 227.

intuitions regarding divine immutability and timeless eternality as well as the passibilist's intuitions about divine personhood, divine relationality, and Christology. And I want to affirm the sensibilities on both sides pertaining to divine omniscience and Scripture.

Is a reasonable compromise between these conflicting views possible? I believe so, and to see what such a view amounts to we need only apply some ingenuity in combining the attributes emphasized above. Let us grant the essence of divine passibilism, that God experiences real emotions. The Lord really feels sorrow, joy, anger, humor, grief, pain, affection, and so on. But let us also affirm the impassibilist's point that God is both immutable and timelessly eternal, keeping in mind that this claim implies that the divine life is lived, as it were, all at once. As Aquinas notes, "Something can be present to what is eternal only by being pres-ent to the whole of it, since the eternal does not have the duration of succession."[22] Taking these two points together, then, we arrive at the notion that God experiences all of his emotions at once, that is, eternally. If God is immutable and the inner life of God is one of absolute simultaneity—everything "all at once"—then if God has any feelings whatsoever, they must be eternal. So on this view, divine feelings, like God's knowledge, are ever constant and unchanging. He experiences all emotions and does so for all eternity. God, we might say, is *omnipathic*.

What I am proposing, then, is the possibility that both sides of this debate are correct, at least as regards their *positive* claims about God's nature, viz. that God is immutable and timelessly eternal, on the one hand, and that God is personal and fully relational, on the other. I am, of course, implying that both sides have been mistaken as well, specifically in their *negative* claims that God's immutability and timeless eternality and God's personality and relationality are mutually exclusive. From a rhetorical standpoint, the advantage of proposing a mediating position like this is that I can simply appeal to arguments on both sides of the debate as favoring my position. The disadvantage is that such a theory is naturally to be questioned for its coherence.

---

[22] Thomas Aquinas, *The Disputed Questions on Truth*, 1:219. Richard Creel insightfully comments on this passage, noting, "those events in time that do not exist simultaneously with one another nonetheless exist simultaneously with the whole of God as he is in himself. Events may exist later than one another, but they cannot exist earlier or later in relation to God because God does not exist earlier or later in relation to anything" (*op. cit.*, 107).

Can this view really incorporate the insights on either side of the conceptual divide and, at the same time, avoid internal contradiction? Unfortunately for me, to show that this is so is not something that can be achieved with a few cogent arguments. It can be done only by developing the model, in this case through explication of the concept of omnipathos. Thus my method will be essentially abductive, making the case for the theory based on its internal coherence and overall explanatory power.

Thus far I have claimed that divine omnipathism affirms some major claims of both passibilism and impassibilism. This is only the first stage of my abductive case for the model. It remains for me to: (1) demonstrate how divine omnipathos compares to and complements other classical divine attributes, (2) show how it fits with some standard theories of emotion, and (3) illustrate other virtues of the theory, both theoretical and practical in nature. I hope the cumulative effect of my carrying out these tasks will be persuasive. For those who remain unconvinced, perhaps the concept of divine omnipathos will prove useful anyway, if only as a heuristic device.

In the next section I will continue to develop my model by discussing the classical divine attributes. In some cases I will use a standard interpretation of the divine attribute as a sort of conceptual guide, allowing it to steer our intuitions about divine omnipathos in one direction or another. In other cases, where such would be problematic, I will take another course. But in these instances I will justify the path I take with arguments. The result will be a coherent set of divine attributes that includes divine omnipathos as a very natural component. However, I should note by way of disclaimer that due to the breadth of territory that must be canvassed, our discussion of the divine attributes must be cursory and schematic, at least as compared to the level of sophistication that discussion of these issues has reached in contemporary philosophical theology.

Omnipotence and Omniscience

I have chosen the term *omnipathic* to describe God in the context of divine emotion not only because it is an accurate description of the view I am proposing, but also because it is intended to make the doctrine of divine passibility parallel some of the other divine attributes. Just how close those parallels are, however, will possibly be a contentious matter, depending upon one's views of those other divine attributes.

Let us begin with the doctrines of divine power and knowledge. Consider these definitions:

Omnipotence =df the ability to do anything that is logically possible[23]

Omniscience =df the knowledge of all true propositions[24]

In formalizing our understanding of omnipathos, we might begin by defining the concept in a way that is strictly parallel to either of these, as follows:

$[O_1]$: Omnipathos1 =df the capacity to experience all emotions

$[O_2]$: Omnipathos2 =df the actual experience of all emotions

Now O_2 is much more robust than O_1. I prefer O_2, since O_1 appears to make the notion of divine omnipathos trivially true. If God merely has a *capacity* to experience all emotions, this in no way implies that God *actually* experiences *any* emotions. Unlike the case of omnipotence, where the very existence of the world demonstrates God's use of power, omnipathos understood analogously, or O_1, has no such parallel implications. So O_1 constitutes a rejection of a critical passibilist insight that my theory is designed to accommodate, namely that God genuinely experiences emotion. For example, if God merely *can* be sorrowful or exuberant but never really is, then we don't have a God who existentially identifies with us in these ways. So it seems that the better route is to model omnipathos after our definition

---

[23] This is a general definition of omnipotence, traditional since Aquinas. For a good discussion of more nuanced renderings of this basic idea, see Richard Swinburne, *The Coherence of Theism* (Oxford: Oxford University Press, 1993), Chapter 9.

[24] Perhaps a preferable definition of omniscience is the knowledge of all facts (where a fact is some state of affairs to which a true proposition corresponds). I have chosen to use the definition I am using for simplicity's sake. Also, as in the case of omnipotence, there is much debate as to what is (and is not) entailed by so general a definition of omniscience (e.g., knowledge of future contingents, such as free human choices and actions). Again, I skirt these matters only because they are not crucial to the present discussion.

of omniscience, at least if we are going to take the passibilists' arguments seriously.[25]

There is one more recommendation for modeling omnipathos after omniscience rather than omnipotence. Emotions are, arguably, a kind of awareness. (Explication of this point will have to wait until later.) Some have even argued that emotions are a means of acquiring knowledge or accessing truth.[26] In any case, if to have an emotion is to be aware in some special way, or if emotion in any way involves awareness, then this seems to make emotion more similar to knowledge than to power. After all, knowledge is, or involves, a certain kind of awareness. Or, to make the case more cautiously, emotion has an essentially cognitive component, as does knowledge. Power does not. Since emotion shares this essential feature with knowledge, then, it seems wise to take my approach.

So let us opt for O_2 and affirm the notion that God actually experiences all emotions. Now there is a further decision to be made with regard to the modal scope of the term "all" in our definition. The distinction may be made as follows:

[O_2a]: Omnipathos2a =df the actual experience of all real emotions in this world

[O_2p]: Omnipathos2p =df the actual experience of all emotions in all possible worlds

Using omniscience again as our model, the issue is whether or not God's emotions are analogous to his knowledge of just this world (WA)

---

[25] If we look more closely we will see that there are at least two senses in which the classical definition of omniscience may be conceived:

[Os_1]: Omniscience1 =df knowledge of all truths, where S has knowledge of p if S is ever-presently aware of p

[Os_2]: Omniscience2 =df knowledge of all truths, where S has knowledge of p if S has the capacity to recall p

Notice that Os_2 is patterned after our definition of omnipotence. Deciding which of these, if either, is adequate to an understanding of divine knowledge will be at least as tricky as deciding which conception of omnipathos one should accept. Certainly the fact that Os_1 provides a more robust conception of omniscience will find favor with some. Another consideration in its favor might be the fact that attributes of knowledge and power are different in a crucial way: In ordinary usage we regard power as essentially a capacity of a certain kind (viz. to do certain things), while we typically regard knowledge as something presently possessed. However, it may be replied, in favor of Os_2, that in ordinary usage we regard a person as possessing knowledge about all sorts of truths, in spite of the fact that he or she is not now thinking about those truths.

[26] See Robert Roberts, "Emotions as Access to Religious Truths," *Faith and Philosophy* 9:1 (January 1992): 83-94.

or his knowledge of all possible worlds (WP), including this world. Many philosophers affirm that, in addition to knowing everything there is to know about the actual world, God knows all that would obtain in every possible world. So for the O_2 omnipathicist the question is whether God's emotional life is similarly transworldly in the modal sense. Does God only experience all emotions actually experienced by creatures in this world? Or does he also experience all logically possible emotions, that is, all emotions that *could* be experienced by creatures in all possible worlds?

To complicate the matter yet further, there is one more distinction—or four more, depending on how one counts—to be made regarding the content of the divine emotional life. Specifically, does God experience all emotion tokens—each particular emotion experienced by each particular person (whether in WA or in WP)—or does God only experience all emotion types—every kind or category of emotion (whether in WA or in WP)? While the model I am proposing is compatible with any combination of responses to these questions, it will become clear in the next section why I believe the former position fits more comfortably with a classical conception of God.

Omnipresence

What does it mean to say that God is omnipresent? Since God is not an embodied being, any plausible account of the concept will have to involve divine mental attributes. Accordingly, I would propose that the concept be unpacked in terms of awareness. For a spirit (a non-embodied being) to be omnipresent entails that this being is aware of the physical cosmos from every spatially locatable perspective. That is, every point of view that someone *could* have within the cosmos, an omnipresent spirit *in fact* has. One might say, then, that an omnipresent being is omniperspectival. Some, such as Aquinas[27] and Richard Swinburne,[28] have also included conative aspects within the concept of omnipresence so that the attribute also entails the capacity to directly control every physical component of the cosmos. This seems to me, how-

---

[27] Thomas Aquinas, *Summa Theologica*, I.8.
[28] Richard Swinburne, *op. cit.*, 106-107.

ever, to confuse the concept with an aspect of omnipotence. At any rate, here, for simplicity's sake, I will take a minimalist approach:

Omnipresence =df the possession of every spatially locatable perspective[29]

Now just as divine omnipresence entails that God's experience exhausts all cosmic points of view, we might say that divine omnipathos entails that God's experience exhausts the whole range of emotions. God is, on this model, emotively complete. Just as there are no novel spatial perspectives that may be added to the divine perspective to improve God's perception of the cosmos, so there are no new emotions God could experience to increase his awareness of creaturely feelings.

To apply this to a concrete case, suppose someone suffers a grief of some kind, such as the loss of a loved one. On the omnipathic view, God knows, in the deepest existential sense, just what she experiences. God not only knows her point of view on the world spatially, but God also shares her emotive perspective. Now to faithfully model omnipathos on our definition of omnipresence we must affirm that God is not merely empathetic in the sense that he feels *some* pain much like hers, but rather that God feels *this* pain of hers. Notice how this parallel between omnipathos and omnipresence entails that God experiences all emotion tokens, as opposed to mere emotion types (per the question posed at the end of the previous section).

Given the classical doctrine of omnipresence, it is curious that only relatively recently have theists readily affirmed that God is passible. If one supposes that God "looks out" on the world from every perspective, then it seems natural to suppose that God should also feel, as it were, from every emotive "perspective." Here the passibilist argument from omniscience is applicable. If God really knows all truths, then God must know what it is like to experience a particular emotion X, wherever and however that emotion is felt. To have an emotion is a fact about the world, and how it feels to actually *experience* emotion X is a significant aspect of that emotive fact. So it seems God must not only be aware

---

[29] This definition is a cognate of those found in Richard Swinburne, *op. cit.* and Charles Taliaferro, "The Incorporeality of God," *Modern Theology* 3:2 (1987): 179-188.

that X is experienced by a person. God must be aware of what it is like to actually *experience* X.

Divine Omnitemporality

This brings us to a further question. Must God also know what it is like to have emotion X *at time t_1*? That is, does God experience X in a tensed way? The subject of God's relation to time is controversial these days, with some philosophers opting for divine atemporalism, some affirming divine temporalism (or sempiternalism), and still others taking a moderate position that affirms elements of both. Here I will explain these views and consider the doctrine of divine omnipathos in light of each.

I will begin with the classical position on the issue, divine atemporalism, which is also the view that might seem to present the most serious challenge in being reconciled with the concept of divine omnipathos. Those who affirm this view maintain that God is a purely timeless being:

Atemporality =df the absence of experience of time (timeless existence)

To be atemporal, of course, is not simply a privative state. To put it in positive terms, as Plotinus and Aquinas do in some passages quoted earlier, an atemporal God experiences the whole of the divine life, including all of human history, as *now*. The whole of reality is simultaneously present to God. Hugh McCann puts it as follows: "God exists timelessly . . . and his life and experience, while they may concern the world of change, are themselves unchanging. . . . God knows . . . everything . . . in a single, timeless act of awareness that encompasses all of heaven and earth, in its complete history."[30] It is true that theists often speak of God as foreknowing or foreseeing certain events, but this is but a manner of speaking, in this view. John Calvin, explains: "When we attribute foreknowledge to God, we mean that all things always were, and perpetually remain, under his eyes, so that to his knowledge there is nothing future or past, but all things are present."[31] Calvin's (and Aquinas's and McCann's) concern, as is typically the case for atempo-

---

[30] Hugh McCann, "The God Beyond Time," in *Philosophy of Religion: An Anthology*, second edition, ed. Louis Pojman (Belmont, Calif.: Wadsworth, 1994), 232.
[31] John Calvin, *Institutes of the Christian Religion*, trans. Ford L. Battles (Philadelphia: Westminster Press, 1960), 2:926

ralists, is to protect the immutability and perfection of God. If God experiences time, it would seem that God changes. But to change is to become either better or worse. So God must not experience time.

Sempiternalists reject this implication by qualifying the doctrine of divine immutability. There is a distinction to be made here between *ontological* and *moral* immutability. Sempiternalists such as Nicholas Wolterstorff affirm that the latter and deny that the former is true of God, notwithstanding what Christian theologians have often inferred from the biblical references to the changelessness of God: Malachi 3:6 ("I the LORD do not change") and Psalm 102:27 ("you remain the same, and your years will never end"). Says Wolterstorff, "God's ontological immutability is not a part of the explicit teaching of the biblical writers. What the biblical writers teach is that God is faithful and without beginning or end, not that none of his aspects is temporal. The theological tradition of God's ontological immutability has no explicit biblical foundation."[32]

Sempiternalist Stephen Davis argues that atemporalism is incoherent. Take the Boethian notion that for God all times are eternally present. For God, then, any two dates, say 3021 B.C. and A.D. 7643, are simultaneous. According to Davis, this can only be the case if time is illusory. "But since I see no good reason to affirm that time is illusory and every reason to deny that it is illusory, I am within my rights in insisting that the two indicated years are not simultaneous and that the doctrine of divine timelessness is accordingly probably false."[33] Like Wolterstorff, Davis conceives of God as essentially temporal, existing everlastingly within time.[34] Both argue that the simple fact that God has created the world and interacts with it in sundry ways is sufficient grounds for concluding that God is essentially temporal.

Notice that both atemporalists and sempiternalists see divine atemporality and God's genuine temporal interaction with the world as mutually exclusive. But might not God be essentially atemporal and yet enter into time to interact with his creatures? Or, otherwise put, might

---

[32] Nicholas Wolterstorff, "God Everlasting," in *Contemporary Philosophy of Religion*, eds. Steven Cahn and David Shatz (Oxford: Oxford University Press, 1982), 97.

[33] Stephen Davis, "Temporal Eternity," in *Philosophy of Religion: An Anthology*, second edition, ed. Louis Pojman (Belmont, Calif.: Wadsworth, 1994), 228.

[34] Davis writes, "time was not created; it necessarily exists (like numbers); it depends for its existence on nothing else. Time, perhaps, is an eternal aspect of God's nature rather than a reality independent of God. But the point is that God, on this view, is a temporal being" (ibid., 229).

not God be atemporal when considered independently of creation and temporal in relation to creation? Such seems to be the view of William Lane Craig, who argues, "given a dynamic theory of time [the view that tensed facts are objectively real], it follows from God's creative activity in the temporal world and his complete knowledge of it that God is temporal. God quite literally exists now. Since God never begins to exist nor ever ceases to exist, it follows that God is omnitemporal. He exists at every time that ever exists."[35] According to Craig, then, God enters time with the creation of the world. Since the cosmos is a contingent thing, God's dwelling within time is also contingent. God is not essentially a temporal being, but God does experience time—the whole of it, in fact. Thus, we arrive at the following definition:

Omnitemporality =df the experience of all times that ever exist

Since creating the world, God exists in time, but not at any time exclusively. Thus, Craig's view strikes a compromise between the sempiternalist and atemporalist perspectives. God really experiences time, as sempiternalists insist. However, as atemporalists maintain, God is not temporally bound but transcends time.

This seems to me to be a reasonable position. It affirms that God's temporal interactions with the world and the people in it are genuine, but it denies that temporality is intrinsic to God's being. An advantage of this view, at least from the standpoint of atemporalists, is that it preserves some sense of divine ontological immutability. And, of course, the sempiternalist will appreciate the fact that it takes seriously the temporality of God and the sense this makes of divine relations with the world. For this reason omnitemporalism naturally complements the omnipathic conception of divine emotion, since both views affirm divine relationality and (ontological and moral) immutability. Each provides a conceptual framework for conceiving God as both transcendent and maximally immanent.

Divine omnipathos may be conceived analogously to this concept of divine omnitemporality as follows. God experiences emotion but not any particular emotion exclusively. God experiences all emotions and

---

[35] William Lane Craig, "Timelessness and Omnitemporality," in *God and Time*, ed. Gregory E. Ganssle (Downers Grove, Ill.: InterVarsity Press, 2001), 153.

does so in a temporal way, as we humans do. Emotional experiences wax and wane, have a beginning and an end. So they must occur in a temporal way, and it is reasonable to suppose this must be true for God as well. Or, to use the argument from omniscience again, since temporally tensed experiences are a basic fact of the world, and the *having* of such experiences is a significant aspect of these facts, it follows that if God knows the world entirely, God must know what it is like to have temporally tensed experiences. That is, God has such experiences. But the omnipathicist may deny that having experiences as such, emotional or otherwise, is essential to God. So conceived, there are close parallels between omnitemporalism and the omnipathic model of divine emotion. The latter resembles the former in that: (1) God's emotions are merely *contingent* facts about him, (2) God's emotional relations with his creatures are *extrinsic* facts about him, and (3) God experiences all emotion tokens and no emotions exclusively (where emotion tokens may be understood as analogous to moments in the world's time metric).

So the omnipathic conception of God fits with the omnitemporalist view on God and time. But, we might ask, can divine omnipathism be squared with atemporalism and sempiternalism? In the case of atemporalism, there is nothing incoherent in the notion that God experiences all emotions eternally, granting a certain conception of experience, of course. But, one might ask, how might a timeless being have genuine experiences or experientially participate in human emotions in particular? The atemporalist may account for this by appealing to divine imagination. Although God is a timeless being, presumably he is capable of imagining what it is like to be any among various sorts of finite beings, including those whose experience is temporally tensed. The atemporalist may submit that it is due to human finitude that we experience events in time. However, God's infinite cognitive ability makes temporal processes of thought unnecessary for him. He can think about everything all at once and does not need ideas spread out in time. And his infinite cognitive power also enables him to imagine what it is like to be a finite being who thinks, wills, and perceives temporally. Similarly, may not God imaginatively experience emotions even if these are indeed states of consciousness that are essentially temporal in nature? This seems quite reasonable. Moreover, it is intelligible to suppose that through his infinite imaginative power God may experience *all* emotions (tokens and types). So God's experience of emotion appears to present no special problems for the atemporalist. And, in particular, divine omnipathism seems to be perfectly compatible with atemporalism.

As for the sempiternalists, the matter of the compatibility of omnipathos with their doctrine of God and time is problematic. If God dwells everlastingly within time, then the concept of divine experience generally is immediately intelligible. So, too, is the special instance of divine emotional experiences. So that God has genuine pathos is not problematic for the sempiternalist. Indeed, it was to make sense of divine emotions, among other things, that this view was conceived in the first place. The difficulty for the sempiternalist, however, arises as we try to make sense of God's being *omni*pathic. What sense can be made of God's experience of *all* emotion tokens on the sempiternalist scheme? Notice, first, that the term *all* is ambiguous here. It can be understood to denote each and every emotion token ever experienced by all people throughout human history, past, present, and future. Call this the strong sense of the term. Or *all* can be interpreted in a weak sense, denoting just those emotion tokens experienced by all people up to and including the present moment. Sempiternalists may readily affirm that God shares all emotions in the weak sense of the term. But it seems they could not affirm that God is omnipathic in this strong sense, since sempiternalism affirms the future is not real for God or anyone else. Future emotions simply do not exist, in this view, so the only emotions with which God has to identify are those that have already occurred or are presently occurring among his creatures.

One option is open for the sempiternalist who wants to affirm omnipathism in this strong sense. Recalling O_2p above, he might try to account for God's experience of future emotions by appealing to divine acquaintance with all possible emotions via the divine imagination. A sempiternalist could conceive of God's emotive awareness in this modal fashion and thus square his view with an omnipathic conception of God. But, of course, such a move would concede too much for most sempiternalists, since it acknowledges that divine imagining is a sufficient means of securing God's emotive completeness. Sempiternalists have typically maintained, in alliance with divine passibilism, that divine emotions come through divine temporal experiences of the world. Thus, this approach would be awkward, to say the least, for the sempiternalist. It appears, then, that sempiternalism is less amenable to omnipathism than are atemporalism and omnitemporalism. Ironically, a God who is temporally bound might in fact be *less* capable of emotion than a God who transcends time.

So what may we glean from the foregoing discussion? First, the concept of divine omnipathos is a hopeful compromise between the standard passibilist and impassibilist approaches to divine emotion. It incorporates the major insights of both views and avoids most of the problems inherent in each. Omnipathism can be conceived in terms that parallel some of the classical attributes of God, such as omniscience and omnipresence. In fact, it fits comfortably within a classical theistic concept of God. But it also affirms God's genuine relationality, thus affirming the insight of many critics of classical theism. While divine omnipathism is not without its conceptual difficulties, it does seem to be an improvement on both passibilism and impassibilism. Second, omnipathism offers a fruitful means of reconciling the high view of providence with belief in a deeply passionate God. Since an omnipathic God is maximally emotive, this model achieves the aims of sempiternalists who are (rightly) concerned to preserve genuine divine relationality. But since omnipathism fits with atemporalism and omnitemporalism at least as well as—if not better than—sempiternalism, a central argument for the latter is removed. And since sempiternalism plays a crucial role in the low view of providence, omnipathism reduces motivation for this doctrine as well.

THEORIES OF EMOTION AND DIVINE OMNIPATHOS

Having explicated this idea of God as omnipathic, it is about time that we look more closely at the concept of emotion itself, to clarify what it is we are saying when we ascribe emotions to God and determine which, if any, of the major conceptions of emotion are compatible with divine omnipathism. Also, this explication of the doctrine of divine omnipathism will further develop the "expression" component of the E-C model of the world as divine art. The concept of divine emotional expression is that aspect of the model most in need of clarification. Much work has already been done on the topic of divine communication,[36] but

---

[36] For one of the more innovative recent treatments of this subject see Nicholas Wolterstorff, *Divine Discourse: Philosophical Reflections on the Claim That God Speaks* (Cambridge: Cambridge University Press, 1995).

just what it means to say that God expresses emotion is comparatively virgin territory. In order to explore this matter, however, we must first look more closely at the more basic question, what *is* emotion? After summarizing the major theories, I will apply one eclectic account to divine emotion and, more specifically, to an omnipathic God.

Major Theories of Emotion

Some philosophers have proposed that emotions are essentially internal sensations, analogous to sensory perceptions. Descartes, for example, regarded an emotion as a subjective response to physiological disturbance. A passion is a certain feeling within the soul, an introspective perception of a particular sort. Thus, a distinguishing feature of Descartes's view is that it makes emotion essentially passive, much like sensation. The perception of a dangerous animal approaching, for instance, "excites the passion of apprehension in the soul and thereupon that of boldness or that of fear and terror."[37] David Hume, another early modern advocate of the feeling theory, regarded emotions as "[s]econdary or reflective" impressions that proceed from the original sensory perceptions arising from sense organs.[38] Emotions, says Hume, come in two basic forms: calm and violent. Calm emotions are aesthetic, "the sense of beauty and deformity in action, composition, and external objects," while violent emotions include love, hatred, joy, pride, and humility.[39] Like Descartes before him and feeling theorists after him, such as William James,[40] Hume sees emotion as basically passive and, in this case, quite literally a sensation within the soul.

Critics of the feeling theory often point out that it fails to account for the impact that beliefs have upon emotions. It is not mere perception that causes an emotion such as fear or desire but rather the *beliefs* formed on the basis of a perception. Thus, the cognitive theory of emotion places special significance on this element as a causal factor in the occurrence of emotion. Accordingly, Aristotle analyzes numerous emotions in terms of the beliefs that give rise to them. For instance, he says,

---

[37] Rene Descartes, *The Passions of the Soul*, trans. Stephen H. Voss (Indianapolis: Hackett, 1989), 39.
[38] David Hume, *A Treatise of Human Nature*, second edition, ed. L. A. Selby-Bigge (Oxford: Oxford University Press, 1978), 275.
[39] Ibid., 276.
[40] See James's *The Principles of Psychology*, Vol. 2 (New York: Henry Holt, 1896), Chapter 25.

"fear is felt by those who believe something to be likely to happen to them, at the hands of particular persons, in a particular form, and at a particular time."[41] The opposite of fear, confidence, is "the expectation associated with a mental picture of the nearness of what keeps us safe and the absence or remoteness of what is terrible."[42] And so it goes for all of the emotions, according to Aristotle, each essentially arising from some belief or other.

Spinoza developed a version of the cognitive theory that is Aristotelian in the sense that he analyzed particular emotions in mental terms. His account of emotion, like the whole of his philosophy, builds upon some basic concepts, in this case joy and sorrow. Joy, he says, "is man's passage from a less to a greater perfection," while sorrow is "man's passage from a greater to a less perfection."[43] Various emotions are then definable in terms of a combination of some mental state with joy or sorrow. So love, for instance, "is joy with the accompanying idea of an external cause," while hatred "is sorrow with the accompanying idea of an external cause."[44] Similarly, Spinoza analyzes emotions including confidence, despair, gladness, remorse, commiseration, contempt, self-satisfaction, despondency, and shame as consisting in either joy or sorrow combined with some mental process, such as ideation, imagination, or contemplation. The basic intuition shared by Aristotle, Spinoza, and other cognitivists, such as Alexander Shand[45] and William McDougall,[46] is that an emotion is not merely caused by cognition of some kind, but that an emotion in large part *is* a cognitive state in at least two senses. For one thing, it is an intentional state, directed to an object, person, or event in the world. Additionally, an emotional state involves belief. To have a certain feeling about a thing is to have made a rational judgment about it.

Another standard approach agrees with cognitivists on these general points but adds that the particular judgment essential to all emotions is evaluative in nature. Jean-Paul Sartre offers a phenomenological

---

[41] Aristotle, *Rhetoric*, trans. W. Rhys Roberts, in *The Basic Works of Aristotle*, ed. Richard McKeon (New York: Random House, 1941), 1390-1391.

[42] Ibid., 1391.

[43] Benedict de Spinoza, *Ethics*, ed. James Gutman (New York: Hafner Press, 1949), 175.

[44] Ibid., 176-177.

[45] See Shand's *The Foundations of Character* (New York: Macmillan, 1914).

[46] See McDougall's *An Introduction to Social Psychology* (London: Metheun, 1908).

version of this account, conceiving emotion as a particular mode of reflective consciousness that seeks "a transformation of the world," which consists in an attempt "to live as if the connection between things and their potentialities were not ruled by deterministic process, but by magic."[47] In the face of some difficulty the sad or fearful person naturally wants to alter the situation but realizes this is impossible. And the joyful person exhibits a kind of impatience when contemplating the object he or she desires. In such cases the "magical attitude" that constitutes emotion appears, seeking change of the present situation, either by refusing or grasping for the object of his or her consciousness.

A more straightforward and analytical version of the evaluative theory has recently been developed by William Lyons. He says, "X is to be deemed an emotional state if and only if it is a physiologically abnormal state caused by the subject of that state's evaluation of his or her situation."[48] Lyons's view, then, is rather complex, involving diverse elements: (1) a cognitive component (belief), (2) a physical component (physiological change), and (3) the crucial evaluative component, which is typically but not necessarily cognitive in nature. He conceives of the evaluation involved in emotion in the ordinary sense of "relat[ing] something already known or perceived to some rating scale."[49] But the evaluative component in emotion is not always a mental occurrence. It is sometimes merely dispositional—a particular inclination or tendency to make an explicit evaluation of an object, event, or person. The physiological component in Lyons's analysis, he admits, is a way of empirically grounding such dispositions.

Proponents of behaviorism give primacy to the physical aspect of emotion. Among behaviorists there is variance as to whether emotion ought to be conceived in terms of simple bodily changes or operant behavior. Taking the former view, J. B. Watson proposes that "an emotion is an hereditary 'pattern-reaction' involving profound changes of the bodily mechanism as a whole, but particularly of the visceral and glandular systems."[50] Thus, it seems for Watson that any physical

---

[47] Jean-Paul Sartre, *The Emotions: Outline of a Theory*, trans. Bernard Frechtman (New York: Philosophical Library, 1948), 58-59.

[48] William Lyons, *Emotion* (Cambridge: Cambridge University Press, 1980), 56-57.

[49] Ibid., 59.

[50] J. B. Watson, *Psychology from the Standpoint of a Behaviorist* (Philadelphia: J. B. Lippincott, 1919), 195.

response to a stimulus may count as emotional. In contrast, B. F. Skinner analyzes all aspects of the human self, including emotion, into behavior patterns.[51] So the emotion of anger may consist in one's actually pounding the table with her fist or in the tendency to behave in such ways given certain circumstances.

Gilbert Ryle provides a thorough philosophical analysis of such dispositional emotional states, noting that they may be expressed in descriptions that take the general form "Whenever X occurs, S always or usually responds by doing Y." Just as sugar has the dispositional property of being soluble, meaning that *if* placed in water it will enter solution, these sorts of generalizations signify propensities, not particular occurrences. "They are," says Ryle, "elliptical expressions of general hypothetical propositions of a certain sort, and cannot be construed as expressing categorical narratives of episodes."[52] This qualification enables Ryle and other behaviorists to resist the criticism that their view implies the counterintuitive notion that emotions cannot be stifled, that if a person does not *act* on her anger, then she in fact did not have this emotion. So the fact that on some occasions an angry person appears calm and at ease doesn't necessarily falsify the description of her as angry. Still, behaviorism is commonly criticized for ignoring the internal, subjective quality of emotions that is apparent upon introspection.

Roberts's Eclectic Theory of Emotion

Each of the major theories of emotion has its strengths and weaknesses. And, it seems to me, no one of them is a sufficient account by itself. For this reason I favor an eclectic theory that affirms major elements of the feeling, cognitive, evaluative, and behaviorist accounts. I will next expound on such a theory and will apply it to the subject of divine emotion. This will not only provide what I believe to be a more accurate account of divine emotion but will also conserve space in our discussion. Rather than showing how each of the standard accounts of emotion can be applied to God, I can accomplish the same end by applying this sin-

---

[51] Skinner writes, "A self or personality is at best a repertoire of behavior imparted by an organized set of contingencies" (*About Behaviorism* [New York: Vintage Books, 1974], 164). Regarding emotion terms, such as "sad" or "excited," Skinner dismisses these as perhaps "little more than metaphors" as opposed to terminology that really refers to an intrapsychic life of the mind (p. 28).
[52] Gilbert Ryle, *The Concept of Mind* (New York: Barnes and Noble, 1949), 85.

gle multifaceted account. The eclectic theory to which I refer is Robert
Roberts's account of emotion as concern-based construal. As I noted, his
view seems to incorporate elements of all four of the major theories discussed above. And all of them are readily applicable to an omnipathic
God. I will attempt to demonstrate each of these claims in turn.

The basic features of Roberts's theory may be summarized as follows. First, emotions are intentional states. They "have propositional
objects in the sense that what the emotion is about, of, for, at, or to can
in principle be specified propositionally."[53] But emotions are not mere
judgments, for this would not account for irrational emotion, cases in
which the judgment (e.g., "there is a prowler in the house") corresponding to my emotion (e.g., fear of a prowler) may be known to be
false while the emotion persists. As Roberts notes, "a mental state is no
less an emotion for being irrational."[54] So emotions must be more than
mere judgments.

Roberts specifies the nature of emotional intentionality with the
concept of "construal," which he understands as "a mental event or
state in which one thing is grasped in terms of something else," where
the "grasping in terms of" relation can take any of a variety of forms,
including a perception, a thought, an image, or a concept.[55] Thus, one
may *perceive* one person's face in terms of another's or regard it *conceptually* as rugged or kind or *imagine* one's living room in terms of the
furniture one perceives in a store showroom. These are all instances of
construal. What distinguishes emotions is that they are *concern-based*
construals. By "concern" Roberts intends "desires and aversions, and
the attachments and interests from which many of our desires and aversions derive."[56] These may be biological, such as the aversion to bodily
damage, or they may be psychological, or practical in some other sense.
Such concerns involve an evaluative component, namely, an implied
sense of importance for the person who has them. To be concerned with
X is to regard X as important in some way. This is not to say that X *is*
important but only that it seems so to the concerned person.[57]

---

[53] Robert Roberts, "What an Emotion Is: A Sketch," *Philosophical Review* 97 (April 1988): 183.
[54] Ibid., 195.
[55] Ibid., 190.
[56] Ibid., 202.
[57] Robert Roberts, "Emotions as Access to Religious Truths," 89.

So an emotion, according to Roberts, "is a kind of perception of whatever it is about, in terms of propositions, in which the import of those propositions is also perceived."[58] But there is a bit more besides to emotion. Typically, though not always, emotions are felt, and often they have physiological concomitants and "beget dispositions to kinds of actions."[59] Because of special cases of emotion in which feelings and physical factors are absent, Roberts stops short of making these factors essential to his account. Rather, he says, in *paradigm cases* emotions involve feelings of some kind. And although the physiological event of weeping and the act of raising one's voice are natural characteristics of grief and anger, these emotions may occur without them.

In Roberts's view, then, an emotion is a concern-based construal, which is essentially a kind of perception that is analogous to sense perception in that both are intentional and have experiential content. There are two crucial differences between the two, he notes. One is that sense perception has a causal condition of satisfaction that emotions do not—namely, involvement of one or more of the subject's sense organs. The second difference is epistemic in nature; in the case of sense perception the subject's visual experience of, say, a purple gerbil is "*prima facie* grounding for the belief" that there is a purple gerbil in front of her. Emotions, as construals, do not provide such *prima facie* grounding for beliefs.[60]

If we apply this approach to divine emotions, we see that making sense of them is no more difficult than accounting for simple divine perception of the world (i.e., perception of the colors, shapes, textures, sounds, tastes, smells, etc. of all the physical objects that make up the cosmos). In each case there is an intentional mental state of the divine mind that features some qualitative experiential content, whether it takes the form of ideas, propositions, or feelings. And each may be seen as a particular kind of divine awareness. However, to apply Roberts's account, in the case of divine emotion such perception features a concern-based construal, a reckoning of the object of emotion in terms of divine interests, be they eternal or local and contextual. The will of God may be thought of as constituted, at least in part, by various desires and aversions. Thus, God's construals will be so colored by import of these

---

[58] Ibid., 90.
[59] Robert Roberts, "What an Emotion Is: A Sketch," 204.
[60] Robert Roberts, "Emotions as Access to Religious Truths," 91.

factors. Divine emotion, of course, will differ from human emotion in that his construed importance of X will always match the real importance of X. There can be no discrepancy between God's sense of an object's importance and its real importance. However much something seems important to God is just how important it actually is.

It should be obvious that this account is applicable to an omnipathic God. For a God who has all emotions eternally, his concern-based construals would have to be conceived as grounded in the combination of his eternal interests and his eternal knowledge of particular events that occur in the world (and in all possible worlds per O_2p omnipathism). As for atemporalists, they face the same sorts of conceptual problems when it comes to divine emotion as they do when accounting for God's simple perception of the world. Of course, for sempiternalists and omnitemporalists accounting for this is not easy either. But, alas, when it comes to dealing with an infinite mind, we should expect such challenges.

As noted earlier, I see omnipathos as roughly analogous to omniscience, where in each case there is a simultaneous and complete perception of some kind. Omnipathos may be compared as well to omnipresence, which is the attribute of perceiving from all spatial locations simultaneously. And if God's relationship to time is understood in terms of omnitemporality, existing at all times, omnipathos is analogous to this attribute as well. Respectively, an omnipresent and omnitemporal God is neither spatially nor temporally localized but perceives from all places and moments. Similarly, the concept of omnipathos entails that God is not *passionally* localized. No particular feeling dominates the emotive aspect of the divine consciousness to the exclusion of others. God's concern-based construals remain constant. The importance with which he construes an object remains unchanging, just as (and because) his interests do.

APPLICATIONS AND CLARIFICATIONS

The doctrine of divine omnipathos allows us to affirm the classical divine attributes of eternality and immutability while also developing a robust concept of divine pathos. While I have cast this view in original terminology, the view itself is not altogether new. Hints and precursors of my model are to be found in the works of some divine passibilists. Hartshorne notes that "the consequent or concrete nature of God . . . embraces all the positive predicates actualized anywhere. This follows from the primordial attributes themselves, since to be omniscient is to include in one's experience all that is, whatever it be."[61] This, of course, would seem to include all emotions. Marilyn McCord Adams addresses the matter of eternal divine suffering specifically when she muses, "perhaps—*pace* impassibility theorists—the inner life of God itself includes deep agony as well as ecstatic joy."[62] Presumably, Adams would allow for inclusion in the divine inner life the whole spectrum of emotions that range between agony and joy. This, too, points in the direction of my proposal. Even a leading impassibilist has made omnipathicist intimations, albeit qualifiedly. Paul Helm writes,

> Necessarily, human beings experience emotions or passions as affects. (They are 'affections'). But it is conceivable that what are necessarily experienced by human beings as affects are, as a matter of logic, capable of being experienced, or possessed, in non-affective ways. . . . Suppose we call any such a state had by God a *themotion*. (A themotion X is as close as possible to the corresponding human emotion X except that it cannot be an affect.)[63]

Helm then proceeds to suggest that it is possible that "God has all those themotions which are consistent with his moral character to an unsurpassed degree."[64] What he hints at here seems to be something very much like what I have proposed. But, like Hartshorne and Adams, Helm leaves his suggestion undeveloped. These writers seem to intuitively recognize that a compromise between the standard positions of divine passibilism and impassibilism is possible, though they do not spell it out as such. My model can be seen as one attempt to work out some of the details of their general proposals with a view toward such compromise.

Although the practical benefits of a theological position are not independently decisive grounds for its acceptance, such considerations

[61] Charles Hartshorne, *Man's Vision of God*, 321.
[62] Marilyn McCord Adams, "Redemptive Suffering: A Christian Solution to the Problem of Evil," *Rationality, Religious Belief, and Moral Commitment*, eds. Robert Audi and William J. Wainwright (Ithaca, N.Y.: Cornell University Press, 1986), 264.
[63] Paul Helm, *op. cit.*, 140.
[64] Ibid.

are not irrelevant either. Accordingly, it is fit to ask what practical benefits omnipathism may yield. One outstanding feature, as mentioned earlier, is therapeutic in nature. An omnipathic God experiences all emotions that ever have been or will be experienced by human beings. In all human pain and suffering, God emotionally participates. And this is no mere cognitive awareness of facts or abstract propositions. He doesn't just know we are in pain—he literally sorrows with us. Our suffering *is* his suffering, regardless of how demeaning or severe. This is an obvious source of psychological comfort for the believer who suffers. If one affirms no distance between God and our suffering, then any sense of divine aloofness or apathy will naturally diminish. Additionally, the believer will be more assured of divine providence. Recognizing the emotional immanence of God in even the most difficult of circumstances, one will be more, not less, inclined to affirm his sovereignty over them. So omnipathism reinforces the believer's confidence in both divine goodness and sovereignty. In these respects, then, omnipathism seems to be a boon to faith.

Omnipathism also offers an expansive perspective on what it means to "participate in the divine nature," as Peter so cryptically puts it (2 Pet. 1:4). When it comes to participating in another's emotion, the operative term is *empathy*, which refers to shared feeling or literally "in-feeling." Jung Young Lee, like many others, has noted the significance of God's empathy with human beings as particularly manifest in the suffering of Christ. He writes, "the meaning of the divine empathy as the participation of divine feeling or pathos into human feeling is none other than the unity of the divine and human experience in its complete sense. The unity of experience between God and man is, then, possible through the empathy of God."[65] Lee calls pathos the "vector" of that shared experience, the means by which God participates in human emotion. Now empathy is a symmetrical relation. That "X feels with Y" implies that "Y feels with X." So any exposition of God's empathy with human beings can be made in the other direction as well, whereby our suffering is a means of empathizing with God. If God's pathos is a vector for sharing human experience, then our pathos is similarly a vector for sharing divine expe-

---

[65] Jung Young Lee, *God Suffers For Us: A Systematic Inquiry Into a Concept of Divine Passibility* (The Hague: Martinus Nijhoff, 1974), 13.

rience. Now to believe in an omnipathic God is to recognize that every emotion one feels serves this vector function. There are no emotions that any human being may experience that are not inroads to the divine psyche. From this perspective, then, every emotive feature of one's conscious life brims with discovery about the life and experience of God. All feelings one has are pregnant with possibility for gaining theological insight and deepening one's personal relationship with God.

Some will have reservations about such complete divine sharing of the human experience, particularly those who believe, like von Hugel, Creel, and others, that suffering is an intrinsic evil. This misconception, it seems to me, is due to sloppy thinking about the nature of suffering. It is the psychic paralysis and negative behavioral consequences that sometimes ensue from suffering that are evil, not the suffering itself. This becomes clear when we concentrate our attention on the phenomenological core of suffering, which is essentially a qualitative feature of our mental life rather than a thing in and of itself. Nicholas Wolterstorff insightfully fastens on this point:

> We must not think of the connection between some facet of our experience, on the one hand, and joy or suffering, on the other, as the connection of efficient causality. The suffering *caused* by pain is not some distinct sensation caused by the pain sensation. Suffering and joy are, as it were, adverbial modifiers of the states and events of consciousness. . . . A fundamental fact of consciousness is that the events of consciousness do not all occur indifferently. Some occur unpleasantly, on a continuum all the way to suffering. Some occur pleasantly, on a continuum all the way to joy; and some, indeed, occur in neither mode.[66]

Indeed, it is the fact that suffering is essentially unpleasant that entices some to see it as essentially evil. But this is a *non sequitur.* There seems to be no good reason to believe that God should not find certain things displeasing from an emotional standpoint. In fact, that God finds some states of affairs displeasing in a moral sense—which even the most austere impassibilists will allow—lends *prima facie* credence to the notion that he should experience displeasure in other ways as well, including emotional displeasure.

---

[66] Nicholas Wolterstorff, "Suffering Love," 216.

Other considerations, from the standpoint of Christian theology, undermine the notion that suffering is intrinsically evil, not the least of which are that Jesus really suffered and that God intended him to suffer. Moreover, as I will note in the next chapter, there is much good that can and does come of suffering. Only through suffering to some extent can a person develop such virtues as patience, forgiveness, and compassion. And atonement for sin, at least in Christian theology, essentially involves suffering, as does the beatific vision of God, on most accounts. So to say that suffering is intrinsically evil is inaccurate. On the contrary, it is vital to moral growth. So one might even say it is a means of grace.[67]

Omnipathism might appear to pose another sort of threat to God's goodness. Certain particular emotions seem necessarily linked to evil or moral failure, such as shame and remorse. If God is omnipathic, then he experiences these emotions as well. But one might object that they are inappropriate for a morally perfect being.[68] To this objection I have a dual response. First, I see no reason why God could not experience such feelings as shame and remorse without the moral status of guilt that ordinarily accompanies them in humans. Feelings—as the pop psychology dictum goes—are never wrong, so there is no inherent problem with a divine being experiencing shame and remorse. But now one might ask whether it even makes sense for God to have such feelings in the absence of guilt. I think sense can be made of such feelings in reference to the sorts of divine imaginative experiences discussed earlier. If God can imagine what it is like to be a human who has sinned and feels bad about it, and surely he can, then he can also have the feelings that attend such an experience, namely, shame and remorse.[69] Second, from the standpoint of Christian theology, one theory of atonement is directly relevant to this issue and may help as a further response to the objection. Many

---

[67] Charles Taliaferro has offered a similar sort of argument, maintaining that some sorrows, such as the "noble sorrow" at witnessing tragedy, are intrinsically good. See his "The Passibility of God," 221.

[68] I have Eric Johnson to thank for this objection.

[69] A further objection, pertaining specifically to Christian theology, is as follows: How does this view account for the very local and limited feelings of Jesus, God incarnate? In reply, I would note that I need not be able to give a complete explanation regarding this aspect of Christological doctrine any more than one does regarding Jesus' knowledge, which, too, seems limited and focused, yet we nonetheless affirm Christ's divinity. Having made that disclaimer, I would distinguish between limited and local feelings of Jesus the man from the unlimited and comprehensive feelings of the eternal second person of the Trinity. Still, how these two pathic scopes are coherently reconciled in Jesus of Nazareth I cannot explain. But again, this is a problem in Christology that is precisely analogous to the problem of omniscience in Christology; so it should not be rejected by the orthodox on these grounds.

regard the redemptive work of Christ as essentially a vicarious act, whereby his suffering and death serve a penal-substitutionary function for believers. According to this interpretation, God treated his son *as if* he were guilty of sin and punished him accordingly. Concomitantly, God treats believers *as if* Christ's righteousness were theirs. Hence, Christians exchange their sin and guilt and the punishment that goes with it for Christ's moral perfection and the rewards that go with it. Now this perspective, which does enjoy some significant biblical support, may be extended into the emotive realm to provide help in dealing with the issue at hand. If Christ can assume the status of moral guilt and be treated accordingly by God, then it seems a small matter by comparison that Christ should participate in the emotions that naturally attend this status—namely, shame and remorse.

Those who grant that divine omnipathism can avoid these problems associated with evil might not be so convinced that the doctrine can avoid the problem of implying divine limitation and, hence, imperfection. After all, human experience of pain nearly always involves frustration of will, a thwarted desire to avoid the pain. While this is a legitimate concern, concluding for this reason that God experiences no pain is unjustified, because the analogy between the human and divine experiences is imperfect, the crucial difference between us being that we are limited and he is not. Painful emotions characterize our own limits (physical and psychological), but for an omnipathic God these are but features of his psychological completeness, for they are all perfectly directed at various objects and events occurring in time both to and within finite beings such as ourselves (and all creatures in all possible worlds on the O_2p version of omnipathism). Suffering is (typically) regarded by us as a sign of imperfection and limitation because it supplants or negates our joy, peace, and other pleasurable (or in some other sense positive) emotional states. But since God is *omni*pathic, his suffering does not detract from any aspect of his eternal pleasure and joy. His painful emotions are just particular modes of divine experience that when occurring in a finite being do so in a way that tends to dominate its consciousness. I would suggest that for God a pleasurable emotion, such as joy, is always dominant. And since a significant aspect of God's pleasure is derived from the mercy, healing, forgiveness, and compassion he shows to persons in pain, it is appropriate, even necessary, that divine joy should be informed by painful feelings. So although the suffering of the Godhead is eternally real, divine pleasure is real as well, but dominantly so. In Christian theology the theme that joy prevails over suffering is reflected in the history of the cosmos and human civilization. I propose that this is a theme within the mind of God as well. Thus, omnipathism affirms a parallel between God's public and private life, so to speak.

CONCLUSION

My proposal that God is omnipathic may be conceived as a compromise between (or perhaps a synthesis of) the two traditional views on divine emotion. I have tried to show that this perspective takes seriously the main arguments on either side of the debate and incorporates the most compelling elements of each in an intuitively satisfying way. The result, I hope, achieves a satisfying balance. I am sure plenty of tensions remain in my position—but perhaps not nearly so many as plague each of the standard views. I have also tried to show how the main elements of each of the standard theories of emotion can be applied to God, both in a general sense and when God is conceived as omnipathic. Finally, the whole discussion of this chapter serves to underscore an overarching point as regards the doctrine of providence. It is this: one need not take the low view of providence in order to affirm that God is emotional or, more generally, that he is fully relational. The high view of providence offers resources for conceiving the emotive life of God that are equal to or better than those available in the low view.

6

THE PROBLEM
OF EVIL

Traditionally, the problem of evil has been regarded as the most serious objection to theism and to Christianity in particular. As Dostoyevsky once said, "the earth is soaked from its crust to its center" with the tears of humanity.[1] This can be a difficult thing to reconcile with belief in a perfectly good and powerful deity. The Augustinian view of providence, it is commonly believed, is especially vulnerable to objections from evil. After all, in this view God's responsibility for all that goes wrong in the world is active rather than merely passive, and this seems more directly incriminating. Other versions of the high view do not fare much better, some argue, as they acknowledge that God created the world knowing in advance all of the evils that would occur. Such thinking appears to be the chief impetus for many who take the low view of providence. The writings of open theists, for example, are filled with illustrations and arguments from evil, aimed at persuading their readers that openness theology better shields God from accusations of cruelty, injustice, or malevolent apathy. But is the high view of providence really more susceptible to objections from evil than the low view? In this chapter I will show why this notion is egregiously mistaken. On the contrary, it is precisely in the complete sovereignty of God that we find the best resources for dealing with evil, both philosophically and practically.

---

[1] Fyodor Dostoyevsky, *The Brothers Karamazov*, trans. Constance Garnett (New York: William Heinemann, 1945), 224.

DEFINITIONS AND PROBLEMS

Sadly, we are all well acquainted with evil. It visits us regularly and in myriad ways. Evil is typically categorized as "moral" or "natural." The former refers to the wrongful actions of free beings, such as rape, murder, theft, slander, and child abuse. Natural evil, on the other hand, includes pain and suffering that are not attributable to immorality, such as occur in earthquakes, famines, congenital defects, and infectious diseases.

To define evil generally is no easy task, but the most influential definition in the West sees evil as essentially privative, specifically a lack of being. Augustine maintained, in agreement with Plotinus before him, "that which we call evil [is] but the absence of good."[2] Along these lines Aquinas writes:

> Being and the perfection of any nature is good. Hence it cannot be that evil signifies being, or any form or nature. Therefore it must be that by the name of evil is signified the absence of good. . . . For since being, as such, is good, the absence of one implies the absence of the other.[3]

This conception of evil also has been widely affirmed outside philosophical and theological circles, such as by Emerson, who declares that "Good is positive. Evil is merely privative, not absolute: it is like cold, which is the privation of heat. All evil is so much death or nonentity."[4]

While I affirm this traditional Augustinian definition of evil, nothing that follows depends crucially upon it. One may prefer to define evil more generally as any departure from the way things ought to be, whether morally as in the case of sin or naturally as in the case of pain and suffering. The main point to recognize here is that something has gone terribly wrong in this world, and those of us who are theists have

---

[2] Augustine, *The Enchiridion*, trans. J. F. Shaw (Chicago: Henry Regnery, 1961), 11. This follows from the fact that "All things that exist . . . seeing that the Creator of them all is supremely good, are themselves good. But because they are not, like their Creator, supremely and unchangeably good, their good may be diminished and increased. But for good to be diminished is an evil, although, however much it may be diminished, it is necessary, if the being is to continue, that some good should remain to constitute the being" (ibid., 12).

[3] Thomas Aquinas, *Summa Theologica*, trans. English Dominican Fathers (New York: Benziger Brothers, 1947), 1:248.

[4] Ralph Waldo Emerson, *The Works of Ralph Waldo Emerson* (New York: Bigelow, Brown and Co., n.d.), 4:87.

some explaining to do. Or, as some might dare to put it, the God in whom we believe has some explaining to do.

There are really two problems of evil, one philosophical and the other practical. An early statement of the philosophical problem was made by Epicurus:

> God either wishes to take away evils and he cannot; or he can and does not wish to, or he neither wishes to nor is able, or he both wishes to and is able. If he wishes to and is not able, he is feeble, which does not fall in with the notion of god. If he is able to and does not wish to, he is envious, which is equally foreign to god. If he neither wishes to nor is able, he is both envious and feeble and therefore not god. If he both wishes to and is able, which alone is fitting to god, whence, therefore, are there evils, and why does he not remove them?[5]

The tension to which Epicurus points arises at the interface of evil and the divine attributes of omnipotence and omnibenevolence. If God is all-powerful, then presumably he *could* eliminate evil. If he is all-good, then he *would* eliminate evil.[6] Yet evil persists; so God must not be both all-powerful and all-good. It seems the theist must abandon one of these divine attributes or else deny the reality of evil. But none of these options are compatible with classical theism generally or biblical Christianity in particular.

The other problem of evil is less formal and more existential in nature. It pertains to the practical difficulty of relating to God, given the abiding presence of evil in our lives. How can I trust a God who allows such rampant injustice and suffering to continue from day to day? From an emotional standpoint, how can I relate to such a God? And if God somehow intends some or all of the evil in the world, then what am I to make of biblical directives for human beings to oppose evil? In this chapter, our primary focus will be the philosophical problem. Although I will address the practical problem to some degree as well, I will discuss this at greater length in the final chapter. I intend to show that the best strate-

---

[5] Quoted by Lactantius, *On the Anger of God*, in *Lactantius: The Minor Works*, trans. Mary F. McDonald (Washington, D.C.: The Catholic University of America Press, 1965), 92-93.

[6] This intuition is pivotal in most atheistic arguments from evil. See, for example, J. L. Mackie, *The Miracle of Theism* (Oxford: Oxford University Press, 1982), 150-176 and William Rowe, "The Problem of Evil and Some Varieties of Atheism," *American Philosophical Quarterly* 16 (1979): 335-341.

gies for dealing with these problems assume an Augustinian view of providence. Far from exacerbating the problems of evil, the Augustinian perspective actually provides better resources for handling them than are available to those who affirm the low view of providence.

THE PHILOSOPHICAL PROBLEM OF EVIL

To solve the philosophical problem of evil one must propose a satisfactory explanation as to why God would permit evil. To attempt to justify God's ways of governing the world is known as a *theodicy*. Christians have offered many different theodicies over the centuries, and I will review some of the more prominent of these.

The Counterpart Theodicy

Some respond to the problem of evil by insisting that without evil there would be no goodness. Everything is defined by its opposite; so goodness presupposes evil. One cannot exist without the other. Sometimes this theodicy is articulated in epistemic terms, where evil is seen as necessary in order for us to *understand* what is good. Things are best known by their opposites, it is argued, and evil is the opposite of goodness. So bad things must happen in order for us to recognize life's blessings. Were there no starvation, we would not appreciate the goodness of adequate nutrition; were there no broken relationships, we would not understand the goodness of harmonious ones; and so on.

There are problems with both versions of this approach. To say that goodness demands evil as a counterpart implies that God cannot be good without evil. But to make God's goodness contingent upon evil is unacceptable. Clearly God would be good even if he were the only being in existence. As for the notion that evil exists to make goodness known to us, this defies common sense. One may experience and enjoy many good things without understanding them fully. Surely a toddler experiences the good of vibrant health, even though he or she has no understanding of the reality of disease and nutritional deficiencies. Even granting that it is a greater good to understand, by contrast with evil, how fortunate we are to experience many good things, this does not explain why there is so much evil in the world. Do we really need earthquakes and holocausts to reveal our blessings?

The Natural Law Theodicy

Here some appeal to the laws of nature to explain both why evil occurs and why there is so much of it. To arrange the world in an orderly way God had to set up some law-like regularities such as the inverse square law in physics and the ideal gas law in chemistry. We noted in an earlier chapter how such regularities have many practical benefits, as we are able to learn from experience what sorts of natural events lead to others. Ultimately, we have been able to exploit such laws of nature to do everything from build automobiles to make dialysis machines. But our reliance upon natural laws is even more basic than this, as Bruce Reichenbach explains:

> Without the regularity which results from the governance of natural laws, rational action would be impossible. Without regularity of sequence, agents could not entertain rational expectations, make predictions, estimate probabilities, or calculate prudence. They would not be able to know what to expect about any course of action they would like to take. . . . Hence, agents could not know or even suppose what course of action to take to accomplish a certain rationally conceived goal. Thus, rational agents could neither propose action nor act themselves.[7]

However, a necessary consequence of such laws is that through misuse, ignorance, or carelessness we sometimes harm ourselves. The same law of physics that keeps objects from simply floating around also guarantees that falling off a rooftop will cause serious injury; and the same laws that enable us to make cars also make car accidents possible. It is not God's fault that we make mistakes that lead to injury and death. If we were more careful, we could avoid these evils. And as for natural disasters, such as droughts, earthquakes, hurricanes, and mudslides that have killed millions of people, these are unavoidable negative consequences that attend a world arranged according to strict natural laws.

In response to this theodicy, we may ask, why did God make the laws of nature as he did, if he knew the kinds of suffering to which they would give rise? Could he not have made the regularities different, so that, say, falling from rooftops generally resulted in only mild injuries

---

[7] Bruce Reichenbach, *Evil and a Good God* (New York: Fordham University Press, 1982), 103.

and collisions in automobiles were typically not very harmful? Or, if one is dubious about the prospects of even an almighty being making such adjustments, consider the amount of suffering that would be avoided if God had simply made nervous tissue regenerative so that paralysis was only temporary. And couldn't he have made our other tissues much more regenerative so that gross disfigurement and disability from severe burns and even amputations were only temporary? If he could endow urodele amphibians with the capacity to regrow lost limbs, then why not also mammals such as ourselves? Surely these are things that an omnipotent deity could accomplish without forfeiting order and predictability in the physical world.

The Divine Retribution Theodicy

Another approach appeals to the concept of divine retribution to explain the existence of evil in the world. Pain and suffering are the result of God's judgment on human sin. As Paul says, "a man reaps what he sows" (Gal. 6:7). This principle is affirmed repeatedly in the Old Testament, such as in the book of Deuteronomy, where the Lord warns Israel,

> If you do not obey the LORD your God and do not carefully follow all his commands and decrees I am giving you today, all these curses will come upon you and overtake you: You will be cursed in the city and cursed in the country. Your basket and your kneading trough will be cursed. The fruit of your womb will be cursed, and the crops of your land, and the calves of your herds and the lambs of your flocks. You will be cursed when you come in and cursed when you go out. (Deut. 28:15-19)

From here the writer continues to itemize numerous specific curses awaiting Israel if they disobey, including diseases (boils, tumors, sores, rashes), mental torture (madness, confusion, fear, despair), agricultural disaster (drought, blight, locust swarms), oppression by others (rape, theft, defeat in battle), all of which will culminate in poverty and starvation, driving the Israelites even to the point of cannibalism (vv. 20-68). The retribution theodicy extends such curses to the entire human population, such that all of us can be seen as suffering just punishment for the sin of our race. Even those who are innocent of actual sins (infants and animals) are regarded as proper recipients of God's wrath, for Scripture says, "he does not leave the guilty unpunished; he punishes the children and their children for the sin of the fathers to the third and fourth generation" (Exod. 34:7).

This theodicy has the merit of being biblically grounded. Even if the curses described seem overly severe and the principle of cross-generational punishment appears unjust, the fact remains that these are biblical truths, and we must reconcile ourselves to them accordingly. Notwithstanding this concession, however, there remains a significant limitation to the usefulness of this theodicy. It fails to explain why God would permit evil in the first place. Given the moral fallenness of the human race, the concept of divine retribution makes perfect sense. But why did we have to fall? After all, God could have prevented this from happening and, in so doing, barred all of the horrific evils that have followed. But he did not. Why not?

The Free Will Theodicy

Currently, the most popular response to this question appeals to human freedom. In short, the Fall occurred because human beings abused their freedom, and evil continues unabated to this day for the same reason. People make evil choices. We have no one to blame but ourselves. Alvin Plantinga explains this theodicy as follows:

> A world containing creatures who are significantly free (and freely perform more good than evil actions) is more valuable, all else being equal, than a world containing no free creatures at all. Now God can create free creatures, but He can't *cause* or *determine* them to do only what is right. For if He does so, then they aren't significantly free after all; they do not do what is right *freely*. To create creatures capable of *moral good*, therefore, He must create creatures capable of moral evil; and He can't give these creatures the freedom to perform evil and at the same time prevent them from doing so. As it turned out, sadly enough, some of the free creatures God created went wrong in the exercise of their freedom; this is the source of moral evil.[8]

Clark Pinnock puts it this way:

---

[8] Alvin Plantinga, *God, Freedom, and Evil* (Grand Rapids, Mich.: Eerdmans, 1974), 30.

We can say that God did not ordain moral evil but that it arose from
the misuse of freedom. . . . God may be responsible for creating a
world with moral agents capable of rebelling, but God is not to blame
for what human beings do with their freedom. The gift of freedom is
costly and carries precariousness with it. But to make a world with
free beings is surely a worthwhile thing to do.[9]

These expositions well represent the free will theodicy. Several
important features of this approach are worth highlighting. First, notice
the high premium that is placed on self-determination. Proponents of the
free will theodicy typically assume, often without justification or argument, that personal autonomy is so valuable that it makes the risk of
moral evil worthwhile. But it is not really self-determination itself that
is of ultimate value. The ultimate good for which such autonomy is a
critical means is genuine loving relationships between God and human
beings. Second, and most important, this theodicy is presented in libertarian terms, where freedom is seen as incompatible with causal determination of the will. As discussed in an earlier chapter, the libertarian
conception of freedom sees the human will as essentially a miniature
unmoved mover, capable of choosing independently of external causal
determinants. A person enjoys the power of contrary choice in all free
actions, such that no antecedent conditions guarantee that he or she
either will or will not perform the act.

As attractive as this approach is to many people, it is replete with
problems. Let's begin with the two assumptions just highlighted. First,
is human autonomy really so valuable that it makes God's risking cosmic catastrophe worthwhile? It is safe to assume that an omniscient
being would be able to anticipate just how devastating our evil choices
might (or would likely) turn out to be, including the massive proportions
of rapes, tortures, murders, and other cruelties that human history has
seen. Such misery presents a strong presumption against the idea that
personal autonomy justifies it all. I do not mean to declare with finality
that personal autonomy cannot justify the risk (or reality) of such evils.
I am only saying that an argument is needed here. Now perhaps a case
for this claim can be made successfully, but notice that to do so one
would have to show that even the most horrific evils can be *justified by*

---

[9] Clark Pinnock, "God's Sovereignty in Today's World," *Theology Today* 53:1 (April 1996): 19.

appealing to higher goods, in this case human autonomy and the genuine relationship with God that this makes possible. This is an important point to keep in mind, as will become clear later.

As for the libertarian conception of freedom, we noted the problems with this perspective in Chapter 2. I won't rehearse those criticisms again here, but to summarize, we saw that libertarianism suffers from an incoherent conception of causality of the will, an inadequate account of personal responsibility, and a failure to account for predictions and explanations of human behavior. Suffice it to say that libertarianism is deeply problematic in its own right, and a theodicy that appeals to this view of human freedom inherits all of those difficulties.

But the problems with the free will theodicy run even deeper. Even granting the premises of this approach, we may still reasonably ask why God has allowed so much evil. Couldn't he at least have diminished the harmful effects of our sins in ways that I have already suggested above? Even in allowing us to run headlong into the many vices we do, surely God could have curbed the painful ramifications somehow. And couldn't he have simply made us more intelligent, such that we could more keenly anticipate the negative fallout of our wrong choices? And giving us a stronger moral imagination would have helped, so that we would have a more acute sense of what it is like to be other people. This, too, would have provided a powerful buffer against evil without compromising our freedom.

To push this line of thinking even further, why couldn't God keep us from doing evil altogether? According to libertarians, this would negate our freedom. But this is not true. Much real freedom would remain for us within the domain of goodness, since there are myriad good actions one may perform in any given situation. Right now, for instance, God could build a moral hedge around me so that I could not sin in any way, yet I would still be free to do thousands of different things, from continuing my writing, to taking a walk, to starting a conversation with some students down the hall. Granted, freedom is a good thing. But must my freedom entail the capacity to rape and murder? Compare the situation with physical freedom. I am limited by my body in such a way that there are many physical actions I cannot perform, such as safely inhale water or jump to the moon (or even dunk a basketball on a ten-foot goal for that matter), but these limits don't imply that I am not physically free. On the contrary, I am still free within a significant range of physical activity. Neither, then, should we conclude that my not being able to perform moral evils would imply that I am not morally free. If so constrained that I could not do evil, I could still freely choose among countless virtuous and morally neutral deeds to perform.

Some will take issue with this claim and insist that in order to be genuinely morally free one *must* be able to perform evil actions. But this contention flies in the face of the Christian doctrine of heaven. Orthodox Christians affirm, among other things, each of the following regarding our promised heavenly condition: (1) we will enjoy genuinely free and personal relationships with God and other beings (human and angelic), and (2) we will be perfectly moral (i.e., we will not fall into sin at any time). This second point is an aspect of the biblical doctrine of glorification, the teaching that those who are saved will be perfected in their humanity when they arrive in heaven. Now if (1) and (2) are correct, it follows that an important pillar of the free will theodicy, and the libertarian view of freedom generally, is false. Remember that libertarians hold that in order for creatures to be free, their actions cannot all be morally steered away from evil. As Plantinga asserts in the passage quoted earlier, the capacity for moral goodness implies a capacity for moral evil. Or, in the words of another free will theodicist, David Basinger, "God cannot unilaterally ensure that humans exercising free choice will make the decisions he would have them make (and thus act as he would have them act)."[10] But in heaven, contra Plantinga, we will *not* be capable of moral evil, and, contra Basinger, God *will* make sure that we make the right sorts of decisions and perform the sorts of actions he wants us to. In short, God will guarantee that we will not sin in heaven (whew!), yet we will be free nonetheless. So the central idea behind the free will theodicy, viz. the notion that God could not have prevented moral evil without violating our freedom, is mistaken.

THE GREATER GOOD THEODICY

Given the formidable problems with each of these traditional theodicies, the outlook for finding a solution to the problem of evil seems grim.

---

[10] David Basinger, *The Case for Freewill Theism: A Philosophical Assessment* (Downers Grove, Ill.: InterVarsity Press, 1996), 36.

None of the considerations discussed thus far can justify God's allowance of evil, not to mention the scale of evil the world has seen. So where do we turn? I propose that we look for a solution that is both *biblically based* and *essentially Christian*. Notice that only one of the above theodicies—that which appeals to divine retribution—is scripturally based, but even this one fails to explain why the innocent suffer. Nor does it account for God's allowance of evil to begin with. An adequate theodicy must explain these things. Moreover, we must ask whether there are any resources for dealing with this problem that derive from a uniquely Christian point of view on the matter. Disappointingly, many contemporary Christian philosophers who have written on the problem of evil fail to inform their theodicies biblically or to offer an account that is distinctively Christian.[11] Happily, there is an approach that is both recommended by Scripture and, in its most mature form, distinctively Christian. The "greater good" theodicy, as it is commonly known, also has the merit of explaining the suffering of the innocent and why evil came to exist in the first place, thus overcoming the limits of appealing to divine retribution.

In developing this theodicy, I will divide the discussion into two parts, based on the distinction between natural evil (human suffering) and moral evil (human sin). I will proceed in this way for two reasons. First, although suffering and sin are alike as departures from good, they are crucially different in the *kind* of departure from good they constitute. Casually mingling these concepts when discussing evil can be misleading in many ways; so I want to avoid potential confusion by dealing with them separately. Second, from a philosophical standpoint the problem of moral evil is largely contingent upon the problem of natural evil. That is, human sin would not be such a philosophical headache if it

---

11 For example, treatments of the problem by Daniel Howard-Snyder, Bruce Reichenbach, and Richard Swinburne ignore or minimize use of relevant biblical resources. Marilyn McCord Adams, John Edelman, and Eleonore Stump, on the other hand, richly inform their accounts with biblical ideas and specifically Christian concepts. See Daniel Howard-Snyder, "God, Evil, and Suffering," *Reason for the Hope Within*, ed. Michael J. Murray (Grand Rapids, Mich.: Eerdmans, 1999), 76-115; Bruce Reichenbach, *Evil and a Good God* (New York: Fordham University Press, 1982), Richard Swinburne, *The Existence of God* (Oxford: Oxford University Press, 1979), 200-224; Marilyn McCord Adams, "Redemptive Suffering: A Christian Solution to the Problem of Evil," *Rationality, Religious Belief, and Moral Commitment*, eds. Robert Audi and William J. Wainwright (Ithaca, N.Y.: Cornell University Press, 1986), 249-267; John Edelman, "Suffering and the Will of God," *Faith and Philosophy* 10:3 (July 1993): 380-388; and Eleonore Stump, "Providence and Evil," *Christian Philosophy*, ed. Thomas P. Flint (Notre Dame, Ind.: University of Notre Dame Press, 1990), 51-91.

weren't for its painful consequences. It is hard to imagine that anyone would be prompted to question God's existence (or goodness or power) just on the basis of human immorality if no suffering resulted from it. In the end, human sin is philosophically problematic because of the misery it brings. So to address the issue of suffering is, in the main, to address the problem of evil generally. That being said, the matter of moral evil must be addressed in its own right, which I will do as well.

Let us begin with two key New Testament passages that address the matter head-on, the first of these coming from the apostle James: "Consider it pure joy, my brothers, whenever you face trials of many kinds, because you know that the testing of your faith develops perseverance. Perseverance must finish its work *so that* you may be mature and complete, not lacking anything" (Jas. 1:2-4). And Peter, writing of the wonderful eternal inheritance we have in Christ, says, "In this you greatly rejoice, though now for a little while you may have had to suffer grief in all kinds of trials. These have come *so that* your faith—of greater worth than gold, which perishes even though refined by fire—may be proved genuine and may result in praise, glory and honor when Jesus Christ is revealed" (1 Pet. 1:6-7). I have highlighted the phrase "so that" in each of these texts to emphasize their intent to explain *why* it is that we suffer. James and Peter are telling us here that there is a purpose to our pain. Its occurrence is not an unpleasant residue or peripheral nuisance in our lives. No, our trials are essential means for the attainment of precious goods, including (1) our maturity and completeness, most significantly as regards our faith, and (2) praise, glory, and honor for Jesus Christ. So we suffer for the sake of our growth and God's glory. Could there be two more worthy purposes?

The Soul-Making Theodicy

John Hick's "soul-making" theodicy comes the closest to capturing the essence of this approach. He maintains that we can look at God's creative activity in two stages. The first of these is initial creation, where humans are made in the divine image, endowed with certain ultimate capacities for reason, will, and imagination. This is followed by the second stage, in which we are currently living, as humans struggle and suffer, all the while developing character traits that bring us into a closer conformity to God's likeness. This process, Hick maintains, makes for a better world overall. He writes that

> one who has attained to goodness by meeting and eventually mastering temptations, and thus by rightly making responsible choices in concrete situations, is good in a richer and more valuable sense than would be one created *ab initio* in a state either of innocence or of virtue. In the former case, which is that of the actual moral achievements of mankind, the individual's goodness has within it the strength of temptations overcome, a stability based upon an accumulation of right choices, and a positive and responsible character that comes from the investment of costly personal effort.[12]

Thus, argues Hick, "human goodness slowly built up through personal histories of moral effort has a value in the eyes of the Creator which justifies even the long travail of the soul-making process."[13] There are greater moral goods to be achieved in this way than could ever be achieved by God's simply giving them to us at creation. Our trials and afflictions do serve a good purpose, the betterment of our souls.

There are, in fact, numerous moral virtues that cannot be achieved except by struggling against or in the midst of evil. These include patience, courage, sympathy, forgiveness, mercy, perseverance, overcoming temptation, and much greater versions of faith, hope, love, and friendship. What sense could be made of the trait of courage in a world in which there was no danger and nothing to fear? How could one show sympathy to others were there no sorrow or affliction with which to sympathize? How might one forgive where there has been no offense? And how can one be said to persevere through perfectly pleasant circumstances?

Now these characteristics—courage, sympathy, forgiveness, perseverance—are not just good traits. They are among the greatest of all character traits. When we consider those people we admire most, these are just the sorts of virtues that stand out to us. From the apostle Paul and Justin Martyr to Martin Luther and Mother Teresa, all of our heroes attained that status because of their struggles against and in the midst of evil. Indeed, Jesus Christ himself is our moral exemplar precisely

---

[12] John Hick, *Evil and the God of Love* (New York: Harper and Row, 1978), 255-256.
[13] Ibid., 256.

because he endured so much shame, humiliation, and torture, the very worst things that a human being can experience, and did so with perfect moral comportment. It was the evil he successfully endured that marks him as maximally virtuous. Surely, he was morally impeccable before he went through a single trial. But the fact that he lived flawlessly through a lifetime of temptation and vexation warrants his exaltation to the greatest heights of glory.

Now this syncs well with the biblical writers' attitude toward suffering. As we noted, James and Peter link our trials with the growth of our faith and overall maturity. Other biblical texts point in the same direction. Through the prophet Isaiah the Lord declares, "See, I have refined you, though not as silver; I have tested you in the furnace of affliction. For my own sake, for my own sake, I do this" (Isa. 48:10), thus emphasizing again the dual purposes of human moral refinement and divine glory. And elsewhere the same prophet asserts, "Although the Lord gives you the bread of adversity and the water of affliction, your teachers will be hidden no more; with your own eyes you will see them" (Isa. 30:20).[14] This is a remarkable statement, equating adversity and affliction with *nourishment*. Our hardships, paradoxically, are a primary source of moral sustenance, drawing us closer to God and to our fellow human beings, and even serving to give us hope. As Paul writes, "we . . . rejoice in our sufferings, because we know that suffering produces perseverance; perseverance, character; and character, hope. And hope does not disappoint us, because God has poured out his love into our hearts by the Holy Spirit, whom he has given us" (Rom. 5:3-5). On top of this, most Christians readily testify to the fact that their most significant moral maturation has occurred during their most severe trials. So this oft-repeated biblical teaching is also borne out in experience.

The moral-psychological dimensions of this dynamic of growth through trials are worth exploring in some depth. John Edelman has noted the usefulness of suffering for imparting to us a particular kind of wisdom, namely that consisting "in the recognition of the limits of human power."[15] Our trials force us to acknowledge that we are not ultimately in control of our own lives, even at a very basic level. Thus, suf-

---

[14] The *New American Standard Bible* translates the key phrase as "bread of privation and water of oppression."

[15] John Edelman, *op. cit.*, 383-384.

fering turns out to be a form of divine grace, enhancing our understanding of our own contingency and our basic reliance upon God. From a Christian point of view, this realization must not be a merely cognitive matter, as one would, say, acknowledge the truth of heliocentrism. Rather, it must be expressed in personal surrender to God. This, of course, is the virtue known as faith, a living act of trusting God in his governance of our life and its circumstances. Not only is faith a Christian virtue, it is a very crucial one, even decisive when it comes to the matter of a person's eternal destiny. The vice that opposes this virtue is the lust for control over all of one's life circumstances.[16] Our trials curb that lust by existentially proving how impractical it is. As our lust for control is curbed, our inclination to trust God's control is strengthened, if only by default. Foolish as we humans naturally are, it often takes a great deal of pain to prompt us to look upward rather than within to find someone worthy of our trust. But any earthly suffering is a small price to pay for this, relative to the riches garnered by faith.

Solidarity with Christ

So suffering is a critical means of prompting recognition of one's contingency and curbing the lust for control.[17] But suffering yields something even more fundamental in the building of Christian faith: *solidarity with Christ*. To unpack this idea, we must first reckon with the crucial fact that God intended Christ to suffer. As Isaiah says in a messianic prophecy, "It was the LORD's will to crush him and cause him to suffer" (Isa. 53:10). In fact, the Messiah was identified by the prophet

---

[16] Here on the matter of faith and the lust for control I am very closely following Robert Adams's account in *The Virtue of Faith* (Oxford: Oxford University Press, 1987), 18-20.

[17] Note the implication of this point for sadomasochism, the self-infliction of pain for pleasure's sake. Sadomasochism is an expression of the natural human desire to transcend. And to this extent it coheres with a Christian perspective. But sadomasochism departs from a Christian view in at least two critical ways. In sadomasochism the individual maintains control of his suffering, whereas suffering as a Christian is not properly dictated by the sufferer's will. Most importantly, sadomasochism is self-centered and self-indulgent. The sufferer is totally focused on himself when self-inflicting pain. The Christian, on the other hand, is properly focused on Christ, whether directly or indirectly by serving others in a way that is painful or, for the sake of knowing Christ better, enduring the pain that others inflict upon him. Of course, this is not to say that the Christian's suffering is not self-interested. Indeed, it is. Even Christ endured the cross "for the joy set before him" (Heb 12:2). But there is a difference between selfishness and self-interest. The sadomasochist suffers selfishly, having only his own pleasure in view. The Christian suffers for Christ's sake and as a consequence is blessed. The initial outward, service-oriented focus of a Christian's suffering redounds upon him in ways that advance his own good and make him happy in the Aristotelian sense of *eudaimonia* (complete well-being), as opposed to merely pleasant feelings.

as "a man of sorrows" who was "familiar with suffering" (Isa. 53:3). He was "despised," "rejected," "stricken," "smitten," "afflicted," "pierced," "crushed," "wound[ed]," and "oppressed" (Isa. 53:3-7). And, of course, God planned all of this suffering for a good purpose.[18] Now here is the pivotal question: Are we to be like Jesus in this way or not? Before reading on, think about it for a moment.

Even many Christians will balk at the notion that God wants his people to suffer. Yet the message is clear from Scripture that this is essential to being a Christ-follower. Paul writes, "I want to know Christ and the power of his resurrection and the fellowship of sharing in his sufferings, becoming like him in his death, and so, somehow, to attain to the resurrection from the dead" (Phil. 3:10-11). And elsewhere he says, "if we are children [of God], then we are heirs—heirs of God and co-heirs with Christ, if indeed we share in his sufferings in order that we may also share in his glory" (Rom. 8:17). Two points are abundantly clear from these passages: (1) we must share in Christ's sufferings, and (2) this suffering has profound benefits, qualifying us for our own resurrection and sharing in Christ's glory. To unite to Christ is to accept the whole package, from preliminary agony to final glory. This is the gospel, notwithstanding the cavils of many contemporary quasi-theologians. We cannot share in the resurrection and glory of Christ without also sharing his pain; we cannot share in his joy without also knowing his sorrow. Like him, we must descend in order to rise. It is easy to overlook the implication of Jesus' metaphor about spiritual rebirth. Being born *hurts*. Growing is painful. But it is a necessary condition for emergence into new life and maturity in that new life.

How did Christ suffer? Remember that the pain of Jesus was not limited to his final days. Rather, it characterized his entire life. As the "man of sorrows," he was troubled and tempted daily, and he endured the sins of others on a more or less constant basis. What, then, does this entail regarding our solidarity with Christ in the fellowship of suffering? Presumably, it implies that we, too, must regularly endure troubles and temptations and also suffer from the sins of others. But how are we to make sense of this, especially given the fact that Jesus is supposed to have atoned for our sins?

---

[18] See Luke 18:31-33, Mark 10:33-34, and Acts 2:23-24.

Many atonement models provide theoretical accounts as to how the work of Christ graciously unites us with God.[19] I will not review them all here. But it seems to me that the one that best accounts for the biblical teaching of the believers' fellowship of suffering with Christ (while overcoming the problems with the other standard theories) is the Thomistic model.[20] Roughly, this model pivots on the concept of the church as a body (Rom. 12). And, as Paul teaches in Ephesians 5 and 1 Corinthians 12, Christ is the head of that body. We who are in Christ are united with him as members of the body, quite analogous to a physical body, which is a real unit featuring diverse parts with various functions. The result, according to the Thomistic account, is a mystical body, analogous to a physical body. Being part of that mystical body, the Christian partakes in the atoning work of Christ, his obedience, passion, death, and resurrection. The whole of this work is graciously infused to us. Christ's righteousness becomes ours, as does his physical resurrection. However, this also entails that we share in his passion and death and that we do so always for a good purpose. Thus, Richard Purtill explains:

> Christ's mystical body suffers not only in Christ's own sufferings but also in the sufferings of the starving baby, the old man dying of cancer, and the woman who is raped and murdered. And *all* this suffering is redemptive; the crucifixion of Christ is going on right now in the children's wards of hospitals, in Mother Teresa's hospices for the dying, in the streets of our cities.[21]

Our solidarity with Christ combined with the perfectly redemptive nature of his work guarantees that none of our pain or sorrow is wasted. The whole of Christ's suffering achieved good, and so, it follows, must our suffering. This, of course, includes our suffering the moral wrongs

---

[19] The principal models are the penal-substitutionary theory, the ransom theory, and the exemplar theory. For concise but penetrating criticisms of each, see Richard Purtill's "Justice, Mercy, Supererogation, and Atonement," in *Christian Philosophy*, ed. Thomas P. Flint (Notre Dame, Ind.: University of Notre Dame Press, 1990), 37-50.

[20] See Thomas Aquinas, *Summa Theologica*, 3.8.1-8 and 3.48.1-6.

[21] Richard L. Purtill, *op. cit.*, 47 (emphasis his). For another superb discussion of the Thomistic model, see Eleonore Stump, "Atonement According to Aquinas," in *Philosophy and the Christian Faith*, ed. Thomas V. Morris (Notre Dame, Ind.: University of Notre Dame Press, 1988), 61-91.

of others. Membership in Christ's mystical body necessarily involves us in the severe grace of bearing one another's sins.[22]

Beatific Vision

The fellowship of suffering in Christ entails a further benefit that warrants highlighting, specifically that captured in the traditional concept of beatific vision. Sharing in the pain of Christ is valuable for the direct knowledge of God that it imparts. Marilyn Adams considers how "our deepest suffering as much as our highest joys may themselves be direct visions into the inner life of God, imperfect but somehow less obscure in proportion to their intensity."[23] From this perspective, each trial or sin endured is yet another portal into the mind and glory of God. And, Adams notes,

> The good of beatific, face-to-face intimacy with God is simply incommensurate with any merely non-transcendent goods or ills a person might experience. Thus, the good of beatific face-to-face intimacy with God would engulf . . . even the horrendous evils humans experience in this present life here below.[24]

To know the beauty of the Lord in an intimate fashion is an incomparable good, says Adams, and suffering is a vehicle for close divine acquaintance. We should only expect that this be so, since Christ was a suffering servant.

Of course, in human experience there are other pointers in the direction of this concept of beatific vision. One of these is the simple fact that so many people report the experience of drawing closer to God through their trials. Suffering, even in extreme forms, is unique in its capacity to

---

[22] Dietrich Bonhoeffer recognizes this implication of our union with Christ when he says, "since he has suffered for and borne the sins of the whole world and shares with his disciples the fruits of his passion, the Christian also has to undergo temptation, he too has to bear the sins of others; he too must bear their shame and be driven like a scapegoat from the gate of the city. . . . As Christ bears our burdens so ought we to bear the burdens of our fellow-men. . . . My brother's burden which I must bear is not only his outward lot, his natural characteristics and gifts, but quite literally his sin. And the only way to bear that sin is by forgiving it in the power of the cross of Christ in which I now share. Thus the call to follow Christ always means a call to share the work of forgiving men their sins. Forgiveness is the Christlike suffering which it is the Christian's duty to bear." From *The Cost of Discipleship*, trans. Kaiser Verlag Munchen (New York: Macmillan, 1963), 100.

[23] Marilyn M. Adams, "Horrendous Evils and the Goodness of God," in *The Problem of Evil*, eds. Marilyn M. Adams and Robert M. Adams (Oxford: Oxford University Press, 1990), 219.

[24] Ibid., 218.

clarify perception of divine reality and, accordingly, inspire adjustment of one's life values and commitments. Further clues lie in the area of art and aesthetics. In Chapter 3 I expounded upon the aesthetic applications of an Augustinian view of providence, noting the centrality of the concept of beauty in a Christian worldview that sees all of creation as basically a divine artwork. Let us continue that application here. First, note that beauty always carries with it an element of sorrow. This is a common feature of intense aesthetic experiences. A sublime photograph or painting emotionally stirs us. A profound narrative is heart-rending. An exquisite melody moves us to tears. An animal, flower, or natural setting evokes emotions of pathos. In each case, if we introspect carefully, we find yearning, an intensified desire for something that is not yet within our grasp. Even where there is no sad content, so long as there is significant beauty there is bound to be a degree of pathos as well. Christian aesthetician Edward Farley notes, "pathos is an ever-present and intrinsic element in beauty."[25]

Furthermore, the sorrowful commonly turn to art. The pursuit of beauty, whether in the form of appreciation of art or original creative endeavor, provides considerable comfort and release in times of sadness. That most great artists suffered severely—whether from personal losses or internal psychological struggles—testifies to this fact. There is something undeniably therapeutic about experiencing or creating art, and this goes beyond the capacity of art to powerfully communicate truth. Even if no one hears or sees the art we make, the creative process may still satisfy. Even when the content of an artwork has nothing to do with the nature of our particular affliction, experiencing it may nonetheless please us. And those who suffer often turn not to human art but to nature in order to experience its therapeutic benefits. As the romantic poets Wordsworth and Coleridge emphasized, the beauty of the natural world has an uncanny capacity to soothe the aching soul. Since nature is divine art, this too exemplifies the inclination to experience beauty that is prompted by sorrow.

So beauty is tinged with sorrow, and sorrow inclines us to beauty. What explains this seemingly reciprocal relationship between the two? A properly Christian explanation lies in the fact that God is most beau-

---

[25] Edward Farley, *Faith and Beauty: A Theological Aesthetic* (Burlington, Ver.: Ashgate, 2001), 105.

tiful and the living source of all other beauty. Since this is so, beauty in nature and human art evoke sorrow by arousing our natural, subconscious longing for God. I believe that even in the unbeliever beauty awakens intuitions about and sensitivity to aspects of the divine that otherwise lay dormant. This explains why so many atheists and otherwise nonreligious people make art their life passion and why so much of the art world is imbued with a sort of religiosity. This is no surprise, given that great beauty exalts the mind and alerts us to transcendent realities. What artists and connoisseurs of art are searching for and striving to mimic is the consummate beauty embodied in the triune God. Whether or not they realize it, they are responding to the glory of the Lord that calls to them in all things beautiful.

And, of course, suffering does the same thing in a different way. Whenever we experience trials and temptations, something in us recognizes that things have gone awry, that this is not ultimately the way the world should be. As bearers of the *imago Dei*, we naturally long for reunion with God and a reestablishment of the close fellowship we humans had before the Fall. Our hardships ensure our continued longing for God and, hopefully, prompt constructive action on our part, such as seeking to understand and obey God. Christian commitment does not immediately cure our sorrow any more than it brings an end to our suffering. But ours is, as Paul says, a godly sorrow rather than a worldly sorrow (2 Cor. 7:10). It is hopeful, resting in the knowledge that our longing for God will one day be satisfied.

So beauty and sorrow have this in common: they both stir longing for God. Alike, they remind us that we are not yet home. Through so much splendid art—human-made and natural—and the trials of life, beauty and sorrow call us home and inspire us to do what is necessary to ensure our eventual safe arrival.

Other Functions of Suffering

Whether or not the "greater good" account of evil I have sketched here is precisely correct, I should emphasize again that the biblical writers assume that the pain we endure is worthwhile. As Paul says, "I consider that our present sufferings are not worth comparing with the glory that will be revealed in us" (Rom. 8:18). Elsewhere, in the same vein, Paul declares, "our light and momentary troubles are achieving for us an eternal glory that far outweighs them all" (2 Cor. 4:17). So as children of God we have a glorious destiny awaiting us, and our suffering is not an obstacle but a *means* to the realization of this destiny. I have tried to demonstrate in various ways *how* this is the case. If I have failed, it nonetheless remains *that* it is the case. God's promises are no less true for our not being able to make sense of them.

To this point I have noted many benefits yielded by our trials, as identified in Scripture—namely, character building, solidarity with Christ, and a beatific vision of God. But what about those who are not Christians? What good is served by the evils visited upon them? Two such purposes, both with biblical grounds and precedent, come to mind. One of these is the *punitive function* that natural evils sometimes serve. Although it is not a popular teaching these days, even in Christian circles, we cannot ignore the plain biblical teaching that God punishes the wicked by afflicting them in various ways. For instance, a proverb says, "the LORD works out everything for his own ends—even the wicked for a day of disaster" (Prov. 16:4). And Paul says, "the wrath of God is being revealed from heaven against all the godlessness and wickedness of men who suppress the truth by their wickedness" (Rom. 1:18).

Admittedly, this is dangerous hermeneutical territory, subject to abuse and exploitation by those who pretend to more knowledge than they actually have. The Bible, of course, also refers to many instances of affliction of the righteous (e.g., Joseph, Job, and Paul, not to mention Jesus). And sorting out which trials are or are not punitive is a messy business, to say the least. But this epistemic problem does not justify throwing out the category altogether, especially since Scripture repeatedly sanctions the notion of divine wrath displayed on earth (as opposed to its being wholly reserved for the afterlife).

Let me make a potentially helpful distinction. In Chapter 3 I elucidated an Augustinian conception of the laws of nature, which sees such laws as simply the regular workings of providence. From this perspective, the "natural consequences" of any human action are properly seen as providentially arranged. And what we call miracles are really no more divinely orchestrated than the usual workings of nature. But because they are exceptions to the rule and so stand out to us, they deserve special designation. Now along somewhat parallel lines, we might distinguish between two forms of divine wrath—"natural" and "special." It is safe to assume that God acts wrathfully only when sin is involved. Now a particular sin (or set of sins) will often have a natural negative consequence (e.g., sexual promiscuity and venereal disease, gluttony and heart disease, etc.), where by "natural" is meant something like "predictable," "probable," or "common." When severe enough to warrant the appellation "wrath," such may be termed instances of *natural divine wrath*. In other cases of sin God might dispense a unique form of severe pain or difficulty aimed at punishing the sinner (e.g., anything from a bad toothache to torment a glutton to paralysis to plague a pornographer). Such would be uncommon and unpredictable and therefore instances of *special divine wrath*.

This distinction will be of some help when dealing with the epistemic problem: How does one *know* when a particular instance of suffering is a consequence of sin or when instead the victim is enduring the suffering of the righteous? Given the three possibilities—(a) righteous suffering, (b) natural wrath, or (c) special wrath—two of these are usually easy to spot, at least for those well acquainted with the sufferer. If the victim is a person of obvious moral integrity, then one can be confident that she suffers righteously and is to be comforted and encouraged accordingly. If she is given over to some sin, such as drug abuse, promiscuity, or habitual gambling and predictably contracts HIV, suffers from gonorrhea, or goes bankrupt, then one can be confident she suffers from natural divine wrath and may be admonished accordingly. It is cases of special divine wrath that are most difficult to ascertain and are, therefore, controversial. Even strong acquaintance with the person(s) involved might prove to be of little help. Years ago a friend of my family developed a unique and peculiarly grotesque tumor shortly after leaving his wife of many years to marry another woman (who also divorced her husband in order to marry him). Within months he was dead, as was their short-lived romance. Was this a case of special divine wrath? On a broader scale, some have asked whether the 9/11 terrorist attacks were instances of special divine wrath. (Some Christians publicly declared, in appallingly unseemly fashion, that they indeed were.) Like miracles, acts of special divine wrath are exceedingly difficult to verify, and for many of the same reasons. Most obviously, confirmation in both cases usually demands thorough understanding of the context and meticulous causal analysis. Most of us don't have the time or patience to do this. So convictions about special divine wrath are usually best kept private. Here the analogy with miracles breaks down, since there is less risk of personal offense by spouting off claims about an event being miraculous (as my students sometimes do about their own test performances).

Another major purpose of trials for the unbeliever overlaps somewhat with the punitive role they play. Natural evils may also serve a *warning function*. C. S. Lewis writes, "God whispers to us in our pleasures, speaks in our conscience, but shouts in our pains: it is His megaphone to rouse a deaf world."[26] Since the Fall, human beings suffer from a corruption of both judgment and will. But the pain sin brings has the power to get through to us despite this basic warping of human faculties. Regarding our judgment, sin skews a person's perceptions and values, disabling his or her ability to tell right from wrong. By ordaining unpleasant consequences to immoral living, God has provided a clear, natural, and regular statement about sin: avoid it. Since we are naturally selfish, he speaks to us if, even when deeply immersed in vice, we still have ears to hear. We will listen to our own pain, even when we are impervious to everything else.

As for steering the will, pain is a powerful motivator. In behaviorist terms, pain serves as negative reinforcement, turning our desires away even from what we naturally prefer—living just to please ourselves. Pain from immoral choices also points beyond itself, not just to further pain that awaits us if we continue to indulge in sin but also to a painful afterlife, where we reap the consequences of our ultimate life commitment. In this way, earthly pain, one might say, is a preview for hell and thus serves as a daily warning of that terrible possibility. (Of course, the opposite of pain—satisfaction and enjoyment—serves as positive reinforcement for virtuous living. It is the clear, natural, and regular reminder to pursue goodness and that we have much to hope for. These earthly rewards are hints of the riches that await the faithful in the next life.) Notice that the cautionary function of pain applies to both the believer and unbeliever. It keeps the believer *on* and calls the unbeliever *to* the right path, in each case warning them of the dire consequences of choosing the way of rebellion.

---

[26] C. S. Lewis, *The Problem of Pain* (New York: Macmillan, 1962), 93.

Sin is not just wrong. It is impractical, making life much more difficult than it otherwise would be if we were obedient. As my father-in-law likes to say, "the way of the transgressor is hard." Jesus promised us that his yoke would be easy and his burden would be light (Matt. 11:30). Of course, this does not mean that the Christian life involves no sacrifice. On the contrary, the Christian life is very costly. But what Jesus asks us to give up is only what will harm us anyway. The righteous must forsake much, but nothing that is crucial for the growth and development of their souls. And he assists us in the forsaking we must do, encouraging us along the way. Finally, he preserves us through the storms that come into our lives. As the psalmist says, "a righteous man may have many troubles, but the LORD delivers him from them all" (Ps. 34:19). Unrepentant sinners, on the other hand, enjoy no such comfort. And their immoral choices disrupt and complicate, sometimes even making their lives miserable. This is the warning function of pain.

The Free Will Theodicy (Again)

The foregoing illustrates a variety of positive functions of suffering, which I have gathered under the rubric "greater good." The theodicy I favor, then, is really a package of considerations, rather than a singular explanation, as to why we suffer. Crucially, each good purpose is explicitly grounded in Scripture, and the central considerations of this compound approach are distinctively Christian, focusing as they do on the purpose of suffering in contributing to our character development and union with Christ.

Consider, by contrast, the rationale for divine allowance of evil on the free will theodicy. In that view, massive amounts of evil are justifiable for the sake of respecting human autonomy. Granting that this is a worthy end (though it is not explicitly recognized as such in Scripture), how much more so are evils justifiable for the sake of greater goods, such as building Christian character, establishing union with Christ, and deepening intimacy with God. The greater good theodicy proves more attractive still when we consider the punitive and warning functions of suffering, which, too, are recognized in Scripture.

The overarching theme of the greater good approach is that *all suffering has a purpose.* My aim has been to illustrate some of the more significant of these purposes and to highlight biblical grounds for this perspective. That all suffering is purposeful is a fundamental point of disagreement between proponents of the free will and greater good theodicies and, more generally, for proponents of the low and high views of providence. By implication, it is important to note, the greater good theodicy denies the existence of gratuitous evil in the lives of God's children. In this view, that is, we are assured that there is no pointless and unproductive evil in the world. The free will theodicy, however, offers no such guarantees. In fact, we may expect with this view, as its open theist proponents often declare, that there is indeed much gratuitous evil in the world. I shall have more to say about this in the final chapter.

So the advantages of a greater good theodicy over the free will approach are twofold. For one thing, the former provides a fuller *philosophical* account of suffering than the latter, offering greater justification for God's making a world in which hardships of all kinds occur. Second, and most significant, the greater good theodicy, at least the version presented here, is more *theologically* informed than the free will theodicy, as it is grounded in and in fact inspired by the direct teaching of Scripture on the subject of suffering. Moreover, again as presented here, this theodicy contains a strong Christological element, thus distinguishing it as a uniquely *Christian* response to the problem of suffering.

THE PROBLEM OF MORAL EVIL

Having dealt with the problem of suffering, we must now look specifically at the problem of moral evil. It is one thing to affirm God's complete control over human suffering, but can one reasonably maintain that God governs even human sin? If God ordains human sin, then doesn't this imply that God himself is culpable for that sin? We have already dealt with the compatibility of divine sovereignty and human freedom, so we need not be distracted here by that issue. The present problem is how God can be guilt-free if his providential control extends even to human immorality. But regarding this issue my approach will parallel the approach I took on the matter of providence and human freedom. Here, as there, it is instructive to note that several biblical texts explicitly (and many more, implicitly) affirm God's sovereignty over moral evil. Let us examine some of these.

The Joseph Paradigm

The life of Joseph, as recounted in the book of Genesis, provides a particularly vivid portrait of how moral evil can redound to great good. Jacob loved Joseph more than his other sons, and Joseph's brothers hated him because of this. Their resentment grew especially bitter when one day Joseph told them of some dreams he had, which suggested he would one day rule over them (Gen. 37:5-11). So they plotted to murder him. Instead, they sold Joseph into slavery and feigned his death by soaking his clothes in goat's blood. Jacob was devastated by the news of his son's apparent fate, and he mourned even as Joseph took up service for Potiphar, an official of the Egyptian Pharaoh. Soon Joseph earned Potiphar's respect. But when Joseph refused the sexual advances of Potiphar's wife, she slandered him. So Joseph landed in prison, now twice waylaid. While in prison, Joseph earned the warden's respect, who put him in charge of the inmates. He also became known for his gift of interpreting dreams. So when Pharaoh was troubled by some dreams, he called upon Joseph to interpret them, which he succeeded in doing. Consquently, Pharaoh rewarded Joseph by making him second-in-command in Egypt.

Now the dreams that had troubled Pharaoh pertained to an impending famine in the land that, on Joseph's recommendation, the Egyptians successfully prepared for by storing up grain prior to its onset. Back in Canaan, however, they were unprepared. Desperate for food, Jacob sent his sons to Egypt to obtain grain, since the abundant supply there was well-known. Ironically, Joseph's brothers appeared before their brother (whom they did not recognize), bowing to him as they made their request. Eventually Joseph revealed his identity to his brothers. They were all joyfully reconciled, and together they wept. Jacob, too, returned to his son, and the entire family took up residence in Egypt (where, of course, they grew into a great nation of people). But Joseph's brothers feared that he would take revenge for what they had done to him. They threw themselves before him saying, "we are your slaves," thus fulfilling Joseph's prophetic dream that had so provoked his brothers in the first place. But Joseph responded with grace, saying, "Don't be afraid. Am I in the place of God? You intended to harm me, but God intended it for good to accomplish what is now being done, the saving of many lives" (Gen. 50:19-20).

I take the time to recount this story in some detail because it so powerfully illustrates my basic claim about God's sovereign and good use of moral evil. On the Augustinian view of providence, there is a double intention when it comes to sinful choices, a fact to which Joseph testifies when responding to his brothers. They made choices with evil intentions, but God purposed those same events with good intentions. And so it goes for all our sins, as is further evidenced in the great promise of Romans 8:28. When Paul tells us that "in all things God works for the good of those who love him," presumably this includes the sinful as well as the virtuous actions that we and others perform. What we viciously intend, God virtuously intends. He purposes our moral evils to advance his own purposes and bring him glory, a pattern of providence that we might call the Joseph Paradigm.

Of course, the story of Joseph is ultimately a type of the gospel story. Jesus, too, was a special son, disparaged for his prophecy, resented for his goodness, abused, slandered, (in a sense) sold into slavery, only to persevere in righteousness and ultimately rise to glory. And all of this was a means to "the saving of many lives." Moreover, it was all intended by God, as Peter testifies in an early speech in Acts, saying about Jesus: "This man was handed over to you by God's set purpose and foreknowledge; and you, with the help of wicked men, put him to death by nailing him to the cross" (Acts 2:23). God used the wickedness of Jesus' murderers to accomplish the greatest of all goods. If the Joseph Paradigm applies to acts so sinister, might it not also apply universally to moral evils? This certainly seems to be Paul's message in Romans 8:28.[27]

An a Fortiori *Argument for Divine Sovereignty over Moral Evil*

But, one might ask, aren't some acts too morally vile even for God to redeem in any way? How could the Joseph Paradigm apply to such things as the rape of a small child or extreme torture and dismemberment of an innocent person? What possible good could God intend in

---

[27] Someone might complain that this approach invites us to do evil intentionally in order to bring about even greater good. This is a tempting objection, so much so that Paul anticipated a version of it in Romans 6 in the context of his exposition of how our sin affords the occasion for God's grace. His answer: "By no means! We died to sin; how can we live in it any longer?" (v. 2). Our sin is reprehensible, notwithstanding the fact that God always uses our mistakes to procure other goods.

such horrors? Admittedly, some evils are so horrific that sufficient goods to justify their occurrence defy the imagination. We have heard chilling accounts of moral evils that are so disturbing that we can only shake our heads and murmur, "Why?" Here it is imperative that we keep in view the limits of our understanding. Just as there are mysteries in the physical world about which we should take care to avoid bold pronouncements, there are moral and theological mysteries about which we should take similar care. Just because *we cannot imagine God's purposes*, it does not follow that *there are no divine purposes* when it comes to particular instances of moral evil. This is an instance of a more general *non-sequitur* fallacy: "X is inconceivable; therefore it is impossible." Human ignorance is no grounds for concluding a thing doesn't exist. Furthermore, to declare boldly that an action or event is unredeemable is to assert that one knows the limits of God's power to redeem. Such an attitude subjects the power of God to the limits of our own finite imaginations. This is presumptuous and arrogant, to say the least.

That said, I believe we have *a fortiori* biblical grounds for believing that God has good purposes in all moral evils and that we are just blind to these reasons. My reasoning may be presented in the form of an argument, as follows. God ordained the murder of Christ, the singularly worst moral evil the world has ever seen. God redeemed this worst evil to bring about a great good, in fact the greatest good the world has ever seen: the redemption of the human race. Thus, God is capable of redeeming even the worst moral evil. Moreover, the divine reasons for the murder of Christ were not clear to anyone until God made them clear to us. So if God is capable of redeeming the worst of all evils—which, as a matter of historical fact he already has—then how much more is he capable of redeeming the lesser moral evils that continue to occur in the world? And if we were blind to the higher (and now obvious) good that Christ's tortures served, then how much more might we be blind to the higher good served by the sundry other moral evils that vex us? The point here is that given what we know about God's proven ability to redeem the worst moral evil, we should trust his ability to redeem other moral evils.

The reasoning here actually features two *a fortiori* ("from the stronger") inferences. One is ethical: If the worst moral evil can be justified, then even more so may lesser evils be justified. The other is epistemic: If we can fail to recognize the highest goods achieved through the greatest evil, then even more so may we fail to recognize lesser goods achieved through lesser evils. These twin *a fortiori* inferences share a common pivot point pertaining to the limits of human reason and imagination. In Chapter 2 we saw that lack of ability to comprehend a proposition is not sufficient grounds for rejecting its truth. The same applies here. And here as regards divine sovereignty over evil, we have similar biblical grounds to believe *that*, though we might fail to comprehend *how* this is so.[28]

The passion of Christ provides the archetypal instance of the Joseph Paradigm, featuring as it does the convergence of the worst evils performed by human beings and the greatest good that God has done in our world. Indeed, it boggles the mind to juxtapose such evil human intentions and good divine purposes. But the biblical point on this matter remains clear. Both human and divine intentions are real; and both are responsible, whether culpable or praiseworthy. One is really evil, while the other is really good. (Yes, this creates some rational tension. But what else are we to expect? We are talking about profound metaphysical mysteries here.) This is the biblical paradigm for all evil that God uses to accomplish his purposes, from the waylaying of Joseph to the torture of Jesus. The *a fortiori* argument simply shows us that there are no acts "too evil" for God to redeem, as he has already redeemed the worst evil our world has seen. If he can redeem the worst, then surely he can redeem lesser evils.

It should be noted that God's perfect rationality implies there must be a sufficient reason for his ordaining all that he does. The point of my argument is not just that we should accept the truth of Augustinian prov-

---

[28] We might even be tempted to shield God himself against the apparent implication that he himself did evil when ordaining Christ's suffering. Thus, some insist that the Lord merely *allowed* Jesus to be tortured and crucified, that God did not plan such awful suffering for him. But Scripture says, "it was the LORD's will to crush him and cause him to suffer" (Isa. 53:10) and Jesus' crucifixion was according to "God's set purpose" (Acts 2:23). To view God's work in Christ in such passive and responsive terms (God only *allowed* Christ to die) dramatically diminishes his glory for the gospel. If he merely responded in a positive way to the cruelty of Christ's murderers, then we cannot be confident that all of the suffering of Jesus has a purpose. And we lose much of the existential comfort otherwise available in Christ's passion. But, the objector continues, if God really intended this bloody torture of Jesus by the wicked people who did it, then is he not implicated in their immorality? How can God not be guilty in ordaining Christ's murder when the murderers themselves are guilty? Must not the orchestrator of a heinous crime be likewise judged a criminal? How dare we suggest that God planned this? Such is the typical language used by those who refuse to accept Scripture's plain teaching on this matter. Our proper response, of course, is to submit to that teaching, though this need not deter us from searching out this mystery (as in fact I have attempted to do in this chapter), so long as we use Scripture as our chief guide.

idence despite our inability to rationally reconcile the doctrine with all the moral evil we experience (though it does entail that). The point is that we should be confident that there *are* good reasons for all that God ordains related to human immorality. So I am not advocating a form of fideism, opposing reason to faith. On the contrary, I am arguing that we have biblical grounds to be confident that our faith *is* rational, based on some significant biblical-historical precedents. Just as some good reasons for (the most) extreme evil were once hidden from us but are now apparent, so might not the divine reasons for some other evils just be hidden from us now?

CONCLUSION

It should be clear that the greater good theodicy as outlined here is available only to those who affirm a high view of providence and is best suited for the Augustinian perspective. This resource for dealing with the problem of evil is another major benefit of a strong affirmation of God's sovereignty. I do not want to be interpreted as maintaining that the greater good theodicy serves as a final *explanation* of every instance of evil. On the contrary, the thrust of the theodicy is its insistence that we accept the biblical *promise* that there are greater goods awaiting us associated with our suffering. It is true that Scripture gives us the broad contours of the purposes of evil, some of which can be elucidated in some detail, as I have tried to do here, but it does not provide a complete account as to how it all works. So although we may be confident *that* all evil is redeemed, we often don't know *how* this is the case. There is much here that remains a mystery. But this is to be expected: "'for my thoughts are not your thoughts, neither are your ways my ways,' declares the LORD. 'As the heavens are higher than the earth, so are my ways higher than your ways and my thoughts than your thoughts'" (Isa. 55:8-9).

7

MORAL AND DEVOTIONAL APPLICATIONS

We have explored the benefits of providence in a variety of contexts, including aesthetics, science, divine emotion, and the problem of evil. The final applications I want to make are essentially moral in nature, pertaining to the day-to-day spiritual life of the Christian. Effectively, in this chapter I will address this common question about the Augustinian view of providence: What *practical* and *personal* difference does it make to believe that God is completely sovereign? What relevance does this view of providence have for one's daily *conduct*? I don't mean to insinuate here that the previously discussed applications are not practical, personal, or relevant to conduct. On the contrary, they certainly are for me and for many others. But of more immediate and universal concern for the Christian is virtuous living. We aim to relate to God personally and, toward that end, practice the spiritual disciplines, so that, in the words of Paul, "the man of God may be thoroughly equipped for every good work" (2 Tim. 3:17). In the end, it is our moral behavior that matters most. According to Scripture, true love and knowledge of God are impossible without obedient conduct (see John 14:15; 1 John 2:3-4), and good works are definitive for faith as well (see Jas. 2:24, 26). So a doctrine of providence should be assessed according to its moral impact. A truly biblical view of providence will help, not handicap, the Christian in this area. So is the belief in complete divine sovereignty a boon to the Christian moral life? Very much so, I believe, at least when properly understood.

MORAL VIRTUE

Jesus says, "If anyone loves me, he will obey my teaching. My Father will love him, and we will come to him and make our home with him" (John 14:23). To be obedient is to display certain kinds of character traits or what are known as virtues. The virtues are specific forms of moral excellence that are appropriate to particular life contexts. They include such traits as kindness, patience, generosity, self-control, peace, diligence, sincerity, faith, joy, gratitude, and wisdom. Paul identifies such traits as "the fruit of the Spirit" (Gal. 5:22-23). Jesus Christ unfailingly displayed these characteristics. In fact, an exhaustive list of the virtues is essentially a profile of Christ's moral character. So to be a mature Christian is to exhibit these traits and to do so in increasing measure.[1] One of the most significant benefits of the Augustinian view of providence is the fertile soil it provides for growth in virtue. Generally speaking, it encourages a submissive attitude, which is crucial for most of the virtues. Much of the moral life is about surrender and "giving in" to God's plan for one's life, however painful that might be at times. An Augustinian perspective also advantages the Christian in the development of particular virtues.

Humility

A humble person is one who is willing to take a low position before others. Although he recognizes his great worth before God as someone who bears God's image, he behaves in such a way as to assume an inferior place, to put others' concerns before his own. Scripture repeatedly emphasizes the importance of this trait. God says through Isaiah: "This is the one I esteem: he who is humble and contrite in spirit" (Isa. 66:2). The psalmist declares that the Lord "crowns the humble with salvation" (149:4). And one of Jesus' constant refrains is that the humble will be exalted.[2] Indeed, Jesus himself embodied radical humility, as Paul summarizes in Philippians 2: "Your attitude should be the same as that of Christ Jesus: Who, being in very nature God, did not consider equality with God something to be grasped, but made himself nothing, taking the

---

[1] For an extended discussion of the virtues, see my *How to be Good in a World Gone Bad* (Grand Rapids, Mich.: Kregel, 2004).

[2] See, for example, Matt. 5:3-5; 20:16, 27; and Mark 10:15.

very nature of a servant, being made in human likeness" (vv. 5-7). Arguably, humility is the core Christian virtue, that trait from which all other moral excellence stems. Andrew Murray calls humility "the root of all virtue and grace" and adds, "the health and strength of our spiritual life will entirely depend upon our putting this grace first."[3]

The Augustinian view of providence is humbling, and it properly spawns an attitude of humility. It leaves no room for any ultimate praise to go to human beings for any good traits they possess. As Paul tells us, even our faith is a gift from God (Eph. 2:8), and it is he who works in us "to will and to act according to his good purpose" (Phil. 2:13). Unlike the low view of providence, the Augustinian perspective affords no room for human credit with regard to our faith and good works. Of course, many people resent the fact that all glory for these things should go to God, but given the obdurate pride of the human heart, this is to be expected. This is why I say that the Augustinian view of providence "properly" spawns humility. To some it only provokes prideful resentment, as it did in me before I submitted to this biblical truth.

The virtue of humility squelches pride and so is unnatural, relative to our fallen condition. We all tend to put ourselves first, seeking foremost our own desires and interpreting all our experiences in light of our own desires. Therefore, to assume a humble perspective, such that I see my own life as no more important than others', is not just a subtle change but a fundamentally different orientation on life, a radical moral paradigm shift.[4] The Augustinian view of providence is unnatural for precisely the same reason. We want to control our own destinies. But to affirm complete divine sovereignty over the world militates against this instinct. So it is not surprising that resistance to the idea would be strong, even among some Christians. It offends our innate egocentrism. Just as personal humility demands a certain submission before others, the Augustinian view of providence demands submission before God's rule of the world and every human heart. Our surrender to the truth of God's sovereignty, and the corresponding check on human pride that this

---

[3] Andrew Murray, *Humility* (New Kensington, Penn.: Whitaker House, 1982), 25, 19.
[4] Norvin Richards characterizes humility as "understanding that one is not special, from the point of view of the universe, not an exception to be treated differently from others." From *Humility* (Philadelphia: Temple University Press, 1992), 189.

involves, will better prepare us to submit to others and check our pride before them.

Faith

The whole matter of submission is relevant to another core Christian virtue: faith. Faith is essentially personal trust, manifested in behaviors consonant with that trust. If we entrust ourselves to someone, then we will act in the interest of that person, doing his bidding and acceding to his wishes. There is certainly a cognitive dimension to faith, as we must believe certain things about God before we can entrust ourselves to him. But mere assent is a far cry from genuine biblical faith, as James makes clear when he says that "faith without deeds is dead" (Jas. 2:26) and that "even the demons believe . . . and shudder" (Jas. 2:19).

As rational beings, we humans naturally seek to manipulate the world around us in order to survive and flourish. We farm the land, erect buildings, build cars, treat the sick, organize institutions, etc., all aimed at making life as pleasant as possible and shielding ourselves from the countless hazards that nature poses. Each of us occupies a unique domain in which we wield particular influences and through which we hope to prosper and help our loved ones do the same. But as we all know, there are limits to our control over the world and even our own lives. Here we arrive at the question of faith: Does anyone control the cosmos and our lives in an *ultimate* sense? To answer that question affirmatively and to live accordingly is to be a person of faith. But to live in such a way as to answer negatively is to lack faith, whatever one might cognitively affirm in response to this question. Robert Adams has proposed that the attitude opposing faith is *lust for control*, the desire to manipulate all of one's life circumstances. This is a strong temptation because

> In Christian faith we are invited to trust a person so much greater than ourselves that we cannot understand him very fully. We have to trust his power and goodness in general without having a blueprint of what he is going to do in detail. This is very disturbing because it entails a loss of control of our own lives.[5]

---

[5] Robert Adams, *The Virtue of Faith and Other Essays in Philosophical Theology* (Oxford: Oxford University Press, 1987), 19-20.

Now the Augustinian view of providence promotes faith, because those who take this perspective believe that God ultimately controls the world and that nothing, in the final analysis, is left to chance. Nor do we have the capacity to override or curtail God's plans. Of course, intellectual assent to this notion does not guarantee the sort of existential trust in God that characterizes biblical faith. But this belief is a crucial precondition for such trust. One may choose to resent or rest in God's sovereignty. Obviously, an Augustinian perspective well prepares a person to do the latter.

Moreover, the humility spawned by the Augustinian view of providence is itself an encouragement to faith. Faith requires humility. As Jesus says, "unless you change and become like little children, you will never enter the kingdom of heaven" (Matt. 18:3). This is because surrendering ultimate control of one's own life is to submit in the most basic (and frightening) sense. Lacking the power and other resources to run their own lives, children have no choice but to depend on others and occupy a low position in terms of authority. Concomitantly, they naturally recognize that someone else is in control and easily entrust themselves to the care of adults. The call to faith is essentially a call to so entrust our lives to the care of God. And to do so we must first, like children, recognize that someone else already ultimately controls things; then we too will more easily entrust our lives to his care. The Augustinian view of providence recognizes this fact and so enhances one's faith.

Courage

Another important virtue bolstered by the Augustinian view of providence is courage. The moral crest between the valleys of cowardice and foolhardiness, courage is the moral skill of acting rightly in the face of danger. Whether taking a risky business venture or confronting a violent alcoholic friend, the courageous person is by no means fearless, but she is not overrun by her fear. Nor is she less aware than others of the potential harm the situation poses. Rather, she sees that the goodness of a course of action warrants risking harm, and she has the self-control to follow through in spite of the possible negative consequences.

From a Christian standpoint, all earthly danger is to be viewed *sub specie aeternitatis* (under the aspect of eternity). The prospect of our heavenly reward puts the temporary pains of this life into proper perspective. Acting wrongly to avoid injury might make things more pleasant for us now, but we will net a long-term loss in the afterlife as a result. Courageous Christians keep this truth in the forefront of their minds, and their behavior is motivated accordingly.

One's view of providence, however, will affect the way one views a dangerous situation. According to the low view, God might not have even anticipated the danger one faces, much less planned for it. Suppose I learn that my boss has been sexually harassing some of my fellow employers. He has freely chosen to perform his vicious actions, so God might not have foreseen them. Nor does God necessarily foresee what will occur if I blow the whistle. Given our libertarian free will, even God might be surprised if I lose my job or worse. In a fit of rage, my boss might turn on me and maim or kill me, and this might be unforeseen even by God. And when God does intervene, there is no guarantee that things will turn out for the best. As we saw earlier, some open theists, in particular, admit their conviction that "sometimes God's plans do not bring about the desired result and must be judged a failure."[6] This doesn't provide a person much comfort when facing a dangerous situation and gives little motivation for doing the courageous thing.

The Augustinian view of providence, however, offers a much different analysis of the situation. Whatever my boss has done, God has been aware of it for all eternity. Moreover, he has planned for all eternity to work the situation out for my good, assuming I have been his faithful servant. This much he has clearly promised in Romans 8:28. The fact that my boss is a free and responsible agent does not preclude God's control over his life, including how it affects me. Thus, as I consider my duty to confront my boss or to report his indiscretions to the appropriate authorities, I can rest in the confidence that God will follow through on his promise by protecting me. And if I do catch the wrath of my boss and am maimed or killed, I can know in advance that this, too, was part of God's design. Nothing can happen to me, as a child of God, that does not contribute to my ultimate good and, most important, the glory of

---

[6] John Sanders, *The God Who Risks: A Theology of Providence* (Downers Grove, Ill.: InterVarsity Press, 1998), 88.

my God. Now this is fertile soil for courage, the strongest possible motivation for acting rightly in the face of danger.

Patience

So an Augustinian view of providence motivates courage because it assures us that even calamitous events contribute to God's purpose for us. For a similar reason, the Augustinian view motivates the virtue of patience. To be patient is to endure discomfort without complaint. A patient person is skilled at waiting through uncomfortable circumstances without grumbling or losing his or her cool. The contexts in which patience is called for are myriad, from waiting in traffic to waiting for desired employment to waiting to find a spouse or to conceive a child. Some waiting is uncomfortable because it is dull or annoying, but other times waiting is physically or emotionally painful. In any case, it is often difficult to endure such discomfort without complaining.

Whatever one's view of providence, the Christian knows that God keeps his promises and that he will grant us salvation and other rewards eventually. But it is one thing to believe this and quite another to recognize that God sovereignly governs even the minute details of one's life. He is the one who knowingly placed me in my situation, however tedious or difficult it might be. So I can rest in the fact that even this will contribute to my long-term good and God's glory. Moreover, I always have grounds to go to him as the sovereign source of my current situation. However, to take the Augustinian view of providence is to recognize that all patience is ultimately *patience with God*. Whether or not my waiting immediately involves other free agents, such as the motorists in front of me on the highway or my teenage son who is maturing far too slowly, I know that God is behind it all. Therefore, I enjoy the right to complain *to* God about my life situation if it is becoming too much for me. I don't have the right to grumble, that is, to complain to others about my life situation, however. I must go to the source as the psalmists do in so many instances. I will say more about this below.

The Augustinian perspective encourages patience because it demands that we see even apparently random and purposeless events as having their place in God's economy. His timing is perfect, and I can rest secure in this. I am spared the torment of trying to ascertain which events fit into God's plan and which do not. Instead, I have the comfort of knowing that literally everything that comes to pass is part of the perfect divine plan for the world and for my own life. This realization is a tremendous source of inner peace, yet another benefit of providence.

THE RIGHT TO COMPLAIN AND THE PRIVILEGE TO GIVE THANKS

In our earlier discussion of the problem of evil, I noted that the low view of providence allows for the existence of gratuitous evil—that is, sin or suffering that serves no good purpose whatsoever. Some evils are neither foreseen by God nor used by him for higher ends. I contrasted this perspective with the Augustinian view, which affirms that even the most despicable evils somehow fit within God's plan to redeem people and glorify himself. Now each of these contrasting points of view will necessarily affect a person's attitudinal responses to evil. With the low view, we cannot be sure whether a particular evil will contribute to a good end, while in the Augustinian view we can rest assured that this is so. Furthermore, when it comes to those events about which we feel special outrage, very different responses will follow. While all Christians reserve what might be called the "right to complain" to God about unpleasant circumstances (as modeled by the psalmists), the exercise of this right will look very different depending upon one's view of providence. God is more or less in control of history and our individual lives, according to the spectrum of views on providence. Accordingly, God will be more or less a proper target of my complaints, depending upon what view I hold and what sorts of events I want to complain about.

The Right to Complain

What exactly is a complaint? Suppose I receive poor service at a restaurant. The waiter is rude and inattentive, and he gets my order wrong not once, but twice. Moreover, after finally returning with the correct order he sneers at me and makes a profane remark. Now I think it is appropriate for me to contact the manager about this mistreatment and to suggest that some disciplinary measure be taken regarding this employee. Such action on my part would constitute a complaint. Now if this case is paradigmatic, there seem to be at least four essential components to a complaint: (1) an expression of dissatisfaction, (2) regarding some culpable agent, (3) based on some purportedly compelling reason, which is (4) directed toward a responsible party.

Someone may experience dissatisfaction for any number of reasons, and dissatisfaction may be expressed in a variety of ways. But one distinguishing feature of any complaint is the claim that some other agent besides the complainer is somehow responsible for one's dissatisfaction. It was the waiter's fault, not mine, that the wrong dish was prepared. And his sneer and profane remark, too, were his fault, not mine. Here, as in any case of complaint, someone other than the complainer is to blame, and on these grounds moral redress is sought.

We typically give reasons for our complaints rather than merely expressing dissatisfaction. The sorts of reasons we cite go beyond the mere fact of unfulfilled desire or personal harm and identify morally compelling considerations such as a broken promise, negligence, or injustice. Such grounds constitute a charge *against* some culpable agent and so assume a burden of evidence for the complainer that mere expression of dissatisfaction does not. And the accused agent is properly considered innocent of the charge until his or her moral guilt has been demonstrated. As it is in the legal world in these respects, so it goes for the moral realm. Moral accusations must be evidentially justified.

Further, a complaint is properly directed to the allegedly responsible agent, whether directly or indirectly. Although most of us tend to express our dissatisfaction in the presence of concerned but not responsible persons, such expressions are usually ineffectual at redressing the grievance for just this reason. And the mere airing of dissatisfaction with no view to moral redress is probably better termed grumbling or venting just because it is unproductive. Thus, in the illustration I take my complaint to the restaurant manager because, although not directly culpable for my mistreatment, he is generally responsible for the conduct of his employees. My assumption is that the manager will confront the waiter about the situation and some appropriate disciplinary action will follow, calling for at least an apology from the waiter. In any case, a complaint must somehow aim toward its object, the accused agent, even if only indirectly.

I have noted that a complaint presupposes a responsible agent and is properly directed toward him. Now in the low view of providence, my suffering does not ultimately come from the hand of the Lord. In fact, it is pointless, as John Sanders insists:

> When a two-month-old child contracts a painful incurable bone cancer that means suffering and death, it is pointless evil. The Holocaust is pointless evil. The rape and dismemberment of a young girl is pointless evil. The accident that caused the death of my brother was a tragedy. God does not have a specific purpose in mind for these occurrences.[7]

Sanders's dogmatic confidence here about the limits of God's sovereignty is remarkable. How can he be so sure of the boundaries of God's purposes? Besides the fact that these assertions flout Scripture, the devotional implications for the Christian are severe. If such evils are pointless, then presumably God had nothing to do with them. Consequently, we have no grounds for complaint *to him* for such events. We can only shake our heads and sigh at the sheer waste of human sorrow.

The corresponding benefit for proponents of the Augustinian view of providence is that they enjoy the right to direct their complaints toward the agent ultimately responsible for such misery. Charges may be brought vigorously and continually before God for the suffering experienced by humans as well as by sentient non-humans every day. In fact, in Scripture prayers of complaint, which recognize God as the source of terrible suffering, are not only permitted but also encouraged. For example, the psalmist writes:

> *You have made us a reproach to our neighbors, the scorn and derision of those around us. You have made us a byword among the nations; the peoples shake their heads at us. . . . All this happened to us, though we had not forgotten you or been false to your covenant. . . . But you crushed us and made us a haunt for jackals and covered us over with deep darkness. . . . Awake, O Lord!*[8]

Such complaints, though stunningly bold in their challenge of divine wisdom, appear repeatedly in the Psalms (see also Psalms 13, 22, 59, 64, 74, 88, and 142). In practice, the benefits of such prayers are plain. First,

---

[7] Ibid., 262.
[8] Psalm 44:13-23.

they are implicit affirmations of faith, thus reassuring fellow believers and the complaining believer that God is the sovereign source of all that befalls us, however sad or tragic our circumstances. In turn, this is comforting, since we know that God is merciful and works to redeem all situations for his people. Second, the theist's complaints serve a cathartic function, purging negative emotions that might otherwise cause stress and emotional debilitation. Thus, the prayer of complaint is a salutary feature of the Christian devotional life.[9] The Augustinian perspective guarantees that God is always a proper target of such complaints, since he carefully controls the entire universe. The low view offers no such guarantees.

The Privilege to Give Thanks

Another benefit of providence concerns the human impulse to give thanks for the goods we all experience at one time or another, most significant of which are physical health, emotional well-being, the beauty of nature, and the blessings that come to us through other people. We all have felt gratitude for good fortunes that fall into some or all of these categories. All Christians, regardless of their view of providence, enjoy the privilege of thanking God for such things, as he is their ultimate source. But exactly what is gratitude, and under what conditions is it appropriate? In addressing these questions, Fred Berger's seminal analysis is a good starting place. According to Berger, gratitude is properly an affective response to benevolence, where a benevolent act is understood as being (a) voluntary, (b) intentional, and (c) performed to help someone.[10] Each of these conditions is necessary in order to generate gratitude as a proper response. Providing a benefit in order to gain something for oneself or because one is threatened does not generate a debt of gratitude on the part of the beneficiary. The benefactor must act, or attempt to act, for the sake of the recipient. Thus, Berger says, gratitude "is a response to a grant of benefits (or the attempt to benefit us) which was motivated by a desire to help."[11]

---

[9] The productivity of complaints to which I refer here pertains only to the psychological effect upon the person who complains through the act of prayer. This ignores the benefit that such prayers might produce through divine actions occurring as answers to prayers of complaint.

[10] Fred R. Berger, "Gratitude," *Ethics* 85 (1975): 298-309.

[11] Ibid., 299.

Other significant treatments of the subject, most notably those of
Terrance McConnell[12] and John A. Simmons,[13] agree with Berger's basic
analysis, though in each case they add various further conditions.[14] But
the consensus among philosophers who have explored this virtue is that
gratitude is a proper response to a benefit freely and intentionally
granted to a person for his or her own good. Some have maintained that
when these conditions obtain, the response of gratitude is a duty. Others,
such as Christopher Wellman, argue that while gratitude is a virtue, it is
not a duty.[15] But from a moral standpoint gratitude is, at least, a moral
virtue and, more broadly, a morally appropriate response to benevolence. I would add that gratitude is also psychologically appropriate, in
the sense that it is a normal, healthy response to those who act benevo-
lently toward us.

Now it is just this response to the "natural" benefits of good health,
emotional well-being, and natural beauty that often issues forth in
expression of thankfulness to God on the part of the believer. Indeed,
such an affective response is always appropriate, since God has blessed
us with so many gifts. But, like the right to complain, the Augustinian
view of providence endows the Christian with a much more expansive
menu of items for praise than does the low view. First, in the Augustinian
perspective we can be confident that God had specific intent with regard
to each of our blessings, that our physical and mental health, the food
we eat, and the friendships we form did not simply result from his per-
mitting these things to develop without his interference. He did not just
"allow" us to enjoy these things. He actively ordained them, which is
grounds for a deeper gratitude.

Second, the Augustinian view of providence warrants our thanking
God for the blessings we receive through the free actions of other people, whether it be services provided by our dentist or mechanic or the

---

[12] Terrance McConnell, *Gratitude* (Philadelphia: Temple University Press, 1993).

[13] John A. Simmons, *Moral Principles and Political Obligations* (Princeton, N.J.: Princeton University Press, 1979).

[14] To Berger's basic set of necessary conditions, Simmons adds such conditions as these: (a) "the benefit must be granted by some special effort or sacrifice," (b) "the benefit must not be forced (unjustifiably) on the beneficiary against his will," and (c) "the beneficiary must want the benefits (or would want the benefits if certain impairing conditions were corrected)" (ibid., 178). McConnell essentially affirms these further requirements but tweaks the last of these to read: "the beneficiary must *accept* the benefit (or would *accept* the benefit if certain impairing conditions were corrected)" (McConnell, 44). Emphasis mine.

[15] Christopher Wellman, "Gratitude as a Virtue," *Pacific Philosophical Quarterly* 80 (1999): 284-300. Wellman supports his view on the grounds that there are no reciprocal rights to gratefulness.

grace shown us by our family and friends. A low view of providence, which affirms libertarian freedom, at best only justifies our thanking God for providing the preconditions for such blessings. But in the Augustinian view God decrees even the goods that accrue to us through the free actions of human beings. So we should be every bit as grateful to God for being blessed by others as we are for the "natural" goods that come to us. The Augustinian perspective enables us to see literally every good thing we experience as warranting gratitude to God. Regardless of how it came to us, whether "naturally" or through the work of another person, we can be confident that God had specific intent in so blessing us. Thus, all gratitude is properly directed primarily to him.

As with the right to complain, the privilege to thank brings some beneficial psychological effects. First, as the positive counterpart of the psychological benefit of complaint, divinely directed thankfulness brings psychological release. There is the sense of a "paid debt" of gratitude, a morally appropriate or just expression of that thankfulness. Now the low view of providence does often make sense of this, but not in all instances. When events unanticipated by God (in the low view) unfold to my favor, I have no reason to thank God. And when I am blessed by another person's actions but cannot locate him to show my gratitude, my urge to thank will go somewhat frustrated. But in the Augustinian view, the primary object of my gratitude is always available to receive my thanks, though the secondary cause—the human involved—might be unknown or lost to me.

THE SPIRITUAL DISCIPLINES

We have seen that the Augustinian view of providence is a fecund source of virtue as well as a psychological balm for the Christian. But the benefits extend also to the moral-spiritual training in which Christians engage.

Prayer

The discipline of prayer is fundamental to Christian spirituality. All agree that prayer is an act of conversation with God. But depending upon one's doctrine of providence, the dynamics and purposes of prayer will be viewed differently. Earlier I discussed the matter of petitionary prayer and how the Augustinian view sees prayer as a secondary cause for the accomplishment of God's will in the world. Prayer does not involve persuading God to act differently from how he had planned nor to adopt our perspective on some matter. Rather, God has ordained prayer as a means by which we enter into and take part in his work in the world. Scripture encourages us to make requests of the Lord (Phil. 4:6), but we are to do so with deference to his will.

Jesus' model for prayer begins, "your kingdom come, your will be done on earth as it is in heaven" (Matt. 6:10). The Augustinian view of providence enables the Christian to more readily pray that most humble of prayers. The Lord's Prayer enjoins complete surrender to God's will, submission of our desires, however strong or sanctified they might be, to God's plans and purposes. Any Christian will testify that this is one of his or her biggest existential challenges—simple surrender. To take the Augustinian view of providence encourages us to surrender, to accept whatever befalls us, however painful or unexpected, as contributing to God's perfect plan for us. All that transpires in our lives is ultimately for our own good, assuming that we are lovingly following him. This perspective prepares us to will what God wills, as Jesus commands us to do with his model of prayer.

So what are we to make of the biblical truth that "the prayer of a righteous man is powerful and effective" (Jas. 5:16)? Does this mean that the plans of the righteous are better than God's plans? Of course not. It means that God uses the prayers of the righteous more readily than those of other people. And why? Because *to be righteous is to will what God wills*. God answers the prayers of righteous people precisely because they are more inclined to think God's thoughts after him and so request what God has already planned. The psalmist's promise, "delight yourself in the LORD and he will give you the desires of your heart" (Ps. 37:4) is to be understood in similar fashion. When I delight myself in the Lord, my desires change so as to conform more fully with God's will. Consequently, as God works out his will, my desires are more frequently satisfied.

The very act of prayer is properly humble and submissive. The point is not to conform God's will to mine but to conform my will to his. This realization should provide the background for all our prayers. Last year I was pleasantly surprised to see this attitude illustrated by my four-year-old son, Bailey. It was mid-February, and there had been very little snow to that point in the winter season. This disappointed him, because he wanted badly to build a snowman and do some sledding. So we encouraged Bailey to pray that God would send some snow. The next day it did snow, and Bailey called me at work, exuberantly proclaiming, "Daddy, my prayer fits in the plan! My prayer fits in the plan!" I was thrilled to know that his perspective is already so theocentric.

Those who take the Augustinian view are also better prepared to handle the disappointment when what they ask for does not come to pass. Confident that God's plan for me must be better than whatever I asked for, I can joyfully accept the "no" answer to my petition. So there is no place for anxiety, nervousness, or trumped-up fervency in prayer for those who take an Augustinian view of providence. One may rest in the assurance that God's will is best, come what may. Here someone may object, "But then why pray at all? Either way, whether one prays or not, God's perfect will is accomplished. Why not just forget prayer altogether?" Again, this forgets the important fact that God has ordained prayer as a secondary cause, through which he accomplishes his will, as noted above. But most important, God *commands* us to pray.[16] So whether or not we can make rational sense of how prayer works, we must do it as a matter of simple obedience. Admittedly, prayer is in many ways mysterious. As in so many other aspects of the issue of providence discussed in this book, we must acknowledge the limits of reason to plumb this mystery and proceed to humbly obey.

Evangelism

This last point, of course, applies as well to the practice of evangelism. Even while recognizing God's sovereignty over all things, we must still proclaim the gospel to others. It is a matter of obedience, as Jesus tells us to spread his message abroad (Matt. 28:19-20). Having said that, much of the practice of evangelism by evangelical Christians these days is fraught with problems and is, in short, unbiblical. It is noteworthy that the Roman Catholic Church boasts one billion members worldwide, while evangelical Protestants number about three hundred million. Yet

---

[16] It is interesting to note in this context that when praying for his disciples, Jesus did not bother praying for Judas Iscariot, whom he recognized as "doomed to destruction" (John 17:12).

evangelicals are incomparably more devoted to evangelistic outreach than are Catholics. How is this to be explained? I suspect there is a complex set of factors that account for this differential, but the most fundamental factor pertains to views of family to be found in Catholic and evangelical Protestant circles. Catholics regard the family as the primary vehicle for building the church, and this belief is expressed in the Catholic community in tangible ways, most controversially in their rejection of artificial means of birth control. Evangelical Protestants, on the other hand, do not see family as central to fulfilling the Great Commission, as is evident in the casual attitude toward birth control among evangelicals. Consider: less than a century ago evangelical Christians were largely opposed to artificial birth control. These days most evangelicals see nothing problematic with the practice, nor do they even suspect that there is a moral question to be posed about it.

What changed our minds? What moral-theological arguments won the day for casual use of birth control? Or, more generally, how did the whole notion of "family planning" as we understand it today become such a routine part of the evangelical mind-set? Could it be that evangelicals have simply conformed to this cultural practice without critically evaluating it? Could it be that this is another symptom of our subtle prioritizing of the value of personal autonomy? I think so. The same value that expresses itself in wayward Protestant views of providence also finds practical expression in our approach to birth control and family planning. Indeed, the two are not unconnected, as I will try to explain below.

Instead of focusing on the family to grow disciples, evangelicals have relied on outreach programs (e.g., parachurch organizations, traveling evangelists, short-term missions trips, etc.) as a primary means of building the church. Such an approach is inherently problematic, as it de-emphasizes the kind of deep, long-term involvement with people that Great Commission discipleship entails. Many evangelicals defend hit-and-run evangelism because of the perception that it produces good results. But when one looks at the numbers, one sees that the numbers don't favor the prevailing evangelical approach. And when one considers the many instances in which a "convert" is made but is not followed up with careful discipleship, it proves all the more problematic. The fresh convert left to fend for himself morally and spiritually will eventually be drawn back into his old lifestyle, only to become more cynical about religion and spirituality, concluding, "Well, I tried religion, and it didn't work for me." This, of course, serves as a devastating set-up for hypocrisy. The new convert is typically outspoken about his faith. So if, undiscipled, he slowly slips back into his pagan ways, he will necessarily appear to be a hypocrite. And this does serious damage to the credibility of the Christian worldview.[17] Tragically, this is a common occurrence in the evangelical world.[18]

So what is the alternative? I believe the proper alternative to current evangelical approaches to evangelism is to return to the original, biblical emphasis on discipleship. We must throw off our current mind-set that prioritizes conversion over making disciples (i.e., morally mature and wise followers of Christ). Many evangelicals could be accurately described as "conversion utilitarians," seeing the "decision for Christ" as the primary end of the Great Commission while downplaying the long-term moral-spiritual growth of those converts. And, for the reasons just described, this undermines the true goal of the Great Commission—making disciples.

So how does the doctrine of providence figure in regarding all of this? In short, the Augustinian perspective encourages me to be more patient and less manipulative when it comes to evangelizing others. In fact, I will be less inclined to view my interactions with others in "conversion utilitarian" terms. I will simply be natural with others who don't share my Christian faith, valuing them as persons and getting to know them for who they are, not because they are potential converts. I will let them get to know my faith in a relaxed, organic way, seeing it woven into the various aspects of my life. And I will trust that God will use this to provide a link in the chain toward their entry into his kingdom, perhaps even through explicit conversations about the gospel for which God may provide opportunity.

Also, the Augustinian view of providence encourages me to surrender control of family planning to God and to be willing to accept a large

---

[17] For an extended treatment of the issue of hypocrisy, see my *Hypocrisy: Moral Fraud and Other Vices* (Grand Rapids, Mich.: Baker, 1999).

[18] In fact, this happened to me. I was twice converted, once by a street evangelist, after which I fell back into my old rebellious ways. Later I was "re-converted," this time through the influence of a friend who took care to disciple me in the context of a local church. I don't intend to use my own case as evidence in support of the view I am advocating here, as it is merely anecdotal. But such stories are quite common. And my own experience has made me sensitive to the sorts of problems that popular forms of evangelism create.

number of children (instead of acting as if kids are not a profound blessing!), even if that is not my preference. Am I saying that we Protestants should behave more like Catholics in this matter? Yes, that is what I am saying. From a brute numbers standpoint, their approach is clearly more effective. Even for those who are conversion utilitarians, it should be clear that the Catholic way is the better way. Trust God for the size of your family, and be loath to artificially inhibit the procreative process, as it is inherently sacred. Or at the least, be willing to make natural birth control (e.g., the "rhythm method," fertility awareness techniques, etc.) your default approach.

And am I saying that we should scuttle foreign missions and other attempts to share the gospel with lost people? Absolutely not. I personally support many missionaries and will continue to do so. But I am advocating a less formally programmed and more organic approach, where Christian missionary families commit themselves to communities and focus on discipleship, as opposed to large-scale evangelistic efforts that focus on conversion and de-emphasize true discipleship. Such programs, however well intentioned, ignore the heart of the Great Commission. To make converts is a far cry from making disciples.

Other Disciplines

One's view of providence deeply influences many other aspects of Christian practice. Worship is the adoration and enjoyment of God, especially through public ritual and artistic expression. Since the Augustinian view of providence encourages us to see God as utterly sovereign, formal worship that is founded on this realization makes him and his works the constant center of focus. The worship liturgy, sermon, and music all orbit around God and his attributes. The theme of worship is God's gracious work, not human *response* to this work, however delightful the latter might be. God redeemed us when we were spiritually dead and therefore powerless to choose him without his first choosing us. Our formal worship should reflect this marvelous grace and exalt God to the uttermost.

Outside a context of formal worship, the Augustinian perspective best enables us to see all that is good as proceeding from the hand of God, the source of "every good and perfect gift" (Jas. 1:17). We will see our own talents as implanted in us and sovereignly developed by God, as he has directed our lives. Thus, we will regard every legitimate expression of those talents, in whatever context they may be used, as an act of worship, an offering back to God what he first gave us. Whether I program computers, sell cars, repair roads, or teach middle-schoolers, the good use of my talents serves to adore my Creator, and I may enjoy him in doing so. He is Lord of all the earth, and true worship may therefore take place in the context of any human activity.

The Augustinian view also provides especially fertile ground for the spiritual disciplines of abstinence, such as fasting, secrecy, sacrifice, and frugality. We noted above how the Augustinian view is a boon to humility, which in turn is crucial preparation for engagement in these disciplines. For one thing, the humble person recognizes his or her need to build moral strength, which these disciplines assist us in doing. By denying myself food for a period of time, I train myself to control one of my body's strongest natural urges. By denying myself the right to make known my good deeds and qualities, I train myself to control the urge for attention and admiration from others. By sacrificing valued items or frugally denying myself indulgence in what is not needed, I train myself to resist the desire for earthly possessions. In directing the mind to the perfect sovereignty of God, the Augustinian view of providence accents the lowliness of the fallen human condition. This helps orient the mind toward self-denial and thus prepares us for engagement in self-renunciation of all kinds, including the disciplines of abstinence.

Finally, an Augustinian perspective encourages practice of the disciplines of confession and submission. The humility and self-denial encouraged by this view enable me to subject myself to others and their authority, such as in confessing my sin and volunteering moral accountability to others whom I respect. This goes for submission to governing authorities as well. Scripture teaches that all leaders, even those who are corrupt, have been given their authority by God (see Rom. 13:1; 1 Pet. 2:13-14). Thus, all submission ultimately constitutes submission before God. But perhaps more than any of the spiritual disciplines, the practice of submission is contrary to human nature. Thomas à Kempis writes:

> Nature is loath to die, or to be kept down, or to be overcome, or to be in subjection, or readily to be subdued. But grace studies self-mor-

tification, resists sensuality, seeks to be in subjection, longs to be defeated, has no wish to use its own liberty. It loves to be kept under discipline, and desires not to rule over any, but under God to live, to stand, and to be, and for his sake it is ready humbly "to submit to every ordinance of man" (1 Peter 2:13).[19]

And what view of providence most inclines us to recognize our subjection to God, to sense our utter dependence upon him from moment to moment, and to affirm that all our finest deeds are but the result of his gracious work in our lives? Indeed, the Augustinian view of providence sees supernatural grace as the source of every positive step in the sanctification process. This attitude, when combined with a strong commitment to practice the spiritual disciplines, basically constitutes Paul's balanced maxim: "work out your salvation with fear and trembling, for it is God who works in you to will and to act according to his good purpose" (Phil. 2:12-13). It is God's work, and it is our work. He sovereignly directs, and we freely act.[20]

CONCLUSION

The purpose of this book has been to show that the doctrine of providence, properly understood, is not only biblically sound but conceptually enriching and personally edifying. I have given both a defense of the Augustinian view of providence and an illustration of some of the resources available to those who affirm this view specifically and the high view of providence generally. To see God as utterly sovereign provides numerous benefits to us in diverse domains, ranging from art and science to ethics and philosophical theology. (In most of these areas, I believe Christian history bears out my claim, such that where the Augustinian view has prevailed, there have been the greatest advances artistically, scientifically, philosophically, and theologically. But, of course, demonstrating this historical claim would demand another book-length discussion in itself.)

---

[19] Thomas à Kempis, *Of the Imitation of Christ* (Pittsburgh: Whitaker House, 1981), 200.

[20] For excellent discussions of the spiritual disciplines, see Richard Foster, *Celebration of Discipline* (New York: Harper, 1978) and Dallas Willard, *The Spirit of the Disciplines: Understanding How God Changes Lives* (San Francisco: Harper San Francisco, 1988). For more on spiritual formation, see Lewis Smedes, *A Pretty Good Person: What It Takes to Live With Courage, Gratitude and Integrity* (New York: HarperCollins, 1991).

At the end of the day, most of us opt for a view of providence that makes the most sense to us, all things considered. Like a good scientific theory, a sound theology—or a particular theological doctrine—must display considerable explanatory power to be worthy of acceptance. Unlike a scientific theory, the matter of providence is not only theoretical and practical but deeply personal as well. The doctrine of providence must help us make sense of Scripture and human history, as well as our intuitions about beauty, goodness, and our deepest fears, desires, and hopes. Consequently, depending upon the reader's perspective, the trek through this book has likely been either very exhilarating or somewhat disturbing. In any case, I trust that irrespective of the reader's perspective the discussion has been stimulating and that even those who disagree with me will have found something of value in this book. As strongly as I disagree with those who affirm the low view of providence, my thinking has been fertilized by theirs. And I hope the reverse will be true as well. If my words cannot persuade, perhaps they will nonetheless edify.

BIBLIOGRAPHY

à Kempis, Thomas. *Of the Imitation of Christ*. Pittsburgh: Whitaker, 1981.

Adams, Marilyn M. "Aesthetic Goodness as a Solution to the Problem of Evil." In *God, Truth and Reality*, ed. Arvind Sharma. New York: St. Martin's Press, 1993.

——————. "Horrendous Evils and the Goodness of God." In *The Problem of Evil*, ed. Marilyn M. Adams and Robert M. Adams. New York: Oxford University Press, 1990.

——————. "Redemptive Suffering: A Christian Solution to the Problem of Evil." In *Rationality, Religious Belief, and Moral Commitment*, ed. Robert Audi and William J. Wainwright. Ithaca, N.Y.: Cornell University Press, 1986.

Adams, Robert M. "Middle Knowledge and the Problem of Evil." *American Philosophical Quarterly* 14, No. 2 (1977): 109-117.

——————. *The Virtue of Faith and Other Essays in Philosophical Theology*. Oxford: Oxford University Press, 1987.

Aiken, David W. "Why I Am Not a Physicalist: A Dialogue, a Meditation, and a Cumulative Critique." *Christian Scholar's Review* 33, No. 2 (2004): 165-180.

Allen, Diogenes. *Christian Belief in a Postmodern World*. Louisville: Westminster, 1989.

Anderson, Bernhard. "The Kingdom, the Power, and the Glory: The Sovereignty of God in the Bible." *Theology Today* 53, No. 1 (1996): 5-14.

Anselm. *Basic Writings*, second edition. Trans. S. N. Deane. La Salle, Ill.: Open Court, 1962.

Aquinas, Thomas. *Summa Theologica*. Trans. English Dominican Fathers. New York: Benziger Brothers, 1947.

——————. *The Disputed Questions on Truth*. Trans. Robert W. Mulligan. Chicago: Henry Regnery, 1952.

Aristotle. *The Basic Works of Aristotle.* Ed. Richard McKeon. New York: Random House, 1941.

Arminius, Jacob. *Writings.* Vol. 2. Trans. James Nichols. Grand Rapids, Mich.: Baker, 1956.

Augustine, *Augustine: Later Works.* Ed. John Burnaby. Philadelphia: Westminster, 1955.

——————. *On Free Choice of the Will.* Trans. Anna S. Benjamin and L. H. Hackstaff. Indianapolis: Bobbs-Merrill, 1964.

——————. *The City of God.* Trans. Marcus Dods. New York: Hafner, 1948.

——————. *The Enchiridion.* Trans. J. F. Shaw. Chicago: Henry Regnery, 1961.

Ayer, A. J. "What Is a Law of Nature?" *Revue Internationale de Philosophie* 36 (1956): 144-165.

Baker, Lynn Rudder. *Persons and Bodies: A Constitution View.* Cambridge: Cambridge University Press, 2000.

Barbour, Ian. *When Science Meets Religion.* San Francisco: Harper San Francisco, 2000.

Bartholomew, D. J. *God of Chance.* London: SCM Press, 1984.

Basinger, David. "Can an Evangelical Christian Justifiably Deny God's Exhaustive Knowledge of the Future?" *Christian Scholar's Review* 25, No. 2 (1995): 133-145.

——————. *The Case for Freewill Theism: A Philosophical Assessment.* Downers Grove, Ill.: InterVarsity Press, 1996.

Behe, Michael J. *Darwin's Black Box: The Biochemical Challenge to Evolution.* New York: The Free Press, 1996.

Bell, Clive. *Art.* London: Chatto and Windus, 1914.

Belli, Humberto and Ronald Nash. *Beyond Liberation Theology.* Grand Rapids, Mich.: Baker, 1992.

Berger, Fred R. "Gratitude," *Ethics* 85 (1975): 298-309.

Berkeley, George. *A Treatise Concerning the Principles of Human Knowledge.* New York: Bobbs-Merrill, 1957.

——————. *The Works of George Berkeley.* Ed. A. A. Luce and T. E. Jessop. London: Thomas Nelson and Sons, 1955.

Bigelow, J., B. Ellis, and C. Lierse. "The World as One of a Kind: Natural Necessity and Laws of Nature." *British Journal for the Philosophy of Science* 43 (1992): 371-388.

Boethius. *The Consolation of Philosophy.* Trans. W. V. Cooper. New York: The Modern Library, 1943.

Boff, Leonardo. *Jesus Christ Liberator: A Critical Christology for Our Time.* Maryknoll, N.Y.: Orbis Books, 1978.

Bonhoeffer, Dietrich. *The Cost of Discipleship.* Trans. Kaiser Verlag Munchen. New York: Macmillan, 1963.

Boogaart, Thomas. "Deliberation and Decree: The Biblical Model of Sovereignty." *Perspectives* 12, No. 3 (1997): 8-11.

Boyd, Gregory. *God at War: The Bible and Spiritual Conflict*. Downers Grove, Ill.: InterVarsity Press, 1997.

Brown, Frank Burch. *Good Taste, Bad Taste, and Christian Taste: Aesthetics in Religious Life*. Oxford: Oxford University Press, 2000.

Brummer, Vincent. *Speaking of a Personal God: An Essay in Philosophical Theology*. New York: Cambridge University Press, 1992.

—————. *The Model of Love: A Study in Philosophical Theology*. New York: Cambridge University Press, 1993.

Calvin, John. *Institutes of the Christian Religion*. Trans. Ford L. Battles. Philadelphia: Westminster, 1960.

Carr, Anne. *Transforming Grace*. New York: Continuum, 1988.

Carson, D. A. *Divine Sovereignty and Human Responsibility*. Eugene, Ore.: Wipf & Stock, 2002.

Chalmers, A. F. *What Is This Thing Called Science?* third edition. Indianapolis: Hackett, 1999.

Cobb, John. *God and the World*. Philadelphia: Westminster, 1969.

Collingwood, R. G. *Essays in the Philosophy of Art*. Bloomington, Ind.: Indiana University Press, 1964.

—————. *The Principles of Art*. New York: Oxford University Press, 1958.

Cone, James. "God is Black." In *Lift Every Voice: Constructing Christian Theologies from the Underside*, ed. Susan B. Thistlethwaite and Mary P. Engel. San Francisco: Harper Collins, 1990.

Corcoran, Kevin J. "Material Persons, Immaterial Souls and an Ethic of Life." *Faith and Philosophy* 20, No. 2 (2003): 218-228.

—————. "Persons and Bodies." *Faith and Philosophy* 15, No. 3 (1998): 324-340

—————. "Soul or Body?" In *Soul, Body and Survival: Essays on the Metaphysics of Persons*, ed. Kevin Corcoran. Ithaca, N.Y.: Cornell University Press, 2001.

Cowan, Steven B. "The Grounding Objection to Middle Knowledge Revisited." *Religious Studies* 39, No. 1 (2003): 93-102.

Craig, William Lane. *The Only Wise God: The Compatibility of Divine Foreknowledge and Human Freedom*. Grand Rapids, Mich.: Baker Book House, 1987.

—————. "Timelessness and Omnitemporality." In *God and Time*, ed. Gregory E. Ganssle. Downers Grove, Ill.: InterVarsity Press, 2001.

Creel, Richard. *Divine Impassibility: An Essay in Philosophical Theology*. Cambridge: Cambridge University Press, 1986.

Danto, Arthur. "The Artworld." *Journal of Philosophy* 61 (1964): 571-584.

Davis, Stephen. "Temporal Eternity" in *Philosophy of Religion: An Anthology*, second edition. Ed. Louis Pojman. Belmont, Calif.: Wadsworth, 1994.

Davis, William C. "Why Open Theism Is Flourishing Now." In *Beyond the*

Bounds, eds. John Piper, Justin Taylor, and Paul Kjoss Helseth. Wheaton, Ill.: Crossway Books, 2003.

Dembski, William A. *Intelligent Design: The Bridge Between Science and Theology*. Downers Grove, Ill.: InterVarsity Press, 1999.

—————. *The Design Revolution*. Downers Grove, Ill.: InterVarsity Press, 2004.

Dennett, Daniel. *Consciousness Explained*. Boston: Little, Brown and Co, 1991.

Descartes, Rene. *The Passions of the Soul*. Trans. Stephen H. Voss. Indianapolis: Hackett, 1989.

—————. *The Philosophical Works of Descartes*. Trans. Elizabeth S. Haldane and G. R. T. Ross. New York: Dover, 1955.

Dickie, George. *Art and Aesthetics: An Institutional Analysis*. Ithaca, N.Y.: Cornell University Press, 1974.

Dilby, Frank B. "A Critique of Emergent Dualism." *Faith and Philosophy* 20, No. 1 (2003): 37-49.

Dostoyevsky, Fyodor. *The Brothers Karamazov*. Trans. Constance Garnett. New York: William Heinemann, 1945.

Dretske, Fred. "Laws of Nature." *Philosophy of Science* 44 (1977): 248-268.

Edelman, John. "Suffering and the Will of God." *Faith and Philosophy* 10, No. 3 (July 1993): 383-88.

Edwards, Jonathan. *The Works of Jonathan Edwards*. Edinburgh: Banner of Truth, 1974.

Emerson, Ralph Waldo. *The Works of Ralph Waldo Emerson*. New York: Bigelow, Brown and Co., n.d.

Fales, E. *Causation and Universals*. London: Routledge Press, 1990.

Farley, Edward. *Faith and Beauty: A Theological Aesthetic*. Burlington, Ver.: Ashgate, 2001

Fiddes, Paul. *The Creative Suffering of God*. Oxford: Clarendon Press, 1988.

Flint, Thomas P. *Divine Providence: The Molinist Account*. Ithaca, N.Y.: Cornell University Press, 1988.

—————. "Two Accounts of Providence." In *Divine and Human Action: Essays in the Metaphysics of Theism*, ed. Thomas V. Morris. Ithaca, N.Y.: Cornell University Press, 1988.

Fodor, Jerry. *Psychological Explanation*. New York: Random House, 1968.

Foster, Richard. *Celebration of Discipline*. New York: Harper, 1978.

Fretheim, Terence E. *The Suffering of God*. Philadelphia: Fortress Press, 1984.

Geisler, Norman. *Encyclopedia of Christian Apologetics*. Grand Rapids, Mich.: Baker, 1999.

Gorringe, T. J. *God's Theatre: A Theology of Providence*. London: SCM Press, 1991.

Gutierrez, Gustavo. *A Theology of Liberation*. Trans. Caridad Inda and John Eagleson. Maryknoll, N.Y.: Orbis Books, 1973.

Harré, R. and E. H. Madden. *Causal Powers: A Theory of Natural Necessity*. Oxford: Blackwell Press, 1975.

Hart, David Bentley. *The Beauty of the Infinite: The Aesthetics of Christian Truth*. Grand Rapids, Mich.: Eerdmans, 2003.

Hartshorne, Charles. *Man's Vision of God*. Hamden, Conn.: Archon Books, 1964.

————. *Philosophers Speak of God*. Chicago: University of Chicago Press, 1953.

————. *Reality as Social Process*. Glencoe, Ill.: The Free Press, 1953.

Hasker, William. "A Philosophical Perspective." In *The Openness of God: A Biblical Challenge to the Traditional Understanding of God*. Downers Grove, Ill.: InterVarsity Press, 1994.

————. *God, Time, and Knowledge*. Ithaca, N.Y.: Cornell University Press, 1989.

————. *The Emergent Self*. Ithaca, N.Y.: Cornell University Press, 2001.

Helm, Paul. "God and Spacelessness." *Philosophy* 55 (1980): 211-221.

————. "The Impossibility of Divine Passibility." In *The Power and Weakness of God: Impassibility and Orthodoxy*, ed. Nigel M. de S. Cameron. Edinburgh: Rutherford House, 1990.

————. *The Providence of God*. Downers Grove, Ill.: InterVarsity Press, 1993.

Hempel, Carl. *Aspects of Scientific Explanation*. New York: Macmillan, 1965.

————. "Provisos: A Problem Concerning the Inferential Function of Scientific Theories." In *The Limitations of Deductivism*, ed. A. Grunbaum and W. C. Salmon. Berkeley, Calif.: University of California Press, 1988.

Hick, John. *Evil and the God of Love*. New York: Harper and Row, 1978.

Howard-Snyder, Daniel. "God, Evil, and Suffering." In *Reason for the Hope Within*, ed. Michael J. Murray. Grand Rapids, Mich.: Eerdmans, 1999.

Hume, David. *A Treatise of Human Nature*, second edition. Ed. L. A. Selby-Bigge. Oxford: Oxford University Press, 1978.

————. "Of the Standard of Taste." In *Essays Moral, Political and Literary*, ed. Eugene F. Miller. Indianapolis: Liberty Classics, 1985.

————. *The Essential Works of Hume*. Ed. Ralph Cohen. New York: Bantam Books, 1965.

Hundley, Raymond C. *Radical Liberation Theology: An Evangelical Response*. Wilmore, Ken. Bristol Books, 1987.

Hunt, David P. "Divine Providence and Simple Foreknowledge." *Faith and Philosophy* 10, No. 3 (1993): 394-414.

Jackson, Frank. "Epiphenomenal Qualia." *Philosophical Quarterly* 32 (1982): 127-136.

Jaki, Stanley. *The Road of Science and the Ways to God*. Chicago: University of Chicago Press, 1978.

James, William. *The Principles of Psychology.* Vol. 2. New York: Henry Holt, 1896.

——. *The Will to Believe and Other Essays.* New York: Dover, 1956.

Johnson, Elizabeth. *She Who Is.* New York: Crossroad, 1992.

Johnson, Phillip. *Reason in the Balance: The Case Against Naturalism in Science.* Downers Grove, Ill.: InterVarsity Press, 1995.

Kassian, Mary A. *The Feminist Gospel: The Movement to Unite Feminism with the Church.* Wheaton, Ill.: Crossway, 1992.

Kuhn, Thomas. *The Structure of Scientific Revolutions,* second edition. Chicago: University of Chicago Press, 1970.

Kuyper, Abraham. *Lectures on Calvinism.* Grand Rapids, Mich.: Eerdmans, 1931.

Kvanvig, Jonathan and Hugh J. McCann. "Divine Conservation and the Persistence of the World." In *Divine and Human Action: Essays in the Metaphysics of Theism,* ed. Thomas V. Morris. Ithaca, N.Y.: Cornell University Press, 1988.

La Croix, Richard R. "Omniprescience and Divine Determinism." *Religious Studies* 12, No. 3 (1976): 365-381.

Lactantius. *Lactantius: The Minor Works.* Trans. Mary F. McDonald. Washington, D.C.: The Catholic University of America Press, 1965.

Larmer, Robert A. "Is Methodological Naturalism Question-Begging?" *Philosophia Christi* 5, No. 1 (2003): 113-130.

Lauden, Larry. *Progress and Its Problems.* Berkeley, Calif.: University of California Press, 1977.

——. *Science and Values: An Essay on the Aims of Science and Their Role in Scientific Debate.* Berkeley, Calif.: University of California Press, 1984.

Lee, Jung Young. *God Suffers For Us: A Systematic Inquiry into a Concept of Divine Passibility.* The Hague: Martinus Nijhoff, 1974.

Leibniz, G. W. *Monadology and Other Essays.* Indianapolis: Bobbs-Merrill, 1965.

Lewis, C. S. *Miracles: A Preliminary Study.* New York: Macmillan, 1960.

——. *The Problem of Pain.* New York: Macmillan, 1962.

Luther, Martin. *The Bondage of the Will,* in *Erasmus-Luther: Discourse on Free Will.* Trans. Ernst F. Winter. New York: Frederick Ungar, 1961.

Lyons, William. *Emotion.* Cambridge: Cambridge University Press, 1980.

Mackie, J. L. *The Miracle of Theism.* Oxford: Oxford University Press, 1982.

Mavrodes, George. "Is There Anything Which God Does Not Do?" *Christian Scholar's Review* 16, No. 4 (1987): 384-391.

McCann, Hugh. "The God Beyond Time," in *Philosophy of Religion: An Anthology,* second edition. Ed. Louis Pojman. Belmont, Calif.: Wadsworth, 1994.

McConnell, Terrance. *Gratitude.* Philadelphia: Temple University Press, 1993.

McDougall, William. *An Introduction to Social Psychology.* London: Metheun, 1908.

McFague, Sallie. *Models of God.* Philadelphia: Fortress Press, 1987.

—————. "The Ethic of God as Mother, Lover and Friend." In *Feminist Theology: A Reader,* ed. Ann Loades. Louisville: Westminster, 1990.

McGregor Wright, R. K. *No Place for Sovereignty: What's Wrong with Freewill Theism.* Downers Grove, Ill.: InterVarsity Press, 1996.

McMullin, Ernan. "Plantinga's Defense of Special Creation." *Christian Scholar's Review* 21, No. 1 (1991): 55-79.

Meyer, Stephen C. "Evidence for Design in Physics and Biology: From the Origin of the Universe to the Origin of Life." In *Science and Evidence for Design in the Universe.* San Francisco: Ignatius Press, 2000.

—————. "The Methodological Equivalence of Design and Descent." In *The Creation Hypothesis,* ed. J. P. Moreland. Downers Grove, Ill.: InterVarsity Press, 1994.

Miller, Vincent J. *Consuming Religion: Christian Faith and Practice in a Consumer Culture.* New York: Continuum, 2003.

—————. Interview with Ken Myers. *Mars Hill Audio Journal* 69 (July/August 2004).

Miranda, Jose P. *Communism in the Bible.* Trans. Robert R. Barr. Eugene, Ore.: Wipf & Stock, 2004.

—————. *Marx and the Bible: A Critique of the Philosophy of Oppression.* Trans. John Eagleson. Maryknoll, N.Y.: Orbis Books, 1974.

Molina, Luis de. *On Divine Foreknowledge.* Trans. Alfred J. Freddoso. Ithaca, N.Y.: Cornell University Press, 1988.

Moltmann, Jurgen. *The Crucified God.* New York: Harper and Row, 1974.

Montaigne, Michel de. *The Complete Essays.* Trans. M. A. Screech. London: Penguin Books, 1987.

Moreland, J. P. "Complementarity, Agency Theory, and the God-of-the-Gaps." *Perspectives on Science and Christian Faith* 49, No. 1 (1997): 2-14.

—————. *Scaling the Secular City.* Grand Rapids, Mich.: Baker Books, 1987.

—————. "Theistic Science and Methodological Naturalism." In *The Creation Hypothesis,* ed. J. P. Moreland. Downers Grove, Ill.: InterVarsity Press, 1994.

Murphy, Nancey. "Supervenience and the Downward Efficacy of the Mental: A Nonreductive Physicalist Account of Human Action." In *Neuroscience and the Person: Scientific Perspectives on Divine Action,* ed. R. J. Russell, et al. Berkeley, Calif.: Center for Theology and the Natural Sciences, 1999.

Murray, Andrew. *Humility.* New Kensington, Penn.: Whitaker House, 1982.

Nagel, Ernest. *The Structure of Science.* Indianapolis: Hackett Press, 1979.

Nagel, Thomas. "What Is It Like to Be a Bat?" *The Philosophical Review* 83 (1974): 435-450.

Nietzsche, Friedrich. *The Birth of Tragedy and the Case of Wagner*, Trans. Walter Kaufmann. New York: Random House, 1967.

O'Connor, Robert. "Science on Trial: Exploring the Rationality of Methodological Naturalism," *Perspectives on Science and Christian Faith* 49, No. 1 (1997): 15-30.

Ogden, Schubert. *The Reality of God.* New York: Harper and Row, 1963.

Packer, J. I. *Evangelism and the Sovereignty of God.* Leicester, UK: InterVarsity Press, 1961.

Peacocke, Arthur. *Theology for a Scientific Age.* Oxford: Basil Blackwell, 1990.

Pearcey, Nancy and Charles Thaxton. *The Soul of Science: Christian Faith and Natural Philosophy.* Wheaton, Ill.: Crossway Books, 1994.

Pinnock, Clark. "God Limits His Knowledge." In *Predestination and Free Will*, ed. David Basinger and Randall Basinger. Downers Grove, Ill.: InterVarsity Press, 1986.

———. "God's Sovereignty in Today's World." *Theology Today* 53, No. 1 (1996): 15-21.

———. "Systematic Theology." In *The Openness of God: A Biblical Challenge to the Traditional Understanding of God.* Downers Grove, Ill.: InterVarsity Press, 1994.

Place, U. T. "Is Consciousness a Brain Process?" *British Journal of Psychology* 47 (1956): 44-50.

Plantinga, Alvin. *God, Freedom, and Evil.* Grand Rapids, Mich.: Eerdmans, 1974.

———. "Methodological Naturalism." *Origins & Design* 18, No. 1 (1997): 18-27.

———. "Methodological Naturalism, Part 2." *Origins & Design* 18, No. 2 (1997): 22-33.

———. "Methodological Naturalism?" *Perspectives on Science and Christian Faith* 49, No. 3 (1997): 143-154.

Plotinus. *Enneads.* Trans. A. H. Armstrong. London: William Heinemann, 1967.

Popper, Karl. *The Logic of Scientific Discovery.* New York: Harper and Row, 1959.

Purtill, Richard. "Justice, Mercy, Supererogation, and Atonement." In *Christian Philosophy*, ed. Thomas P. Flint. Notre Dame, Ind.: University of Notre Dame Press, 1990.

Putnam, Hillary. "The Nature of Mental States." In *Materialism and the Mind-Body Problem*, ed. David M. Rosenthal. Indianapolis: Hackett Press, 1987.

Randles, Marshall. *The Blessed God: Impassibility.* London: Charles F. Kelly, 1900.

Reichenbach, Bruce. *Evil and a Good God.* New York: Fordham University Press, 1982.

Reichenbach, Hans. *Experience and Prediction.* Chicago: University of Chicago Press, 1938.

Rescher, Nicholas. *The Limits of Science.* Berkeley, Calif.: University of California Press, 1984.

Reznicek, A. A. and P. E. Rothrock. "*Carex molestiformis* (Cyperaceae), a New Species of Section *Ovales* from the Ozark Mountain Region." *Contributions from the University of Michigan Herbarium* 21 (1997): 299-308

Rice, Richard. "Biblical Support for a New Perspective." In *The Openness of God: A Biblical Challenge to the Traditional Understanding of God.* Downers Grove, Ill.: InterVarsity Press, 1994.

—————. *God's Foreknowledge and Man's Free Will.* Minneapolis: Bethany House, 1980.

Richards, Norvin. *Humility.* Philadelphia: Temple University Press, 1992.

Roberts, Robert. "Emotions as Access to Religious Truths," *Faith and Philosophy* 9, No. 1 (1992): 83-94.

—————. "What an Emotion Is: A Sketch," *Philosophical Review* 97 (1988): 183-209.

Rothrock, P. E. and A. A. Reznicek, "A New Species of *Carex* section *Ovales* Occurring in the Ozark Mountain Region." *Brittonia* 48 (1996): 104-110.

—————. "The Taxonomy of the *Carex bicknellii* Group (Cyperaceae) and New Species for Central North America." *Novon* 11 (2001): 205-228.

Rowe, William. "The Problem of Evil and Some Varieties of Atheism." *American Philosophical Quarterly* 16 (1979): 335-341.

Rust, Eric C. *Evolutionary Philosophies and Contemporary Theology.* Philadelphia: Westminster, 1969.

Ryken, Leland. *The Liberated Imagination: Thinking Christianly About the Arts.* Wheaton, Ill.: Harold Shaw, 1989.

Ryle, Gilbert. *The Concept of Mind.* New York: Barnes and Noble, 1949.

Sanders, John. *The God Who Risks: A Theology of Providence.* Downers Grove, Ill.: InterVarsity Press, 1998.

Sartre, Jean-Paul. *The Emotions: Outline of a Theory.* Trans. Bernard Frechtman. New York: Philosophical Library, 1948.

Sayers, Dorothy. *The Whimsical Christian.* New York: Macmillan, 1969.

Schaeffer, Francis. *The Complete Works of Francis Schaeffer: A Christian Worldview.* Wheaton, Ill.: Crossway, 1982.

Schopenhauer, Arthur. *The World as Will and Representation.* Trans. E. F. J. Payne. New York: Dover, 1969.

Searle, John. *Minds, Brains and Science.* Cambridge, Mass.: Harvard University Press, 1984.

—————. *The Rediscovery of Mind.* Cambridge, Mass.: MIT Press, 1992.

Shand, Alexander. *The Foundations of Character.* New York: Macmillan, 1914.

Sherry, Patrick. *Spirit and Beauty: An Introduction to Theological Aesthetics.* Oxford: Clarendon Press, 1992.

Simmons, John A. *Moral Principles and Political Obligations.* Princeton, N.J.: Princeton University Press, 1979.

Skinner, B. F. *About Behaviorism.* New York: Vintage Books, 1974.

Smart, J. J. C. "Sensations and Brain Processes." *Philosophical Review* 68 (1959): 141-156.

Smedes, Lewis. *A Pretty Good Person: What It Takes to Live with Courage, Gratitude and Integrity.* New York: Harper Collins, 1991.

Sober, Elliott. *The Nature of Selection: Evolutionary Theory in Philosophical Focus.* Cambridge, Mass.: MIT Press, 1984.

Spiegel, James S. "A Berkeleyan Approach to the Problem of Induction." *Science and Christian Belief* 10, No. 1 (1998): 73-84.

—————. "Does God Take Risks?" In *God Under Fire: Modern Scholarship Reinvents God,* ed. Douglas S. Huffman and Eric L. Johnson. Grand Rapids, Mich.: Zondervan, 2002.

—————. *How to Be Good in a World Gone Bad.* Grand Rapids, Mich.: Kregel Books, 2004.

—————. *Hypocrisy: Moral Fraud and Other Vices.* Grand Rapids, Mich.: Baker Books, 1999.

—————. "The Philosophical Theology of Theistic Evolutionism." *Philosophia Christi* 4, No. 1 (2002): 89-99.

—————. "The Theological Orthodoxy of Berkeley's Immaterialism." *Faith and Philosophy* 13, No. 2 (1996): 216-235.

Spinoza, Benedict de. *Ethics.* Ed. James Gutman. New York: Hafner Press, 1949.

Stek, John. "What Says the Scriptures?" In *Portraits of Creation: Biblical and Scientific Perspectives on the World's Formation,* ed. H. J. Van Till, R. E. Snow, J. H. Stek, and D. A. Young. Grand Rapids, Mich.: Eerdmans, 1990.

Stump, Eleonore. "Atonement According to Aquinas." In *Philosophy and the Christian Faith,* ed. Thomas V. Morris. Notre Dame, Ind.: University of Notre Dame Press, 1988.

—————. "Petitionary Prayer." *American Philosophical Quarterly* 16, No. 2 (1979): 81-91.

—————. "Providence and Evil." In *Christian Philosophy,* ed. Thomas P. Flint. Notre Dame, Ind.: University of Notre Dame Press, 1990.

Swinburne, Richard. "The Argument from Design." In *Contemporary Perspectives on Religious Epistemology,* ed. R. Douglas Geivett and Brendan Sweetman. Oxford: Oxford University Press, 1992.

—————. *The Coherence of Theism.* Oxford: Oxford University Press, 1993.

—————. *The Existence of God.* Oxford: Oxford University Press, 1979.

—————. "The Problem of Evil." In *Reason and Responsibility,* ed. Joel Feinberg. Belmont, Calif.: Wadsworth, 1993.

Swoyer, C. "The Nature of Natural Laws." *Australasian Journal of Philosophy* 60 (1982): 203-223..

Taliaferro, Charles. "The Incorporeality of God." *Modern Theology* 3, No. 2 (1987): 179-188.

————. "The Passibility of God." *Religious Studies* 25, No. 2 (1989): 217-224.

Tolstoy, Leo. *What Is Art?* Trans. Almyer Maude. Indianapolis: Bobbs-Merrill, 1960.

Tooley, Michael. "The Nature of Laws." *Canadian Journal of Philosophy* 74 (1977): 667-698.

Toulmin, Stephen. *Foresight and Understanding: An Inquiry into the Aims of Science.* New York: Harper Torchbooks, 1980.

Turbayne, Colin. "Berkeley's Metaphysical Grammar." In *Berkeley: Principles of Human Knowledge,* ed. Colin Turbayne. Indianapolis: Bobbs-Merrill, 1970.

Van Till, Howard J. "Is Special Creationism a Heresy?" *Christian Scholar's Review* 22, No. 4 (June 1993): 381-393.

Veith, Gene. *State of the Arts: From Bezalel to Mapplethorpe.* Wheaton, Ill.: Crossway, 1991.

Von Hugel, Baron F. "Suffering and God." In *Essays and Addresses on the Philosophy of Religion,* Second Series. London: J. M. Dent and Sons, 1926.

Ware, Bruce A. *God's Greater Glory: The Exalted God of Scripture and the Christian Faith.* Wheaton, Ill.: Crossway, 2004.

————. *God's Lesser Glory: The Diminished God of Open Theism.* Wheaton, Ill.: Crossway, 2000.

Watson, J. B. *Psychology from the Standpoint of a Behaviorist.* Philadelphia: J. B. Lippincott Co., 1919.

Wellman, Christopher. "Gratitude as a Virtue." *Pacific Philosophical Quarterly* 80 (1999): 284-300.

Wesley, John. *The Works of John Wesley,* third edition. Peabody, Mass.: Hendrickson, 1991.

Whewell, William. *On the Philosophy of Discovery.* London: John W. Parker, 1860.

————. *The Philosophy of the Inductive Sciences.* London: John W. Parker, 1847.

Whitehead, Alfred North. *Process and Reality.* New York: The Free Press, 1978.

————. *Religion in the Making.* New York: New American Library, 1974.

————. *Science and the Modern World.* New York: The Free Press, 1967.

Willard, Dallas. *The Spirit of the Disciplines: Understanding How God Changes Lives.* San Francisco: Harper San Francisco, 1988.

————. "The Three-Stage Argument for the Existence of God." In *Contemporary Perspectives on Religious Epistemology,* ed. R. Douglas Geivett and Brendan Sweetman. Oxford: Oxford University Press, 1992.

Wolterstorff, Nicholas. *Art in Action: Towards a Christian Aesthetic*. Grand Rapids, Mich.: Eerdmans, 1980.

——————. *Divine Discourse: Philosophical Reflections on the Claim That God Speaks*. Cambridge: Cambridge University Press, 1995.

——————. "God Everlasting." In *God and the Good*, ed. Clifton Orlebeke and Lewis Smedes. Grand Rapids, Mich.: Eerdmans, 1975.

——————. "Suffering Love." In *Philosophy and the Christian Faith*, ed. Thomas V. Morris. Notre Dame, Ind.: University of Notre Dame Press, 1988.

Wordsworth, William. "The Tables Turned." In *Wordsworth and His Poetry*, ed. William H. Hudson. London: George Harrap & Co., 1914.

SCRIPTURE INDEX

GENERAL INDEX